Sylvia's Table

Sylvia's Table

FRESH, SEASONAL RECIPES FROM OUR FARM TO YOUR FAMILY

Liz Neumark

WITH CAROLE LALLI

ALFRED A. KNOPF   NEW YORK   2013

THIS IS A BORZOI BOOK
PUBLISHED BY ALFRED A. KNOPF

Published in the United States by Alfred A. Knopf,
a division of Random House, Inc., New York, and in Canada by
Random House of Canada Limited, Toronto.
www.aaknopf.com

Knopf, Borzoi Books, and the colophon are registered
trademarks of Random House, Inc.

Page 423 constitutes an extension of this page.

Library of Congress Cataloging-in-Publication Data
Neumark, Liz.
Sylvia's table : fresh, seasonal recipes from our farm to your family /
Liz Neumark with Carole Lalli. — First edition.
pages   cm
"This is a Borzoi book"—Title page verso.
Includes index.
ISBN 978-0-307-59513-3 (hardcover : alkaline paper)
1. Cooking, American.   2. Natural foods.   3. Farm produce.
I. Lalli, Carole, 1942–   II. Title.
TX715.N5095   2013
641.5973—dc23
2013004555

Illustrations copyright © Jason Snyder
Cover photographs courtesy of the author;
(checkered fabric) by Maria Toutoudaki/Getty Images
Cover design by Kelly Blair

Manufactured in China
First Edition

DEDICATION

I learned several years ago that tragedy is not something that happens to someone else. Life is both wonderful and terrifying, and it is how we blend the two that defines who we are.

In the summer of 2004 my youngest child died suddenly at the age of six. Learning how to "live on" after losing Sylvia was a mystery. Creating a living legacy so that we could say her name every day and keep her spirit alive, and to honor her by doing the good she dreamed of, was the anchor for me. My very special husband, Chaim, agreed that we would buy a farm and create the Sylvia Center. I am grateful for that every day. Our children, Nell, Katie, and Sam, embraced these two projects from the start. Without their encouragement and support, I don't think we would have been successful. They are the inspiration in my life and for this book, written to bring families together around the table, in conversation or celebration, making meals and moments count.

This book is also dedicated to the many dear friends and pioneering colleagues who gave their support, involvement, creativity, hard work, and passion for helping others to the Sylvia Center; they are making a difference in many young lives.

Over the years, I have met more bereaved parents than I dreamed possible. Sharing our stories and talking about our children (all of them) gave me strength and hope. This book and its stories are for the friends who have traveled this road and understand the balance of what is important in life.

To my precious family and my dearest friends, I dedicate *Sylvia's Table*.

CONTENTS

INTRODUCTION

I left New York at five thirty on a fall morning in 2006, a city girl heading north to meet a farmer. Just four months had passed since we closed on sixty acres in Kinderhook, a small town in the Hudson Valley; settled in 1640, Kinderhook is deep in the American arcadia, legendary for its gentle hills, rich farmland, and abundant streams. Given their location, it was surprising that our sixty acres had never been farmed—that would be for me to do, so I needed a farmer. By seven thirty Bob Walker and I were chatting over breakfast at the West Taghkanic Diner on Route 82, a rural road that links Hudson Valley towns and villages. I knew Bob was the one, even before I'd finished my oatmeal—really, from the moment I first saw him.

Yes, he looked like a farmer—tall, browned from long days outdoors, and with large hands that looked like they were connected to the earth. But beyond that, Bob was an experienced organic farmer, already contentedly at home in the Hudson Valley. We were determined to plant in the spring, which meant that Bob had to hit the ground fast, and he did, studying and planning nearly obsessively through the few short months we had before planting would begin. The exciting things, like choosing crops, were offset by mundane—and expensive—matters, like laying in twenty thousand feet of drainage pipes (to be followed, two years later, by twenty thousand more). Bob had had experience with start-up farm situations, which our Katchkie would be, and he had worked on farms with the kind of dual mission we were planning—farming with a social cause. In our case, the cause was the Sylvia Center. We made our goal, and, because Katchkie had never before been farmed, we qualified for our organic certification with our 2007 harvest—the most delicious crops from what, a year before, had been a field covered with wild brambles.

Accomplishing all this meant far more to me than simply realizing my dream of having a farm; I'd wanted that for a long time, but that longing had taken on new urgency. I was eager to establish the Sylvia Center, a place to inspire children to eat well and to learn where good food comes from. The center had to be on a farm.

Who is Sylvia? Sylvia was the youngest of our four children, a pixie of a girl who wanted to grow up and become a "helpful human." Two months shy of her seventh birthday she died of a sudden brain aneurysm. In picking up the pieces—and in finding a way to create a legacy for Sylvia—several threads of our lives came together.

Our family already had a place in nearby Putnam County, where we have spent summers and weekends for many years, falling in love with the outdoors and surrounding farms. We have shared memories of hours spent as a family picking and eating our way through the seasons, from strawberries and blueberries to apples and pumpkins.

Looking back, it makes sense that in the early phases of mourning, I discovered that the only places where I felt alive were in one of New York's Greenmarkets, or at the farm where I picked up my CSA (community-supported agriculture) share. There was something healing about being surrounded by the earth and its abundance. This land in Kinderhook—Dutch for "children's corner"—was the perfect place for the Sylvia Center, the place to honor her. It would be the legacy she would have created herself. It seemed a minor miracle to find property close to a place we already considered a second home.

We named the farm for our son, Sam, choosing a nickname I had given him as a baby. Katchkie is Yiddish for "duck" and, oddly, a term of endearment. (Although when I want to tease people, I tell them it is an old Indian tribal name, like our other local ones, Taconic or Mohegan!) And the timing could not have been better, just before the locavore and sustainable farming movements were gaining momentum around New York City. I had a

desire to connect to food fresh from the field; that concept is at the core of the Sylvia Center.

The program's mission is to bring children together with good, delicious foods through joyful experiences in the fields and with cooking. It was an immediate success. The children harvest whatever is ready for picking or pulling and turn it into a meal, right there, in our field kitchen. Then they nourish the soil with the trimmings and plant new crops; they learn, hands-on, the relationship between a farm and the food they eat and the entire cycle of growing. We welcomed our first visitors in 2007, children from local communities and a few groups of public school children from New York City.

Katchkie Farm has brought me close to the sustainable farming movement in our region and led to my involvement in food policy with organizations like Just Food, Grow NYC, and the Governor's Council. This movement has also inspired and informed my professional work—from spring to fall, most of what is grown at Katchkie Farm is used by my catering company, Great Performances, at our events or in our cafés; it also gives us a presence at the city's Greenmarkets and is a source for our products.

As much as I yearned for a farm, Katchkie has enhanced my life beyond anything I ever imagined. Today, some of my most cherished moments are in early spring, after Katchkie Farm has slumbered through the winter and our early crops are just beginning to show. The extraordinary Hudson Valley light is still low, and early in the day it touches the undersides of delicate green leaves; everything glows with spring's promise and new life. Above all, Katchkie Farm is where we are keeping Sylvia's name and her memory alive; she is being the "helpful human" she wanted to be. With this book, we reach even wider—sharing Sylvia's memory and our work on Katchkie Farm with all of you.

I also want this book to inspire families to create memories by cooking together. Some of the best times I recall as a granddaughter or mother take place in a kitchen. My little Russian grandma, Nelly, never cooked from a printed recipe (though I have her tattered ancient recipe notebook with unintelligible scribbles); she defined measurements as a "pinch" or a "touch."

Cooking with my own children was a lesson in letting go and embracing the moment. We had the best collection of sprinkles, frosting tubes, and cookie cutters. We made soups, jams, pancakes, cookies, cupcakes, mousses, and, inevitably, lots of tomato sauce, a consequence of my inability to resist tomatoes in their season. Cooking with a child can lead to "teachable moments," combining basic math and reading skills, providing exposure to new flavors and foods, and leading to the pride of accomplishment and the pleasure of eating. Cooking with a child can be a test of patience as well as a labor of love, but almost nothing is as magical. When I cooked with my kids, we made messes, and yes, we made magic. The gleeful chaos, the surrender of discipline to the joy of discovery, it's all the stuff of indelible memories.

The experience has been no different at the Sylvia Center, where the children also have pulled me into their exuberance. We've learned a lot from them, what they are capable of, what can interest and excite them—how open they can be. For instance, there's the legend of "the boy who didn't like beets," who visited with a group from Chatham Middle School, not far from the farm. Most of the kids, being teens, had a bit of a 'tude about participating in the program. Robin, our culinary intern, had made beets with sour cream—the dish was the most exquisite bright pink. Too colorful for the kids, I guess, because none of them would touch it. Only one boy was game. His classmates watched him eat the beets, at first as if they were a bowl of spiders, then with gusto. He went back for seconds and, amazingly, thirds. His friends were cheering him on. And I felt so grateful for this one brave soul who would not buckle to peer pressure, even with his mouth as bright pink as a little girl's purse.

MY BOOK FOR YOU, OR, HOW TO USE THIS BOOK

Sylvia's Table brings together several aspects of my life and how I've thought about food, as a wife and mother and as a food professional. This is a book for grown-ups, but also a book to be shared with children, a family cookbook. Most of all it is a personal collection of recipes, the ones I've prepared for my own family for many years, along with recipes from my company, Great Performances, dishes that have crossed over from events catered for strangers to food I routinely cook at home—and not while wearing party dresses!

Other recipes in this book came to me through the generosity of friends and relatives, and a handful came from colleagues in the food professions—chefs, authors, teachers. These busy people took the time to think about what would be just right for a cookbook aimed at families and were particularly eager to contribute to an effort that will support the Sylvia Center.

In *Sylvia's Table* you also will come upon essays with various themes. As a farmer, I wanted to pass along some tips for crops you might like to grow in your own backyard or on a suburban deck or even in containers on a city terrace—strawberries, carrots, salad greens, herbs—so easy and so thrilling for children. And whether or not you raise your own crops, I thought it would be helpful to know more about particular kinds of produce, such as squashes and apples and peppers and mushrooms, to help

you identify them and learn some of their characteristics and how to use them in easy ways, so there are guides to them. These are exciting times when local farmers are catching on that if they grow it, we will eat it. Some of the big growers are taking notice, too, and following the trends, to the point that we all are finding things we've never seen before, even at our neighborhood supermarkets.

And I thought that other parents would share my interest in some of the nutritional benefits of various foods. That said, I always meant for this to be a book that celebrates good food for its own pure pleasure, because I believe that is the way to instill lifelong healthful eating habits; it all starts with the palate. There is nothing prescriptive or preachy here, aside from my main message: eat unadulterated food, as fresh, local, and organic as you can possibly manage.

The recipes here reflect today's home cook, a person whose tastes have been formed by the diversity of ingredients available to us, but they also are easy to follow and well within the average home cook's skill level and collection of kitchen gadgets. As a busy professional, I've particularly wanted to inspire the kind of cooking that is nearly free-form, the kind of dishes that are built on the season and the market. You will find such dishes throughout this book. I call them Katchkie Favorites—shorthand recipes that barely require measurements; think of them as rough directions and let the season and the market lead you on. Down on the Farm Pasta Salad (page 28) is a good example, versions of which you probably can produce without exact duplication on a weekly basis. Similarly, there is a basic preparation for chicken breasts and variations, as well as the basic preparations for fish for easy everyday meals.

And, as a curious if casual student of food history, I couldn't resist including some of the food lore I've picked up. Your kids will love knowing that the food they eat—things like strawberries and tomatoes and chiles—resulted from more than five hundred years of exploration. They may be learning about the Age of Exploration at school, but knowing that the potatoes on their plates went from here to there and back on sailing ships will make history immediate and personal. So you will find little essays throughout; if you find them interesting your child probably will also.

In a similar way, children love the language of food and the science involved in cooking—unknown words and chemical interactions can be jumping-off points for learning. So I've developed the habit of deliberately using a term and explaining it on the spot; each has a specific meaning that will not only guide a child through a recipe, but add to his vocabulary as well. I always did this at home, and now we do it at the Sylvia Center. "Emulsify" is a good example; the word and the concept can be explained, understood, and instantly stored. And then there are foreign words—the names of pasta shapes, for instance, or French cookware terms that also apply to the dishes made in them. You will find some of these throughout *Sylvia's Table,* but have your kids keep a kitchen dictionary and add to it as they go along; in a subtle way, they will be learning quite a lot about cooking through its terminology.

This is meant to be easygoing, casual information dropped in as you are cooking together or eating together. And that is how you will stumble on information throughout this book, bits I dropped in as they occurred, which is how I hope you will share them with your children: the phrase "Did you know . . . ?" will capture their attention.

On the practical side, I've kept things simple so that the basic ingredients needed will be in your pantry and your fridge: flour is all-purpose; eggs are large (but if yours are a different size, don't let that stop you); salt is kosher unless I say otherwise; onions are yellow unless another type is specifically called for; butter is unsalted.

Salads

1. Farmers' Market Salad

2. Baby Tomato and Fresh Goat Cheese Salad

3. Panzanella with Heirloom Tomatoes and Anchovy-Caper Dressing

4. Rachel's Famous Multigenerational Coleslaw

5. Daikon Salad

6. Spring Radish Salad with Asparagus and Blood Oranges

7. *Katchkie Favorites:* Watermelon Radish "Ravioli"

8. *Katchkie Favorites:* Braised Radishes

9. Katchkie Farm Spinach and Strawberry Salad

10. Salade Monique

11. Herb Salad

12. Fennel, Celeriac, and Parsley Salad in Lemon-Caper Dressing

13. *Katchkie Favorites:* Down on the Farm Pasta Salad

14. Roasted Poblano, Red, and Yellow Pepper Salad with Raisins and Basil

15. Sweet Corn, Fava Bean, and Shiitake Salad

Thinking about salad brings me straight to the connection between food and the growing season; salad moves gracefully through the year, adjusting easily to whatever is fresh. And for kids, salad is fast food at its best: pick it, wash it, dress it, eat it.

Salad can go beyond the green, the raw, and the predictable; salads may indeed be the most flexible of all dishes. Few salads need to be confined to a separate course; they can be the focus of a lunch or an accompaniment to an entrée. A good example in this chapter is my Roasted Poblano, Red, and Yellow Pepper Salad with Raisins and Basil (page 30). At our classes at the Sylvia Center, we've learned that when you trust children with a challenging task, they reward that trust with accountability. Salad making is an ideal place for children to begin to prepare food; they can acquire basic skills, such as chopping and slicing, and rough notions of measures and agreeable combinations of ingredients without much danger of producing a failed dish or getting burned. Only you can judge when your child is ready to use a knife, but seven or eight is a typical safe age. Keep in mind, for yourself as well as your child, that sharp knives are safer than dull ones.

At the Sylvia Center, we have a few basic steps for developing knife skills and safety that will work for you at home.

First, position the child's hand over what's being prepped to demonstrate the two safest hand positions while cutting: the tunnel and the bear claw. Then he can start on something soft, like cucumbers, tomatoes, or peppers. You can cut the vegetables into workable pieces first, and then let your child dice them.

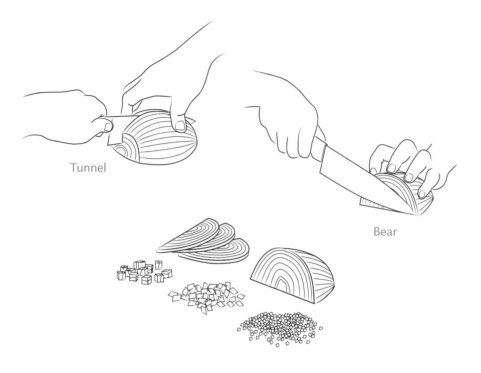

Tunnel

Bear

You can also let the little hands in your kitchen take on other prep steps for salads as well as cooked dishes, such as

- snapping green beans
- shelling peas or fava beans
- snapping asparagus
- seeding peppers and removing the ribs
- cleaning mushrooms
- tearing lettuce leaves off their ribs
- peeling onions
- cutting into chiffonade

THE WINDOWSILL GARDEN

The best kind of salad is one you can watch coming your way—you can grow small pots or cups of microgreens, those tasty little versions of arugula, kale, mizuna, and miniaturized lettuces as well as herbs, on a sunny windowsill. As the greens grow, let youngsters snip them and add them to their salads. Do taste tests, and talk about how they differ. And take daily photographs of the greens as they grow, from planting the seeds and the first exciting glimpse of green pushing up through the earth to the full-grown plant.

1. Farmers' Market Salad

Think of this salad as something to stimulate your own creativity, and vary the ingredients according to what is on hand or in season. For a meal in a bowl, add cheese—a sharp Cheddar or a blue cheese is particularly good—or leftover chicken or shrimp. My favorite addition is a can of sardines or a few anchovies; those little fish deliver lots of protein.

Look for other terrific salad mixes: tender baby lettuces (so pretty), mustard, mizuna, kale, and pea or mustard sprouts. Even in an urban grocery store, one can frequently discover a range of greens appropriate for salad—watercress, radicchio, romaine, baby bok choy, cabbage, and more. Never hesitate to include an herb such as dill, parsley, or basil in your lettuce mix. SERVES 4 TO 6

2 large or 3 medium
   cucumbers
2 tablespoons fresh lemon
   juice or red or white wine
   vinegar
6 tablespoons olive oil
Salt and freshly ground
   pepper
2 tablespoons roughly
   chopped assorted herbs,
   such as chervil, basil, and
   cilantro
2 cups assorted heirloom
   cherry tomatoes, cut in
   halves or quarters
½ cup thinly sliced scallions,
   green and white parts
¼ cup diced red onion
½ cup diced radishes
½ cup sliced snap peas
½ cup fresh peas

Scrub the cucumbers, but do not peel them unless their skins are waxed (see next page), or peel them in strips. Cut the cucumbers in half lengthwise and scoop out the seeds. Slice the cucumbers crosswise about ¼ inch thick, into half moons. Whisk together the lemon juice and olive oil in a salad bowl. Season with salt and pepper to taste. Add the cucumbers and the remaining ingredients, and toss gently; taste and adjust the seasoning.

CUCUMBERS

There are more cucumber choices in the markets than there used to be, including the long slender variety known as English, as well as Persian, Lebanese, and, more recently, some delicious Asian types that are nice and crisp to the bite. These come unwaxed, and most have thin, tasty skin; they need only be washed before using. Pickling or Kirby cukes are usually found in farmers' markets in the summer; they of course do not need to be pickled to be eaten, but their skin can be thick and sometimes bitter, so give them a taste test before throwing them into a salad, and peel them accordingly.

Cucumber seeds can be scooped out with a teaspoon, grapefruit spoon, or melon baller, a chore kids enjoy. Take care with a melon baller that has somewhat sharp edges. Don't forget, cucumbers are such a beloved kid snack that you should plan to have enough on hand for the salad and the snackers. Cucumbers are soft enough to be cut into half-moons with plastic paring knives made for children—the ones we use at the Sylvia Center. They are widely available in stores and through mail order. Some five- or six-year-olds can manage this chore, but you are the best judge of your child's readiness.

The cucumber is good for you in the sense that it has practically no calories, is at least 90 percent water, and delivers some fiber, vitamin C, and trace minerals, including potassium and manganese. You will get more in the way of nutrition if you eat the skin, which means finding unwaxed and, if possible, organic cucumbers. (Commercially grown cucumbers are waxed to keep them fresh and to prevent bruising during shipment, which is a benefit for the big growers and distributors, not so much for the consumer. Various ingredients and compounds go into the waxes used, some benign, but there is no practical way to know, so waxed cucumbers must either be well scrubbed or peeled.)

2. Baby Tomato and Fresh Goat Cheese Salad

This is an early signature dish of my colleague Jonathan Waxman, who has been at the center of the contemporary American food scene since the early 1970s, when he worked at Chez Panisse in Berkeley and at Michael's in Los Angeles. Waxman now presides over Barbuto—he's "the bearded one"—in the far west Greenwich Village, where all-American inclinations meet simple Italian cooking, frequently in the wood-burning oven. Jonathan's cooking has always been defined by its clarity; there are times when I wonder how he has managed to make something as simple as a roasted chicken or a plate of beets seem so special. Top-quality ingredients in season and vigilant preparations are the answers—what I strive for in my own cooking.

This dish is a classic example of the early wave of what was known as the New American Cooking—a movement, if not a revolution, now forty years old and counting. It also demonstrates that a new, even trendy, dish can endure and become a classic—if it has integrity. Nevertheless, you can improvise here. Change the herbs according to what you've got, and the oils for the dressing.   SERVES 4

4 cups baby tomatoes

1 cup (about 8 ounces) fresh goat cheese

1 teaspoon chopped chives

1 teaspoon chopped basil

1 teaspoon chopped oregano

1 teaspoon chopped thyme

1 cup unseasoned fresh bread crumbs or panko (page 218)

Salt and freshly ground pepper

1 egg

2 tablespoons each hazelnut, walnut, and olive oils, or any combination equal to 6 tablespoons

1 tablespoon fresh lemon juice

12 sprigs chervil or flat-leaf parsley

Preheat the oven to 375 degrees.

Cut the tomatoes in half horizontally.

Mix the goat cheese with the herbs and shape the mixture into four 2-inch cakes and chill them for 30 minutes or so.

Season the bread crumbs with salt and pepper to taste. Beat the egg with a pinch of salt. Carefully dip the goat cheese cakes into the egg, then into the bread crumbs to coat lightly. Place the cakes on a buttered cookie sheet and bake them until golden brown, about 8 minutes, or brown them in an oiled heavy skillet over medium-high heat.

Whisk together the oils and lemon juice and toss with the tomatoes. Season with salt and pepper. Arrange the dressed tomatoes on a serving platter. Place the baked goat cheese cakes on the tomatoes, garnish with the chervil, and serve.

3. Panzanella with Heirloom Tomatoes and Anchovy-Caper Dressing

I talian bread salad—*panzanella*—is a glorious dish that was created by thrifty cooks looking for ways to use up stale bread. It is typical of Tuscany, where the traditional bread is a simple country type with a heavy crust, coarse crumb, and no fat that goes stale swiftly. There are numerous versions, but, along with the bread, tomatoes and basil are constants and anchovies are often included. I like this interpretation, where the salad is piled onto toasted French bread and the delicious dressing soaks into it. There are people who don't like anchovies, or think they don't, but I suspect they won't notice their presence in the dressing here. If you prefer, leave them out of the dressing and offer them at the table. But don't forget your best olive oil! SERVES 6

1 loaf day-old French
   baguette or similar crusty
   bread
6 tablespoons extra-virgin
   olive oil
Salt and freshly ground
   pepper
2 tablespoons fresh lemon
   juice
2 tablespoons capers in
   vinegar, drained
2 teaspoons chopped anchovy
   fillets, drained if they are in
   oil, rinsed and patted dry if
   they are packed in salt

1 small garlic clove, minced

2 cups (about 1 pound) assorted heirloom cherry tomatoes, halved or quartered depending on their sizes

2 pounds assorted beefsteak heirloom tomatoes, each cut into 6 wedges

1 cup crumbled feta cheese or ricotta salata

¼ cup thinly sliced fresh basil

3 tablespoons chopped flat-leaf parsley

Preheat your broiler.

Cut the bread in half lengthwise and then crosswise into six pieces. Brush the cut side of the bread lightly with some of the oil and season it with salt and pepper. Toast the bread under the broiler until it is golden brown and crunchy, 2 to 3 minutes; take care that it does not burn.

Combine the lemon juice, capers, anchovies, and garlic in a small bowl; slowly whisk in the remaining oil until well incorporated.

Toss together the tomatoes, feta, basil, and parsley in a bowl and add half the dressing; season with salt and pepper to taste. Place one piece of the toasted baguette on each of six plates and spoon the tomato salad over; spoon the remaining dressing around the plate.

You probably won't want to light a charcoal fire just to toast some bread, but if you happen to be grilling another part of your meal, throw the bread on the grill to toast and to pick up extra flavor and a nice light smoky taste.

TOMATOES

The East Coast arguably produces this country's finest tomatoes. Up and down the middle Atlantic, the tomato is the emblem of summertime. New Jersey certainly has bragging rights, along with the Delmarva Peninsula and eastern Long Island. Katchkie Farm, nestled in the rich Hudson Valley, gives no quarter. We are enormously proud of our tomatoes, and over the seasons, our varieties have increased. This follows the recent trend of small growers working to meet the demands of chefs and consumers for better, different, tastier tomatoes, including varieties that were very near extinction.

I could not be more enthusiastic, but the movement has led to confusion for consumers, as the "heirloom" label gets smacked onto any tomato that qualifies. The fact is, an heirloom may be any one of thousands of varieties that have evolved since the cultivation of tomatoes began about five hundred years ago.

An heirloom is not a particular tomato; to have a sense of the characteristics of different ones, I can't imagine a better tasting project than setting out a selection of tomatoes ranging in size and color and sampling them. There are some as tiny and bright as berries and just as sweet; others that have tart, citrusy flavors; and some that are bright green or dark brown even when ripe. See what's available when you explore the farmers' market and take advantage of the bounty that is moving in, even to supermarkets.

During the Katchkie Farm Tomato Festival we show off the diverse flavors and textures of nine tomato varieties: Sungold, Mountain Fresh, Cherokee Purple, San Marzano, Favorita, Primetime, Black Krim, Sunshine, and Juliet. And within a day or so off the vine, they make their way onto the menus and plates of restaurants and homes all the way downriver to the city.

We get a jump on our tomato season by planting in-ground seedlings in our two greenhouses by April. By mid-May, the plants are almost thigh high with green fruit. By June we are lucky enough to feast on local, luscious tomatoes. It is worth the incredible effort and quite amazing to watch as they grow in vinelike fashion, tethered to string suspended from the ceiling beams; they continue to thrive in the greenhouses through September.

As fanatically devoted as I am to local tomatoes in their season, there are some I find quite acceptable in the off-season. There are cherry, Roma (plum), and grape varieties, sometimes on the vine, from Mexico and Israel and some from Holland. And I have noticed more and more locally grown hydroponic tomatoes in the markets. Some of these may not be truly ripe when they hit the market, so leave them out for a few days to develop their full flavor. My practice is to never put tomatoes into the refrigerator unless they are at the point of becoming overripe; at that point, sauce is on the way.

I use beefsteak types for sandwiches and salads, especially Caprese salad—we get wonderful fresh locally made mozzarella for that, and, of course, we have plenty of basil. A plate of mixed sizes and types, in colors from yellow to streaky green to purple-red nearly as dark as an eggplant, is as beautiful as food can be, and with some really good olive oil and a pinch of sea salt, defines simple elegance. Tomatoes also lend themselves to "putting by"; we have a plum variety that we use in our Katchkie Pasta Sauce and other Katchkie artisanal products, like Katchkie Farm Ketchup (page 311), Tomato Preserves (page 313), and Pickled Green Tomatoes (page 321).

4. Rachel's Famous Multigenerational Coleslaw

Rachel is my sister, and she is the originator of what has become the family coleslaw. In most families, we talk about recipes that have been handed down through generations, with grandmothers looming large, but we rarely realize that we also may be creating our own heirlooms. It's a nice thought.

During the sharing or handing down, the next cook in the line might put her own spin on a recipe. For instance, I sometimes use half red and half green cabbage in this coleslaw; usually both are available. And I might add a cup or two of thinly sliced bell peppers for color and crunch or shredded carrots or celery; scallions or radishes; roughly chopped parsley and minced onion. Caraway or fennel seeds can be tossed in. I've heard of pineapple in coleslaw, but I don't think I can go there.

Yogurt can be substituted for all or part of the mayonnaise.   SERVES 6 TO 8

1 large head green cabbage
   (about 2 pounds)
1 bunch dill, chopped
1 or 2 carrots, shredded
   (optional)
Salt
1 teaspoon sugar
½ cup cider vinegar
½ cup mayonnaise

Cut the cabbage into quarters and remove the core. Place each wedge, cut side down, on a cutting board, then cut into thin slices with a large sharp knife; cut the strips in half.

Toss the cut cabbage in a large bowl with the dill, carrots, if using, a pinch of salt, and sugar, then pour the vinegar over everything. Add the mayonnaise, and toss well.

Taste and adjust the seasonings. The slaw can be served immediately or kept, covered, in the refrigerator for up to 3 hours in advance. (I find that letting it sit for at least an hour or two helps saturate the flavors. And when I do have leftovers, they are relished the next day as well.)

5. Daikon Salad

This is a bright refreshing concoction that I like as a salad or a condiment to serve with fish, grilled chicken, or meat. Its cool flavors make a nice foil to spicy dishes.   SERVES 2 TO 4

1 medium daikon, thinly
   sliced in rounds
1 large Watermelon radish,
   thinly sliced, then sliced
   again in half moons
1 Asian pear, skin on, cored,
   quartered, and thinly sliced
1 orange, peeled and
   sectioned
Juice of 1 orange
3 tablespoons extra-virgin
   olive oil
1 tablespoon rice wine
   vinegar
Salt and freshly ground
   pepper
1 tablespoon chopped
   cilantro
2 chopped scallions, white
   and green parts

Combine the daikon, radish, pear, and orange sections and toss with half the orange juice in a large bowl.

Whisk the olive oil, vinegar, and remaining orange juice together and season to taste with salt and pepper.

Pour the dressing over the daikon mixture and toss. Place the salad in the refrigerator for an hour or two before serving. Garnish with the cilantro and scallions.

The Watermelon radish is pretty in this salad and has a good sharp flavor, but other varieties can be used, including icicles. The Watermelon radish is larger than many others, so if you do substitute smaller radishes, use three or four.

6. Spring Radish Salad with Asparagus and Blood Oranges

At Katchkie Farm, we make this refreshing salad with Easter Egg radishes, small, brightly colored, flavor-packed ones that are among our earliest spring crops, but any variety can be substituted. We also use the tiny "micro" arugula grown at the farm, so look for the smallest, most peppery arugula around. This is a perfect dish to begin a spring dinner.

Depending on where you live, blood oranges may not be available; regular navel oranges can be substituted.   SERVES 4

1 bunch Easter Egg or other radishes
12 slender green asparagus spears
Salt
1 tablespoon fresh lemon juice
½ cup plus 2 tablespoons extra-virgin olive oil
2 blood oranges, peeled and pith removed, sectioned
½ cup raw pistachios
Freshly ground pepper
3 tablespoons blood orange juice
1 teaspoon champagne or white wine vinegar
1 teaspoon minced shallot
1 cup micro arugula or smallest available

Preheat the oven to 350 degrees.

Wash and trim the radishes, cutting off the tail ends and leaves but retaining a little of the green tops. Cut each radish into four wedges and set aside.

Pour about a quart of water into a skillet or shallow pan and bring to a boil. Trim the ends of the asparagus and peel the lower half. Add a big pinch of salt to the boiling water, reduce the heat, and add the asparagus. Blanch the asparagus for about 3 minutes, then drain and quickly plunge the stalks into a bowl of ice water to stop the cooking. Drain and set the asparagus aside.

Meanwhile, spread the pistachios on a baking sheet and toast them in the oven for 4 minutes.

Whisk together the lemon juice and 1 tablespoon of the oil. Combine the radishes, oranges, and pistachios in a bowl and toss with the oil and lemon juice; season with salt and pepper to taste.

Whisk together the blood orange juice, vinegar, shallot, and a pinch of salt; slowly whisk in the remaining ½ cup plus 1 tablespoon olive oil and season to taste with pepper and additional salt as needed. Gently toss the asparagus with this dressing and divide them among four plates. Spoon the radish mixture over the asparagus and top with the arugula. The salad also can be arranged on a platter and served at the table.

RADISHES

The radish display that now appears at farm stands and Greenmarkets can lure any passersby, children included. For most of us, the round red ones, the Cherry Belle and Champion, crisp and medium-sharp, have been with us always. Now you may also find the more peppery White Icicle, the size and shape of a little carrot, or the pretty French Breakfast, also elongated but rosy-red and white-tipped. The French Breakfast is mild enough for, yes, the breakfast table: spread good sweet butter on a slice of baguette or other sturdy bread, top it with thin slices of radish, and sprinkle on coarse salt. The French Breakfast radish is a classic picnic item and particularly nice with hard-cooked eggs.

We have Easter Egg radishes at Katchkie, a mix of different colors—white, pink, red, purple—that all grow together. This is a good candidate for a children's garden; you can buy the seed mix and grow Easter Eggs easily, even in containers, then wait to see what exciting colors pop through the soil.

April Cross, a kind of daikon, is the size and shape of a large white carrot, and mild, crisp, and versatile—it is good raw, steamed, or stir-fried. Purple or Purple Plum is small and vividly colored; it's another medium-spicy type of radish that retains its crispness well.

But nothing, to me, equals the Watermelon radish. This is quite the little flirt (though it can grow nearly to the size of a baseball), with a demure white or whitish-green exterior that reveals a shocking fuchsia interior that may go straight to the edge or be ringed by white. In any case, a peppery Watermelon radish is a delight to slice and combine with thinly sliced onions and a splash of orange juice.

I sometimes add a bit of spice in the form of crushed red chile flakes or minced hot fresh pepper to radish salads, to emphasize the spiciness and to play off the sweetness of both.

If you and your children do come upon a few varieties of radishes at the farmers' market, seize the moment for a tasting and compare the range of sweet, sharp, and peppery tastes. It's not just about radishes, though they make good subjects: every time you do this you build your children's awareness of food and flavor, and the language we use (see page xvi) expands their food understanding.

Finally, don't ignore radish tops. If they are young and tender, they can go into a salad. And look for radish sprouts—they can be quite peppery; they are terrific with chicken or egg salad, on soup or fish dishes, or used as a garnish on a pureed potato, leek, lettuce, or pea soup.

7. Watermelon Radish "Ravioli"

We make these at Great Performances as well as at the Sylvia Center, and they are always a hit: two thin slices of watermelon radish sandwiching a simple combination of fresh ricotta, chopped pine nuts, and basil. This is fun for kids to make. A responsible grown-up should slice the radishes (a mandoline is good for this). Let the kids mix up the filling and spoon a scant teaspoonful on one slice of radish, then place another slice over it. Finally, they can press around the edges to seal the slices. These "ravioli" are nice with lunch or on an appetizer salad, especially one made with lots of fresh herbs.

And why not encourage the children to invent their own fillings—cream cheese and chives, anyone?

8. Braised Radishes

Don't limit your radish dishes to raw ones. Radishes are delicious when gently braised, just long enough to emphasize their complex flavors and to soften them slightly. This treatment was inspired many years ago by Craig Claiborne. Wash and trim a bunch of radishes, cut them in half lengthwise, then sauté them with a minced shallot in a bit of butter, a tablespoon of honey, and some salt and pepper for a minute or so. Add ¼ cup chicken stock, simmer for 5 minutes, and top with chopped parsley or chives.

9. Katchkie Farm Spinach and Strawberry Salad

This salad is pretty, delicious, and nutritious. Even kids who resist any green food as a matter of policy like it, if—at least at first—only for the novelty. It is not a surprise to us to discover how much children themselves are amazed by their enjoyment of spinach. Poor spinach—vilified in cartoons and the media, but actually quite delicious raw, especially when we are eating it straight from the fields.

This recipe is a good example of the versatility of strawberries. We think of them as a fruit and use them mostly in desserts. They are in a category known as "false berry," because they bear their seeds—on average, about two hundred per berry—on their skins, rather than within, like a true berry. Strawberries also are delicious when pickled, which we do when we have a bumper crop (page 322).   SERVES 4

1 tablespoon champagne or
   white wine vinegar
1 tablespoon raspberry
   vinegar
1 teaspoon Dijon mustard
½ shallot, finely chopped
Salt and freshly ground
   pepper
2 tablespoons extra-virgin
   olive oil
½ pound baby spinach, stems
   trimmed and washed
1 cup thinly sliced
   strawberries
⅓ cup sliced almonds,
   toasted
2 ounces feta cheese, diced or
   crumbled

Whisk the vinegars, mustard, and shallot together in a large serving bowl. Add salt and pepper to taste. Drizzle in the oil while whisking.

Add the spinach, strawberries, almonds, and feta cheese to the vinaigrette, toss to combine, and serve.

STRAWBERRIES

Today's garden strawberries were first cultivated in Brittany, France, in 1740, from two strains from the New World—one from North America, the other from Chile. Together these gave the modern strawberry its flavor and size. Earlier strawberries were the little woodland varieties that you still may find locally (in New England perhaps) or in France or Italy, usually in early spring. A delicious kind grows in the hills above Rome that are simply served with a spritz of lemon juice and a touch of sugar. The American Alpine is similar, about the size of your pinkie fingernail and with a bright clean taste. Imagine my surprise to see them growing one particularly mild October, giving the gift of a second season.

Strawberries are very low in calories—only about forty-five in a cup—and high in vitamins, especially vitamin C. They are also easy to grow if you have a sunny spot and well-drained soil. For the home garden there are several strawberries that bear fruit for two or three weeks in June and others that continue through the season; Everbearing, for instance, produces two or three harvests a season, and Day Neutral yields fruit throughout the growing season. Some types of strawberries grow on runners, but others are more contained, making them good candidates for planting in pots on decks and terraces.

The strawberry is an excellent first crop for young gardeners because their efforts will be easily rewarded with a bounty of treats. And a decent strawberry harvest can lead to culinary lessons like biscuit making and cream whipping, and then to the ultimate reward of shortcake.

10. Salade Monique

Monique was the mother of Eric Ripert. By the time he was twenty-nine, Eric was the executive chef of Le Bernardin in New York City and the restaurant had won its four-star rating from *The New York Times;* nearly twenty years and several critics later, those stars still stand. Eric had many brilliant mentors, but the first was Monique. "Be a chef and you can be anything," she told him when he was just a boy. Monique shopped every day at the markets: "I don't think she set foot in a grocery store, ever," Eric says. "Whenever I am pulling the ingredients together in a big bowl—blanched and raw vegetables, apples, avocado, radishes, potatoes, haricots verts, corn, all from a roadside market—I recognize where this salad comes from."

Salade Monique is a terrific first course to just about any meal. With cheese and good bread, it makes a satisfying lunch. It also can accompany cold grilled or roasted chicken or seafood, or a casual supper of sandwiches or soup.

If you don't have enough pots for blanching the vegetables all at the same time, they can be cooked consecutively in the same pot, in fresh batches of water. Using fresh water for each vegetable keeps their flavors distinct.   SERVES 4 TO 6

½ pound small potatoes

Salt

¼ pound haricots verts (see Note), trimmed

¼ pound asparagus tips

1 ear corn, shucked

2½ tablespoons balsamic vinegar

6 tablespoons extra-virgin olive oil

½ pound fresh mesclun

¼ unwaxed cucumber, cut in half and thinly sliced

Place the potatoes and 2 tablespoons salt in a small pot of cold water. Bring the water to a boil over high heat, reduce the heat, and simmer until the potatoes are just tender when pierced, about 15 minutes. Drain and set the potatoes in the refrigerator to cool. When the potatoes are cool, peel and thinly slice them.

Meanwhile, place three more pots of water to boil over high heat (see above). When the water is boiling, add a pinch of salt to each pot, drop the haricots verts, asparagus, and the ear of corn into separate pots, and reduce the heat to a simmer. Cook the haricots verts for about 4 minutes, the asparagus and corn for about 3 minutes; they all should be tender but still a bit crisp. Drain the vegetables and refresh them under cold water or in an ice bath. Cut the corn kernels from the cob.

12 grape tomatoes, halved

2 scallions, white parts only, thinly sliced

2 radishes, thinly sliced

½ ripe avocado, thinly sliced

½ apple, thinly sliced

½ sweet long green ("banana") pepper (see page 113), finely diced

Fine sea salt and freshly ground white pepper

Whisk together the vinegar and olive oil. Place the mesclun in a big bowl, and add the cucumber, tomatoes, scallions, radishes, avocado, apple, and banana pepper. Before serving, add in the cooked vegetables. Season with sea salt and pepper to taste, drizzle with the dressing, toss, and divide among individual plates or serve at the table.

The cooked ingredients can be prepared in advance and kept at room temperature until you are ready to toss them together and serve the salad.

Keep the unused half of the avocado, still on the pit, snugly wrapped in plastic wrap. A drizzle of lemon juice will help keep it from discoloring.

GREEN BEANS

Haricots verts is French for green beans, but the term usually also refers to a slightly longer and thinner variety than the more familiar American sort.

Any good fresh green beans in season can be substituted for the haricots verts in Salade Monique; they can be "filleted" or "Frenched" by slicing them lengthwise if they are thicker than you like,

or cut diagonally in two or three places. You also may find "filet" beans, especially in the spring and summer at farm stands or farmers' markets. They are similar to haricots verts and very delicious; make them your first choice when they are in season.

Haricots verts and their less glamorous cousin the plain green bean provide a great opportunity for little hands—trimming their tops, and nibbling now and then, is easy work.

MESCLUN

The word "mesclun" is the Provençal word for specific combinations of small greens and herbs that are grown together for salads, carefully picked over, and sold already washed. American growers vary their mixtures and usually include a couple of peppery varieties, such as baby arugula and watercress, as well as herbs like basil, parsley, chervil, and sometimes edible flowers like nasturtiums and chive blossoms. I like the notion of using what's in sea-

son and local for mesclun mixes, but I don't like to see those commercial combinations that include what are obviously torn bits from full-size lettuces. So inspect mesclun mixes carefully, especially the ones that come prepackaged. Mesclun can seem expensive, but a fine batch will have no waste and be delicious.

11. Herb Salad

I adore this lovely mixture, which can be served as a salad on its own or can be mixed with lettuces. The formula here is simply a departure point for what you've got in your own herb garden. An herb salad is more than a garnish, and particularly nice on top of grilled fish or a chicken cutlet; alongside smoked fish; sprinkled over a cold or pureed vegetable soup; on a salad of roasted beets with fresh goat cheese; in a sandwich; or with eggs. I like it best if the leaves are left whole.   MAKES ABOUT 4½ CUPS; SERVES 4

Leaves from 1 bunch fresh
   chervil
Leaves from 1 bunch fresh
   flat-leaf parsley
1 bunch fresh chives
Leaves from ¼ bunch fresh
   mint
Vinaigrette or extra-virgin
   olive oil and lemon juice
   to dress

Wash and dry the herbs. Snip or slice the chives about ¼ inch long. Toss everything together and dress gently with your favorite vinaigrette, or just a light sprinkle of good olive oil and a spritz of lemon juice.

12. Fennel, Celeriac, and Parsley Salad in Lemon-Caper Dressing

What a wonderful combination of flavors this is. Various versions of this salad have become popular recently, but I like to grill the fennel to bring out its sweetness and achieve more contrast with the celeriac. This is good on its own and lovely with fish, cooked or cured salmon in particular.

I like to shred the celeriac with a food processor to give it a soft, noodlelike texture. If you do it by hand, strive for the thinnest possible slices.   SERVES 4 TO 6

3 medium fennel bulbs

5 tablespoons extra-virgin olive oil

Salt and freshly ground pepper

1 celeriac, trimmed (see opposite page)

Leaves from 1 bunch flat-leaf parsley

2 tablespoons capers, rinsed

2 tablespoons fresh lemon juice

Fire up a stovetop grill or grill pan or preheat your broiler.

Trim the fennel at both ends and remove any tough-looking or discolored outer pieces. Cut the bulbs into four vertical wedges, then toss with 1 tablespoon of the olive oil and season with salt and pepper. When the grill or broiler is ready, cook the fennel in a single layer, spreading the slices, just a few minutes, until it is tender and becomes fragrant. Set the fennel aside.

Fit a food processor with the coarse shredding attachment. Trim the celeriac to fit into the feed tube and shred; you should have about 1½ cups.

Chop enough of the parsley to make about ¼ cup, along with 1 tablespoon of the capers, until they become a loose paste. (To intensify their flavors, use the side of a chef's knife to smash some of the parsley with some of the capers.) Whisk the remaining 4 tablespoons olive oil and the lemon juice together well, then stir in the parsley-caper mixture and the remaining 1 tablespoon capers.

Toss the fennel, celeriac, and remaining parsley leaves together. Toss again with the dressing. Adjust to taste with salt, pepper, and lemon juice.

CELERIAC, OR CELERY ROOT

Celeriac, also known as celery root, is a kind of celery, but it is not, as some people assume, the root of the familiar celery plant. Celeriac is versatile, good in gratins and stews. We often add it for flavor and body to the vegetable soups we make with the children (they love how weird-looking a celery root is). Celeriac can be sliced or cut into thick sticks and roasted in a 400-degree oven until lightly browned, about 20 minutes, turning once.

Celeriac seems like a bit of a nuisance to clean, but it's worth the effort. The knobby or indented areas can simply be sliced away. (I use a sharp knife, but a sturdy vegetable peeler can work as well.) Unlike some other root vegetables, celeriac is very low in starch as well as calories, and can be kept for a long time, even as long as a couple of months, in a plastic bag to keep it from drying out, and refrigerated.

IDEAS FOR CELERIAC: A classic preparation is celeriac remoulade, a fixture of the French bistro menu. To make it, cut raw celeriac into fine sticks and toss them in a mustardy vinaigrette. Try variations on this theme in dishes like the one here.

Combine some celeriac sticks with carrot and celery sticks in your child's lunch box, or serve them up with a dip, such as the Hummus (page 308) we make at the Sylvia Center, for a nourishing afternoon snack. Another little treat from celeriac is chips! We slice it thinly on the mandoline and then fry the slices quickly in vegetable oil. Or try brushing them lightly with oil and baking them, spread out on a baking sheet, for 10 or 15 minutes in a hot oven—375 to 400 degrees—checking after a few minutes to be sure they don't burn.

Katchkie Favorites

13. Down on the Farm Pasta Salad

This is what I mean by "local": Everything for this dish came from within a stone's throw of Katchkie Farm. We bought wheat from our neighbors at Lightning Tree Farm, ground it into flour, and then used it to make our own whole-wheat fettuccine.

The rest was easy.

We cooked about a pound of the fettuccine and tossed it with what was just then growing at Katchkie: a couple bunches of quartered baby radishes, two seeded and diced cucumbers, two pints of split cherry tomatoes, and a pound of small-leaf spinach (we used Red Bordeaux).

We dressed it all with a vinaigrette made with our own vinegar—made from the nearby Brotherhood Winery's red wine—and crumbled Coach Farm's goat cheese on top (Coach Farm is another Hudson Valley neighbor). It was a hearty, healthy, delicious main course for six.

Even without handmade pasta and vinegar, any home cook can genuinely duplicate this. Whole-wheat pasta is readily available in supermarkets; there even are some organic brands. Short shapes like penne and fusilli also are good for this dish. You can vary the rest of the ingredients as you like with whatever looks most fresh at a farmers' market or the supermarket. Wherever you do it, let your children help with the gathering and selecting of the raw ingredients. Children become quite proprietary when they're in on planning a meal. It makes them want to eat it.

Toss the salad with your own good dressing. I recommend a fresh cheese like the one we used; fresh sheep's milk cheese or grated ricotta salata also would be delicious.

American Cheese

Happily, "American cheese" has taken on new meaning in the last twenty years or so. Slices of unnaturally colorful, bland, and single-wrapped slices no longer define our cheese. Traditional, handcrafted cheeses can be found from where we are in the Northeast to the Pacific Northwest. For example, Vermont is home to some really marvelous artisan cheese makers, and some of these small operations have emerged into sizable companies. The Old Chatham Sheepherding Company is a good example: Old Chatham combines state-of-the-art techniques and a gorgeous setting, near us in Columbia County. Visitors are welcome—children can see the sheep, the baby lambs, the occasional donkey, and, if the timing is right, they may catch the dogs herding the sheep out to the field.

A visit to a cheese farm can introduce children to one of the most fascinating methods of making food. Like bread and wine, cheese making is ancient, and subject to conditions that cannot be fully controlled by humans: the earth, the water, and the bacteria in the air all affect the outcome. There is magic involved. A taste test of cheese samples can be revealing for children as well as adults. Compare cheeses from different animals—cow, goat, sheep—and finish with a couple of processed types. If you've ever enjoyed a cheese plate in a good restaurant, you will know to start with the milder varieties, like a fresh goat cheese, and move on to richer and more aged cheeses, including blue-veined ones.

14. Roasted Poblano, Red, and Yellow Pepper Salad with Raisins and Basil

I love raw peppers best of all—they are so fresh and juicy. But I must admit that roasting enhances the complexity and sweetness of the flesh. The texture is so different, almost meaty, from the crispness of raw peppers.   SERVES 4 TO 6

1 cup dry white wine

2 tablespoons golden raisins

2 poblano peppers

2 red bell peppers

2 yellow bell peppers

2 cups baby arugula

Leaves from 1 large bunch
basil, torn into pieces

2 garlic cloves, minced

Pinch of crushed red chile
flakes, or more to taste

3 tablespoons extra-virgin
olive oil

3 tablespoons balsamic
vinegar

Salt and freshly ground
pepper

Bring the wine to a simmer in a small pot, add the raisins, then remove the pot from the heat and set it aside to let the raisins plump for about 15 minutes.

Char all the peppers, either over an open fire, under your broiler, or directly on the gas flame on your stovetop. After they are charred, place them in a bowl, cover with a towel, and let the peppers cool. Peel and seed the peppers over a bowl to catch any juices; the charred skin comes off easily with a paring knife, but don't worry if you don't get every bit. Cut the peppers into ¼-inch-thick strips.

Drain the raisins and toss them together with the peppers, arugula, basil, garlic, and red chile flakes. Whisk together the oil, vinegar, and any accumulated liquid from the charred peppers; pour the dressing over the salad and season with salt and pepper to taste. Serve immediately.

The raisins and peppers can be prepared in advance and kept at room temperature for several hours before the dish is assembled.

15. Sweet Corn, Fava Bean, and Shiitake Salad

We began to grow fava beans at Katchkie Farm a few years ago, but we do not have a huge crop, so I tend to indulge in them whenever they appear in the garden. When they are very fresh and tiny, favas need no cooking at all. Do as the Italians do: just dress them with really good olive oil and a sprinkle of sea salt. This salad is similarly simple and elegant, with delicate flavors punctuated by a bit of mint and lemon juice. You can use a different kind of mushroom if you like, but the shiitake has a particularly good texture—slightly meaty—that goes well with the corn and fava beans. SERVES 4 TO 6

2 pounds fava bean pods

Salt

4 ears corn

3 tablespoons extra-virgin olive oil

2 cups (about 6 ounces) shiitake mushrooms, stems removed at the cap, sliced about $\frac{1}{4}$ inch thick

1 scallion, white and light green parts, sliced

1 tablespoon chopped mint

1 tablespoon fresh lemon juice

Freshly ground pepper

Put a large pot of water over medium-high heat. When it comes to a boil, throw in the pods and a pinch of salt; drain after 30 seconds and immediately refresh the pods under cold water. Refill the pot and return it to the heat to come to a boil. Prepare a large bowl of ice water.

Remove the corn kernels from the cobs by holding the cobs on their ends and slicing downward. You should have about $1\frac{1}{2}$ cups.

Remove the beans from their pods and then carefully peel away the thin silky covering over the beans themselves. (The beans are formed of two halves that may separate, but don't fret if they do.) You should have about $1\frac{1}{2}$ cups. Depending on their size, the beans may be tender enough to use at this point; try one and if you find it still too firm, drop them, along with the corn kernels, into the boiling water for 30 seconds to a minute, until both are just tender. Drain the corn and the beans and immediately plunge them into the ice water to stop the cooking.

Pour 2 tablespoons of the olive oil into a hot pan and sauté the mushrooms until just tender, about 3 minutes, then let them cool to room temperature. Place the drained beans, corn, and mushrooms in a bowl with the scallion and the mint. Add the remaining tablespoon olive oil and the lemon juice and season with salt and a bit of pepper;

gently combine everything, then taste and adjust the seasonings as you like. Serve at room temperature.

The components of this salad can be prepared a few hours in advance and kept at room temperature, but keep the mushrooms separate from the corn and fava beans. Cover the dishes loosely with paper towels or kitchen towels until you execute the final steps.

Generally speaking, the cooking time for favas will relate to their size, but that time will never be very long, so be on the alert or you will have mushy beans.

FAVA BEANS

Fava beans are one of the oldest cultivated beans, going back thousands of years; wild favas no longer even exist. Favas go by many names around the world, including broad beans, English beans, and field beans. The fava is related to the pea, but delivers a more assertive and distinct flavor. And the fava is incredibly nutritious, packed with phosphorus, potassium, vitamin K, vitamin A, and iron.

Favas also are marketed dry, sometimes even from a local grower when the season is over; try them in a winter soup in place of dried limas or other beans.

Soups

My grandmothers were unlike each other in nearly every way, but they both made soups that I remember fondly. Grandma Nelly came to America from Russia as a young woman. We loved her stories of her early years in New York, especially about singing in the Yiddish theaters that flourished on the Lower East Side. Nelly was a lively woman and a spirited cook, and you could hear her song in her food, especially her soups. For my grandfather, soup could never be too hot, so there was always great concern about the temperature and getting the soup to the table before it began to cool even a little. Nelly's soups were thick and chunky (I guess they would be classified as peasant soups), and I doubt she ever consulted a recipe.

My second-generation American grandma, whom we called Grandma Kramer (though her first name was Sylvia), made the same soup week after week. It was a classic chicken soup with dainty pieces of carrots and celery. The luxurious shimmer of golden stock, with whatever was floating in it, always meant a special treat was just moments away. Along with the soups they made, I enjoyed the different worlds inhabited by my grandmothers equally.

Not surprisingly, soup was my own portal to cooking; my best first experiments in the kitchen involved soup. I also have always been drawn to ingredients as perfect soup makings, from fragrant fresh herbs to the stunning and colorful array of vegetables each season offers. As my love of soup intersected with my addiction to local vegetables and the CSA shares I brought home every week, I discovered dozens of ways to turn my bounty into luscious easy meals.

In the beginning, I followed recipes, learning the basics and useful tricks, like adding some rice or a small potato to thicken pureed vegetable soups. I've been able to apply the principles to my own many variations. The possibilities of soup are endless. They can be hot or cold, thick or clear, meat or vegetarian, elegant or hearty, first course or main dish—or dessert for that matter (page 46). And I think for a beginner or otherwise anxious cook, soup making is pretty forgiving.

At the Sylvia Center, the children love making soup above all else. Whenever they visit, there is a harvest haul that can be turned into a pot of soup. Anna Hammond, the executive director of the center, has a theory about the appeal of soup: though children are often quite adamant about keeping the different foods on their plates separate from one another, they love soup. They love harvesting and chopping up the veggies and through some alchemy turning them into a whole other thing.

STOCK ON HAND

A good, fresh chicken stock is not only essential to endless dishes, such as stews and other braises, it also is dead easy to make. Next time you roast or broil a chicken, keep the bones; they are full of potential flavor and nutrition. I stockpile bones in plastic bags in the freezer until I have enough for a big pot of stock. (We do this at the Sylvia Center as a way of showing children how to avoid wasting good food.) Don't forget to get the backbone when you have a chicken cut up and to cut off wing tips and add them to your hoard. Above all, include giblets, the chicken's innards, along with the neck; these may be in a packet inside the bird that includes the neck; throw everything except the liver into the stock for a big wallop of extra flavor. (A turkey neck and giblets are the best beginning for successful gravy.)

For a basic chicken stock, just add some chopped carrot, celery, onion, a couple of garlic cloves, and parsley—I save the stems for stock. Put everything in a pot, pour in water to barely cover, and that's it; in a couple of hours you will have the beginning of a good pot of soup.

I make my vegetable stock in a similar way, warehousing trimmings from prepping ingredients through the week in plastic bags or in milk cartons with their tops cut off. Trimmings from onions, fresh carrot tops—so full of flavor that it's as though you have carrots in the pot—green leafy vegetables, lettuces, bits from parsley and other herbs are tossed in. Add just about anything except cabbage, which is too emphatic for broth. My secret ingredients are the trimmed tops and cores from bell peppers, which add a lovely sweetness. Add additional vegetables if you haven't enough trimmings, and a bay leaf or two. For me, making vegetable stock is even more important than chicken stock, because it's harder to find good ready made.

Strain and cool stock to room temperature and store it for a few days in the refrigerator or for a few months in the freezer.

Soup is simple, and has humble beginnings. Your own good stock will make it special but one of the good, organic brands now available can also be fine. In any case, I begin a pot by sautéing up the usual chopped ingredients—exact measurements aren't necessary—for four to six servings: one to two stalks of celery, a medium carrot, one half of a large onion, and a clove of garlic and you're on the way. I love to browse through cookbooks and magazines for fresh soup ideas, but don't be hindered by the lack of one ingredient or another. Turn to your larder and grab those split peas, navy beans, or grains like farro and barley and go to your refrigerator for greens. Tomatoes, canned or fresh, are good with many combinations, especially beans, and small pasta can be added toward the end of cooking. Winter squashes are splendid in soup (page 50). And a small piece of bacon or pancetta or an andouille or chorizo sausage can add flavor and richness with just a little meat. Always save the rinds from pieces of Parmigiano to throw in the pot—they also can add lots of flavor.

I think making a lot of soup is pretty much the same as making just enough for one meal, so I usually end up with extra and throw a quart or two into the freezer. Then I have something on hand for busy days when making a pot of soup—or, sometimes, anything!—seems daunting.

1. Autumn Leek and Mushroom Bisque

Children often first learn to like mushrooms when they are delivered by soup or sauce. When my generation was growing up, canned mushroom soup was a lunchtime staple—more elegant if diluted with milk rather than water. It also worked its way onto family dinner menus as a sauce for pretty much anything and it was the magic that held lots of casseroles together, taking the place of white sauces and adding flavor.

This version is special, a genuine celebration of a variety of fresh and dried mushrooms. It isn't particularly difficult to make—once you've acquired the ingredients. Yes, it is a bit of a splurge, but it's a lovely way to begin a holiday meal or a special dinner.   SERVES 4 TO 6

3 tablespoons butter

2 shallots, sliced

1½ cups cleaned and chopped leeks, white part and an inch or two of green (reserve the rest of the stalk for stock, page 38)

2 sprigs fresh rosemary or a few leaves dried

2 sprigs fresh thyme or a few leaves dried

½ cup chanterelle mushrooms

½ cup dried porcini mushrooms

1 cup cremini mushrooms, quartered

1 cup oyster mushrooms, torn into ⅓-inch pieces

5 cups vegetable or chicken stock, homemade (page 38) or good-quality store bought

¼ cup heavy cream (optional)

Salt and freshly ground pepper

1½ tablespoons olive oil

Leaves from 2 or 3 sprigs parsley, roughly chopped

Put the butter in a large pot over medium-high heat. Add the shallots, leeks, rosemary, and thyme and sauté until the leeks and shallots are soft and the mixture is fragrant.

Add all the mushrooms and stir to combine. Reduce the heat, cover the pan, and cook for about 5 minutes, or until the mushrooms are tender. Remove from the heat and discard the rosemary and thyme sprigs. Add the stock, bring to a simmer, then add the cream and simmer until the soup is hot, about 3 minutes, stirring once or twice.

Season to taste with salt and pepper. Drizzle with the olive oil and sprinkle the parsley over the soup.

You can substitute for any of the types of mushrooms, as long as you end up with the total amount here. Cremini or a combination of cremini and white cultivated mushrooms is good.

2. Broccoli Soup

A simple, sturdy soup, this is good for family lunch or makes a cozy supper with cheese and bread. When the local broccoli crop is new, you may find farm stands offering sweet florets, which make this even tastier, and easier.

My kids love cheese melted into soup. Broccoli takes well to this embellishment, as does tomato. Cheddar, Swiss, and Monterey Jack are particularly good; use the coarse holes on a box grater and grate straight onto the bowls of hot soup, or pass a bowl of shredded cheese at the table.   SERVES 4 TO 6

2 teaspoons olive oil

1 medium onion, finely chopped (about ¾ cup)

2 celery stalks, finely chopped (about 1 cup)

1 medium Yukon Gold potato, peeled and cubed

4 cups chopped broccoli, including stems

4 cups vegetable stock, homemade (page 38) or good-quality store bought

1 cup milk

Kosher salt and freshly ground pepper

Fresh lemon juice (optional)

Heat the oil in a large pot over medium heat. Add the onion and celery and gently sauté until the onion is soft, but not browned, 3 to 4 minutes. Add the potato and broccoli to the pot; pour in the stock and milk. Bring the mixture just to a boil, then reduce the heat, cover, and simmer for 20 minutes, until the vegetables are quite tender.

Set the soup aside to cool slightly, then blend it, in batches, in a food processor or in a blender, until it is as smooth as you like. Return the soup to the pot and heat gently before serving, seasoning with salt and pepper to taste. If you like, add a tablespoon or two of lemon juice to brighten the flavor.

An immersion blender, a kind of hand-held food processor, can also be used to puree the soup, although the texture will not be as smooth. An immersion blender lets you puree soup—or anything else—simply by plunging it into the pot or bowl holding your concoction; you can skip the steps and cleanup involved with a processor. There are several good models on the market, some with attachments for whisking or chopping, and even cordless. As with a food processor, always let hot ingredients cool down a bit before pureeing.

3. Hudson Valley Corn Bisque

Wherever corn is grown in this country, the locals are fully convinced that theirs is the finest. That is the point of view of my family and, as far as I can tell, all our Hudson Valley neighbors. I think this just speaks to the magic of summer; everything is so beautiful and special, right there before our eyes.

The typical impulse regarding corn is to have it as often as possible before it goes out of season. For us, this almost always means simply boiled or grilled and eaten off the cob. But we do manage the occasional departure, like this soup.   SERVES 4

4 ears corn
1 tablespoon butter
1 cup chopped celery
1 cup chopped onion
1 small carrot, chopped
3 cups chicken or vegetable
    stock, homemade (page 38)
    or good-quality store
    bought
1 cup heavy cream
Kosher salt and freshly
    ground white pepper
Dash of Tabasco or similar
    hot pepper sauce
1 thinly sliced scallion

Remove the corn kernels from the cobs with a sharp knife. Use the back of the knife to scrape any juices from the cobs into a bowl; reserve the cobs.

Slowly melt the butter in a large pot over medium heat. Add the celery, onion, and carrot. Cook until the onions are translucent. Add the corn juices and the chicken stock and simmer for 10 minutes. Add the corncobs and simmer for 45 minutes longer. Remove and discard the cobs and pour in the cream; simmer for 10 minutes.

Remove the pot from the heat and let the contents cool slightly. Transfer the soup to a blender or food processor, and, working in small batches, blend until smooth. Return the soup to the pot, add the corn kernels, and simmer for 5 minutes before serving. Season to taste with salt and pepper and dashes of hot sauce.

The soup can be prepared in advance to the point of adding the corn kernels; bring it slowly back to the simmer before you do. Sprinkle the scallion on the soup and serve.

The Language of Cooking: *Bisque*

Strictly speaking, this is not a true bisque, which in classic French cooking refers to a rich soup based on a broth derived from the shells of crustaceans. Until about twenty years ago, "lobster" was the word that almost always came before "bisque." The shells were sautéed; broth, wine, and seasonings were added to the pot and then cooked to extract their flavor; the broth was then strained and thickened with cream. At first, bisque was a frugal way to get every bit of flavor from seafood, but in time it became a dish that defined elegant dining, and was a staple of "Continental" restaurants, especially when a few choice bits of lobster meat were added. Today all sorts of thickened soups are referred to as bisques, even when they don't contain cream.

4. Chilled Cumin-Spiked Tomato Soup

A touch of cumin and a dollop of cilantro-spiked yogurt deliver a hint of Indian flavor to this soup; it also is nearly free of fat and very low in calories. This requires no cooking skills whatsoever—or cooking at all for that matter—but fully ripe tomatoes are essential. The rich Greek yogurt thickens the soup slightly and rounds out the flavors.

SERVES 4 TO 6

2 teaspoons ground cumin

2 pounds ripe tomatoes, cored and coarsely chopped (about 5 cups)

½ cup chopped red onion

¼ cup plus 2 tablespoons chopped fresh cilantro

Juice of 1 lime

2 teaspoons kosher salt

1 cup Greek yogurt

1 cup ice water (optional)

Toast the cumin in a small skillet over low heat, stirring, just until fragrant, 1 to 2 minutes; do not let it burn. Combine the tomatoes, onion, and 2 tablespoons of the cilantro in a blender or a food processor and puree until smooth. Transfer the mixture to a large bowl; add the toasted cumin, 2 tablespoons lime juice, and salt and stir to combine. Refrigerate the soup until it is thoroughly chilled, at least one hour.

Meanwhile, puree the yogurt and the remaining ¼ cup cilantro in a blender or food processor until smooth. Cover the yogurt and refrigerate until ready to serve. Before serving, adjust the soup to taste with additional salt and lime juice; add ice water as needed if you would like a thinner texture.

Divide the soup among individual bowls and garnish each with a generous swirl of cilantro yogurt.

5. Katchkie Farm Cool Cucumber Yogurt Soup

This soup is about as easy as opening a can, and it is especially good for lunch on a hot day or poured out of a thermos at a picnic; it is so refreshing and satisfying. And if you have cucumbers in your garden, here is a way besides salad or pickles to use your bounty. This recipe can easily be doubled. SERVES 2 TO 4

2¼ cups plain Greek yogurt
1¼ pounds Kirby cucumbers, trimmed, peeled, seeded, and cut into 1-inch pieces
2 garlic cloves, minced
1½ teaspoons salt
1 teaspoon ground cumin
1½ teaspoons curry powder
¼ teaspoon ground ginger
Thinly sliced radishes

Combine all the ingredients except the radishes in a food processor. Puree until smooth, then strain through a fine sieve into a large bowl.

Refrigerate the soup until it is well chilled, about 2 hours or up to a day before serving. Thin the soup with just a small amount of water if it is thicker than you like. Ladle the soup into bowls, top with the radishes, and serve.

6. Melon Soup

This is an all-day delight in hot weather—add yogurt for breakfast or a scoop of sorbet for dessert. Puree about 3 cups of cubed cantaloupe flesh and 3 cups cubed honeydew flesh with a cup of fresh orange juice and the juice of two or three limes in a food processor, in batches if necessary. Pour the mixture into a large bowl and then, if it is thicker than you like, stir in water to reach your preferred consistency. Chill the soup for several hours, overnight if you want it in the morning, and garnish with roughly chopped fresh mint. This makes about six servings.

You—or anyone over the age of about three—can scoop out the flesh of a melon with a melon baller or even a small ice cream scoop. Or cut the melon into quarters, slice along the skin, and cut the flesh into chunks.

7. Chunky Purple Potato and Leek Soup

When the children visit the Sylvia Center in the fall, they make this soup from our late harvest bounty; they start by pulling the potatoes right out of the ground. As they prep the potatoes, they set the eyes aside, and after lunch, we plant them. Then we bring all the trimmings to the compost heap.

In the spring, the group returns to see that a new crop of potatoes is coming in and, by the evidence of rows of leafy greens, that the compost has nourished the fields. In this simple way, the children involve themselves in the cycle of the growing year.

SERVES 4 TO 6

3 tablespoons olive oil

2 large leeks, white part and about 1 inch green, split lengthwise, cleaned and chopped

1 large celeriac, peeled, cut into 8 wedges, and chopped

2 large carrots, peeled and chopped

1 sprig fresh thyme or 1 teaspoon dried

3 cups vegetable stock, homemade (page 38) or good-quality store bought, or 3 cups water

3 or 4 purple or other variety of small potatoes, scrubbed and chopped into 1-inch pieces

2 tablespoons minced fresh flat-leaf parsley

Kosher salt and freshly ground pepper

Heat the olive oil in a large pot over medium heat. Add the leeks and cook for 3 minutes. Add the celery root, carrots, and thyme. Cook until tender, about 15 minutes longer. Add the stock or water and potatoes, cover, and simmer until the potatoes are just tender, about 20 minutes.

Remove 1 cup of the soup and puree it in a blender or food processor. Stir the pureed soup back into the pot. Reheat, add the parsley, season with salt and pepper to taste, and serve.

8. Onion Soup with Apple Cider and Thyme

This recipe comes from Rozanne Gold. Rozanne is among the people I think of as "friends of Katchkie Farm." We first met as food professionals more than twenty years ago and have been friends ever since; she has incredible knowledge of food and shares it generously. Even more, Rozanne's experiences with children and cooking have guided our work at the Sylvia Center.

This soup is delicious as is, with just some fresh thyme leaves and a sprinkling of Parmigiano-Reggiano on top, but it also can be pureed until silky. Be sure to use fresh unpasteurized apple cider, especially in the fall, when fresh cider is abundant at farm stands and farmers' markets. Buy some on an outing with the kids and then involve them in soup making.

SERVES 6

5 large onions (about 1½ pounds)
2 tablespoons unsalted butter
1½ tablespoons olive oil
3 cups chicken or beef stock, homemade (page 38) or good-quality store bought
1¼ cups fresh apple cider
1 bunch fresh thyme
Salt and freshly ground pepper
½ cup freshly grated Parmigiano-Reggiano

Peel the onions and cut them in half through the root end. Place the halves flat on a cutting board and cut across into thin slices (⅛ to ¼ inch thick).

Put the butter and oil in a 4-quart pot over medium heat. When the butter is melted, add the onions and raise the heat to medium-high. Cook the onions, stirring frequently, for at least 20 minutes, until they soften and become very dark brown, raising the heat if necessary. Pay attention—you want a deep caramel color, but if the onions burn, the soup will be bitter. Add the stock and cider to deglaze, scraping up any browned bits, and bring to a rapid boil.

Reduce the heat and add 5 sprigs of thyme; season with salt and pepper to taste. Simmer over medium heat for 25 minutes; adjust the heat as necessary to maintain the soup at a low bubble. Stir often. When ready to serve, remove the sprigs of thyme and garnish with thyme leaves from the remaining sprigs and a sprinkling of cheese.

The Language of Cooking: *Deglazing*

As onions brown, the bottom of your pot will brown, or glaze, along with them. The sugar in the onions has been caramelizing and will be released—deglazed—from the surface of the pot, when you pour in the broth and scrape up the delicious browned bits. Carefully browned onions deepen the flavor and are characteristic of a well-made onion soup.

Deglazing adds flavor to all sorts of preparations, stews and braises in particular. But it is always important to take care when browning ingredients; if you let them burn, the finished dish will have a bitter edge.

Katchkie Favorites

9. Winter Squash and Root Vegetable Soups

These wonderful cold-weather ingredients make for great soups. They are different varieties, but can be treated similarly, so here is my basic method and some variations. For six servings I suggest around two pounds total of whatever squash or root vegetable you are using.

For squash (see page 127 for varieties): Peel and cut in half or quarters, remove the seeds—but save and roast them (page 129)—and any stringy material, and chop the flesh roughly. (The smaller the pieces, the sooner you will have soup.) Alternatively, roast the squash according to the methods on page 80.

For root vegetables (carrots, turnips, parsnips, potatoes): Peel and roughly chop the vegetables into small chunks.

Sauté about one half cup chopped onion or shallot or a combination and one or two cloves of garlic (optional) in about 2 tablespoons butter or olive oil or a combination; a handful of chopped celery and carrots or sliced leeks can be thrown in as well. Cook until soft, but not browned, about 10 minutes.

Add the prepared squash or root vegetables, then stir and sauté for a minute or two. Season with salt and pepper, pour in 4 to 6 cups homemade chicken or vegetable stock (see page 38), store-bought stock, water, or a combination—enough to cover the vegetables by an inch or so. Bring the liquid just to a simmer, reduce the heat, and cook for about 40 minutes, or until everything is quite soft.

Cool the soup a bit, then puree it in a blender or food processor or use an immersion blender.

VARIATIONS

Here are just a few good combinations:

Celeriac root and Yukon Gold potatoes

Carrots with parsnips or celery root

Jerusalem artichokes, or sunchokes, alone or with potatoes; and celery, leeks, or garlic, garnished generously with roughly chopped parsley

White turnips or parsnips with peas: Divide 2 cups blanched freshly shelled peas or a 10-ounce package defrosted frozen peas among individual soup bowls and top with the hot soup.

Here are some ways to flavor your winter soups:

Milk, half-and-half, or low-fat milk can be substituted for part of the liquid; this can make a more svelte and elegant soup for a first course. (Turnips in particular are very good when partially cooked with milk.)

Add herbs like rosemary, sage, parsley, or thyme at the sautéing stage; the finished soup also can be topped with chopped parsley, sage, chervil, or thyme, thinly sliced scallions, or thinly sliced shallots or leeks braised in butter for 5 to 7 minutes.

A mild curry blend, garam masala or your own mix of cloves, cinnamon, cumin, and turmeric, mace, or fennel seeds lend Indian flavors and are nice with a dollop of yogurt and fresh cilantro on top.

Try cumin, oregano, and chili powder, a pinch of red chile flakes, minced jalapeño peppers, or a dash of hot sauce for a Mexican or Southwestern version.

Ginger and a touch of paprika are particularly compatible with carrots and pumpkins.

Here are some garnishes and additions:

Croutons or toasted bread crumbs can be tossed onto the finished soup; or grill or toast slices of a sturdy bread, rub them with garlic, brush them with olive oil, and float them on top.

Shavings of Parmigiano-Reggiano, Cheddar, or Gruyère; blue cheese or Stilton on turnip soup is a great combination.

Dollops of sour cream, crème fraîche, or yogurt

Spoonfuls of Basil Pesto (page 293)

Bits of Caramelized Onion Relish (page 305)

Drizzle of really good olive oil

Cooked navy beans or cannellini beans (especially good with butternut or pumpkin)

Crisp crumbled bacon

Shredded greens like kale, escarole, or chard

Seeded and minced tomatoes

Cooked wild rice, farro or wheat berries, barley or small pasta

10. Fresh Spring Pea Soup

It's impossible to think of a cookbook author who has done more to advance the glory and simple goodness of produce than Deborah Madison, who sent this recipe for *Sylvia's Table*. Deborah was the original chef at the marvelous Greens vegetarian restaurant in San Francisco, but nothing in her work has ever hinted at proselytizing for a vegetarian lifestyle or prescriptive eating. These are important lessons for parents: if good-for-you food also tastes good, a young palate will develop naturally.

This soup is all about the peas, which are cooked briefly in a light stock made mostly from their pods. Plan to serve it as soon as it's finished for the freshest flavor, unless you prefer to serve it cool. Look for the brightest-colored pea pods, and avoid any that seem dry or shriveled. Deborah suggests adding a drop or two of white or black truffle oil if you want to dress this up for a special, upscale dinner, but take care not to overwhelm the clean and simple flavor of fresh peas. SERVES 4 TO 6

1 bunch scallions or 2 small
    cleaned leeks, white and
    2 inches of the green parts,
    thinly sliced
5 large sprigs parsley
Sea salt
1½ pounds bright green peas
    in their pods
1 teaspoon unsalted butter
½ cup thinly sliced onion or
    young leek
Freshly ground white pepper
½ teaspoon sugar
Black or white truffle oil
    (optional)

Bring 1 quart of water to a boil. While the water is heating, add the scallions, parsley, and ½ teaspoon salt. Shell the peas, setting them aside, and add about 3 cups of the pods to the boiling water. Once the water returns to a boil, reduce the heat and simmer for 20 minutes. Strain the stock into a bowl and discard the cooked vegetables.

Melt the butter in a soup pot and add the sliced onion. Cook over medium heat for about a minute, then add ½ cup of the stock to let the onion stew without browning. After 4 to 5 minutes, add the shelled peas, ½ teaspoon salt, pepper to taste, and the sugar. Add 2½ cups of the stock, bring just to a boil, then simmer for 3 minutes.

Transfer the soup to a blender or food processor and puree at high speed for 1 minute until smooth, adding additional stock to achieve your desired consistency. Reheat briefly, if necessary. Pour the soup into small bowls and serve immediately, with drops of truffle oil, if desired.

11. Roasted Beet Soup

This soup has a borschtlike effect from the sour cream and a warm edge from the spices. The soup can be cooled to room temperature, then refrigerated and served chilled. Eliminate the ginger and allspice if you like; other herbs, such as chopped fresh dill or chives or scallions, can be used for garnish. SERVES 4 TO 6

1 pound red beets
2 sprigs thyme
1½ teaspoons butter
1½ teaspoons olive oil
1 leek, white and light
   green parts, cleaned
   and chopped
1 small onion, thinly sliced
1 celery stalk, chopped
⅛ teaspoon ground ginger
⅛ teaspoon ground allspice
4 cups water
1 small bay leaf
2 sprigs flat-leaf parsley,
   plus more for garnish
Salt and freshly ground
   pepper
1 cup sour cream

Preheat the oven to 350 degrees. Wash, trim, and dry the beets. Place a large sheet of heavy-duty foil on your work surface. Place the beets and one thyme sprig on the foil, cover with another piece of foil, and pinch the edges together to make a package. Place the package in the oven and roast until the beets are tender when pierced with a cake tester or fork, 45 minutes to 1 hour, depending on their size.

Let the beets cool, then peel, and cut about one-quarter of them into very small dice and reserve them for a garnish. Roughly chop the remaining beets.

Melt the butter with the oil in a heavy, medium saucepan over medium-high heat. Add the leek, onion, and celery and cook just until they are translucent and beginning to brown, stirring frequently.

Stir in the ginger, allspice, and chopped beets. Cook until the vegetables just begin to adhere to the bottom of the pot, stirring frequently, about 7 minutes.

Add the water, bay leaf, remaining thyme sprig, and parsley and bring to a boil. Reduce the heat to low, cover, and simmer until the vegetables are very tender, about 25 minutes.

Remove and discard the bay leaf, thyme, and parsley. Let the soup cool to room temperature. Working in batches, puree the soup in a blender or food processor. Season with salt and pepper and adjust the other seasonings to taste; add water or vegetable stock if the soup is thicker than you like.

Reheat the soup before serving. Transfer the soup to individual bowls, then top with the diced beets, a sprinkle of parsley, and a dollop of the sour cream, or pass it at the table.

BEETS

Beets are among my favorite vegetables; I love them any which way—alone or as a side dish, roasted and splashed with balsamic vinegar and a hint of allspice, or thinly sliced and fried into beet chips (our most popular Greenmarket item). Peeled, sliced, roasted beets, dressed with great olive oil and a sprinkle of sea salt, are perfect with goat or sheep's milk cheese; add a handful of my Herb Salad (page 25) for a first course or light lunch.

At Katchkie Farm, beets grow in long lovely rows and are one of the early crops the children harvest at the Sylvia Center. They learn first off that the beets aren't ready to pull until their domes can be seen just beginning to push out of the soil—this is called crowning. And when they identify a harvest-ready beet, they pounce—sometimes competitively!

I can't tell you how many photographs I have of tiny farmers grinning over armfuls of beet tops. The tender tops often become part of the vegetable minestrone the kids make in the Katchkie field kitchen.

Look for these varieties that we grow, or others:

- Golden beets with green leaves, yellow stems, and yellow roots.
- Chioggia beets, incredibly beautiful things, with fuchsia skin and pink and white pinwheel stripes inside; they sometimes go by the nickname "candy stripe" and are, in fact, a little sweeter than other types. When tender, Chioggia greens are especially good.
- Early Wonder Tall Top have tall, bright, glossy green tops with red veins and are slightly flattened at the red roots.
- Bulls Blood have dark red leaves and candy-stripe sections.
- Merlin and Red Ace have medium-tall, red-veined greens and dark red roots.

Generally speaking, beets can be used interchangeably, though there are subtle differences among them; mainly, some are sweeter than others. I sometimes mix them, according to size and color, to make a pretty presentation.

12. Sylvie's Stars and Moon Soup

My friend Dana Cowin, the gifted editor of *Food & Wine* magazine, comes, paradoxically, from "a long line of women who were not good cooks." But she has always said that "food can take over your life in the most wonderful way, which is what I have consciously wanted for my children."

Dana sent me this recipe, which was created by her daughter Sylvie when she was ten years old, because she knows I like to cook with children. Sylvie loves soup and believes it has no season; any time is soup time. I think other children share Sylvie's point of view: her three main ingredients—chicken, pasta, and edamame—are okay on a plate, but far more interesting in soup.   SERVES 4 TO 6

3½ cups chicken stock, homemade (page 38) or good-quality store-bought, organic if possible

2 medium carrots, peeled and cut into coins

¼ cup orecchiette

½ cup elbow macaroni

½ cup mini pasta stars

1 cup frozen shelled edamame

8 green beans, cut into ½-inch pieces

1 cup shredded, cooked chicken

Freshly ground pepper

Pour the stock into a medium saucepan and set over medium-high heat. Add the carrots and bring to a boil. Add the orecchiette and cook for 2 minutes. Add the macaroni and cook for 3 minutes more. Add the stars, edamame, and green beans and cook for an additional 4 minutes. Add the chicken and cook until it is heated through and the pasta is tender, then sprinkle with pepper and serve.

EDAMAME

Edamame is the Japanese name for fresh soybeans ("beans on a twig"), which are harvested when they are still tender and green and then cooked whole, in their pods, usually simply by boiling them in salted water. In Japan, edamame is snacked on with beer; most of us first encounter it similarly, as a presushi item. It has become so wildly popular that it now is easy to find, frozen, in supermarkets, in the shells or even shelled. Get it fresh though, if you can, which is possible in the big Asian markets and in some supermarkets.

I think part of the appeal of edamame for children—and grown-ups, for that matter—is pushing the beans out of the pods and into the mouth. This may not represent the height of table manners, but edamame is such a nutritional powerhouse of complex carbohydrates, protein, fiber, omega fats, and some vitamins and minerals, a breach of etiquette can be forgiven.

13. Traditional Gazpacho

Gazpacho struck hard at the American consciousness with the beginning of our food obsessions in the mid-1960s. It coincided with the small kitchen appliances that suddenly became commonplace: all the grinding could be done in a blender or a food processor, and no pots were needed. Gazpacho became a bit of a dinner-party cliché and now is so familiar you can get it almost anywhere; predictably, poorly made gazpacho is now as common as it was once a novelty.

I think it's time to remind us all that gazpacho really is a treat, and meant to celebrate good fresh ingredients in their season.

My little neighbors, Max and Rosie, who are about seven and five years old, often bring me the gazpacho they make. In return, I hand over veggies from our farm to get them started on their next batch. SERVES 4 TO 6

3 or 4 large ripe tomatoes
1 medium onion, minced
1 green bell pepper,
   minced
1 cucumber, unwaxed
   if possible or peeled
   if waxed, seeded and
   chopped
2 scallions, white and light
   green parts, chopped
1 garlic clove, minced
3 tablespoons fresh lemon
   juice
2 tablespoons red wine
   vinegar
2 teaspoons minced
   tarragon
1 teaspoon dried basil
¼ cup chopped flat-leaf
   parsley
1 teaspoon white sugar
Salt and freshly ground
   pepper

Place a sieve over a bowl. Cut the tomatoes in half crosswise and squeeze them into the strainer to catch the seeds and reserve the juice; discard the seeds. Chop the flesh roughly.

Put the tomato juice and chopped tomatoes into a blender or food processor, along with the remaining ingredients. Season with salt and pepper. Blend, in batches if necessary, until well combined. Take care not to overblend—you might want to pulse to control the outcome. The soup should have some texture, even chunkiness, and not be a smooth puree. Pour the soup into a bowl and chill for at least 2 hours before serving.

The vegetables can be cut into very small dice and tossed together instead of using a food processor, then added to the tomato broth. The texture will be a little different. Last year at our Farm to Table dinner at Katchkie we packed the vegetables into little custard cups and turned them out onto each soup plate of tomato broth. This is pretty to look at, and easy—try it at home.

The dried basil may come as a surprise, but it adds a deep, characteristic flavor and is quite correct for this very traditional gazpacho.

Gazpacho Before Columbus

It is impossible to think of our "modern" gazpacho as anything but a tomato-based soup, but gazpacho is very old, so old that it existed in Spain long before the tomato had made its way from the New World to the Old. "White" gazpacho was a simple soup of water and garlic pounded with dry bread and drizzled with olive oil, and just one of a vast category of soups based on stale bread going back to ancient times.

Today, almonds are characteristically added to white gazpachos, pulverized along with the bread; it is doubtful they were included when this was just a poor farmer's dish. White grapes and diced cucumber are other contemporary interpretations. The cucumber would represent another post-Columbian innovation, another fruit that made the voyage to Europe.

14. Creamy Cauliflower Soup with Chorizo and Greens

My friend Sara Moulton, the popular cookbook author and well-known television personality, is the author of *Sara's Secrets for Weeknight Meals* and *Sara Moulton Cooks at Home.* Sara is a busy mother who finds substantial and satisfying soups like this one great for family dinners. Thick with pureed cauliflower and potato, it is luxuriously creamy without any cream. The chorizo, greens, and paprika give it heat, and the cauliflower florets give it crunch. Serve this soup with a nice green salad, add toasted or grilled bread rubbed with a garlic clove, and you've got a meal.   SERVES 6

2 tablespoons extra-virgin olive oil

8 ounces chorizo, preferably Spanish, halved lengthwise and thinly sliced

1 medium onion, sliced (about 1 cup)

1 medium head cauliflower (about 2 pounds), trimmed

4 cups chicken stock, homemade (page 38) or good-quality store bought

1 small Yukon Gold potato, peeled and coarsely chopped

1 bunch mustard greens, kale, or spinach, or a mixture, rinsed, dried, and thinly sliced

1 to 2 tablespoons fresh lemon juice, or to taste

Kosher salt and freshly ground pepper

Paprika, preferably smoked, for garnish

Grilled or broiled slices of a country or rustic-style bread, rubbed with a cut garlic clove (optional)

Heat the oil in a large saucepan over high heat until hot. Reduce the heat to medium; add the chorizo, and cook, stirring occasionally, until the pieces are lightly browned on both sides, about 5 minutes. Transfer the chorizo with a slotted spoon to a plate. Add the onion to the pan and cook, stirring occasionally, until softened, about 5 minutes.

Meanwhile, cut 2 cups of small florets from the cauliflower and set them aside; chop the remaining cauliflower. When the onion has softened, add the chicken stock, chopped cauliflower, and potato to the saucepan; bring the mixture to a boil over high heat. Reduce the heat to low and simmer for about 8 minutes, or until the cauliflower and potato are very tender. Let cool slightly, then transfer to a blender or food processor in 3 or 4 small batches and puree until very smooth.

Measure the pureed soup and return it to the saucepan. Add water, if necessary, to make 7 cups. Stir in the cauliflower florets and simmer for 4 minutes, or until they are almost tender. If you are using mustard greens or kale, add them to the soup with the florets. When the florets are just tender, stir in the chorizo and lemon juice; season with salt and pepper to taste. If using spinach, stir it in with the chorizo. Taste again and add salt and pepper. Ladle the soup into bowls, sprinkle each with some paprika, and serve with garlic bread, if desired.

CAULIFLOWER

Cauliflower is a cool-season vegetable and nice to look forward to as your summer crops are waning. Pay attention though, because the cauliflower head develops rapidly and can be ready to harvest in seven to twelve days. The heads, which get to be six to eight inches across, must be harvested before they become overly mature; once individual florets can be seen, the quality of cauliflower deteriorates rapidly. Harvest by cutting at the main stem, and leave a few green outer leaves attached to protect the heads.

15. Shabbat Chicken Soup

Everyone talks about handing down recipes from one generation to the next. This is my niece Nannette's version of the soup her mother—my sister—made for their Shabbat dinners. At the core are family memories woven together with food. Nannette says, "My earliest olfactory memory involves my mom's Shabbat chicken soup. Aromas would begin filling our apartment at around ten o'clock every Friday morning. Various ingredients would assert themselves, and the scents would layer, one on top of the other, creating a symphony that became the harbinger of the Sabbath.

"As I grew up and started cooking in my own kitchen, Mom's soup came with me, a staple at our Shabbat dinners and slowly the soup became my own. It is a weekly tradition in our home and is often sent to friends with colds and to new mothers."   SERVES 4 TO 6

2 tablespoons olive oil

1 onion, sliced

3 cups chopped carrots

1 cup chopped celery

1 cup chopped parsnip
   (optional)

4 pieces of chicken, about
   2 pounds (preferably
   thighs)

3 or 4 bay leaves

5 whole cloves

1 teaspoon whole black
   peppercorns

6 to 8 cups water

½ bunch fresh dill

½ bunch fresh flat-leaf
   parsley

Salt and freshly ground
   pepper

Heat the oil in a large pot over medium heat. Add the onion and sauté until the onion is translucent and softened but not browned; add the chopped carrots and sauté for 5 minutes longer. Add the celery and parsnip, if using, and sauté for 10 minutes.

Place the chicken on top of the vegetables, then add the bay leaves, cloves, and peppercorns. Pour in enough water to cover the chicken and spices by about 1 inch. Bring the water just to a boil, then reduce the heat and maintain a low simmer. Add the dill and parsley; cover the pot and simmer for 2½ to 3 hours.

Remove the pot from the heat and let it cool, uncovered, to room temperature. Place a colander over a large bowl, and ladle the soup into it to strain the solids from the broth.

Discard the bay leaves, cloves, peppercorns, and herbs; remove the large pieces of chicken from the bones and set them aside; discard the bones. When it is cool enough to handle, cut or shred the chicken into easy-to-eat pieces and set them aside. Return the vegetables to the broth and puree it in a food processor or with an immersion blender. Return the chicken pieces to the pot, season to taste with salt and pepper, and reheat to serve.

Pureeing the vegetables gives the soup a rich golden color, thanks to the carrots, but you can skip this step if you prefer and leave the vegetables in pieces.

Tying the herbs and spices in a double piece of cheesecloth before adding them to the pot will make it easier to remove them later.

Rice, noodles, or small pasta such as tubettini or elbows can be included.

Vegetables

Do you have a favorite vegetable? What is it? Did you come to love it as a child or was it a grown-up romance?

All my friends know that I have never met a tomato I didn't love. In fact, every year, in spite of our tomato crop bounty, I feel as if I want to interview all the potential tomato buyers who come to the farm to see if they are worthy of our precious red orbs. I would be just as happy to keep all the tomatoes for myself. Of course, that is ridiculous, but it speaks to the passion I feel for vegetables, especially the ones we grow. For my inner eater, vegetables can start, fill, and complete any meal (with some help from seasonal berries, rhubarb, and peaches).

After my tomato obsession comes my love of beets, all varieties of squash, the vast family of greens, asparagus, the vegetables I stuff into my lasagna—and so on down the straight green rows of Katchkie Farm. It is easy to love what you grow, what you cook, whatever you experience on a personal level. This defines our approach to introducing children to the pleasures of veggie eating. It is choreographed and starts with hands-on, interactive moments when curious minds, tactile participation, and, finally, taste adventures connect them to foods they thought they would never eat.

1. Great Greens: My Favorite Everyday Method for Kale, Swiss Chard, Mustard Greens, Collards, and Beet Tops

At the Sylvia Center, we've noticed that greens go over better with kids when they are sautéed, and not for too long, with some olive oil and garlic, than when braised. Braising can bring forth more of the intense, metallic taste of greens, especially if overdone. Sautéing seems to keep the taste brighter and lighter. Once you make this your favorite method, you may apply it to whatever looks good in the market even several times a week with no fear of veggie fatigue setting in. The only thing that may change is the cooking time; more mature leaves or naturally tougher ones like kale take a bit longer—a bite will let you know. SERVES 4 TO 6

1 large bunch leafy greens, as
  above
2 tablespoons olive oil
1 small garlic clove

Pinch of red chile flakes
1 teaspoon butter
Salt and freshly ground pepper

Rinse the leaves thoroughly. Remove the tough bottom third or so of the stalk and discard or reserve it for soup or broth (see page 38).

Roughly chop the leaves into 1-inch-wide strips. Heat a medium saucepan over medium heat and pour in the olive oil. Smash the garlic with the red chile flakes, add to the pan, and sauté for about a minute. Scatter in the chopped leaves and cover the pan.

Check after about 5 minutes to see if the pot seems dry and add a couple tablespoons of water if needed. With tongs or a spatula, flip the leaves over and cook, uncovered, until they are just tender. Stir in the butter, season with salt and pepper to taste, and serve.

2. Kale with Rice and Tomatoes

This recipe is a specialty for Sylvia Center lunches, especially late in the season. The visiting kids harvest the tomatoes and kale and then move into the field kitchen to wash, prep, and complete the meal. Afterward, as always, they carry the trimmings to the compost heap.

Sometimes I turn the rice into the skillet to cook briefly with the other ingredients, or I use brown rice in place of white (keep in mind that it needs to cook longer); a pinch of red chile flakes can be added for a little heat.   SERVES 6

Salt

½ cup long-grain rice

1 large bunch (about 8 stalks)
   kale

1 tablespoon olive oil

1 small garlic clove, minced

6 large plum tomatoes,
   seeded and chopped
   (1½ cups)

Freshly ground pepper

Bring 1 cup water to a boil in a small saucepan; add a big pinch of salt and the rice, cover, and cook over low heat for 20 minutes, or until the water is absorbed.

While the rice is cooking, remove the kale leaves from the ribs and rinse and drain them well. Chop the leaves finely.

Heat the oil in a large heavy skillet over medium-low heat; add the garlic and stir until it is golden, about 1 minute. Raise the heat to medium, add the tomatoes and kale, and cook the mixture for 3 to 5 minutes, stirring, until the kale is tender.

Fluff the rice and combine it in a serving dish with the kale mixture; season to taste with salt and pepper.

3. Asian-Style Kale

Here I've departed from my everyday olive oil and garlic approach. Kale takes nicely to these bright and warm flavors. SERVES 4 TO 6

1 large bunch (about 8 stalks) kale

1 tablespoon sesame seeds (optional)

1 tablespoon sesame oil

1 small shallot, minced

1 large or 2 small garlic cloves

2 scallions, white and light green parts, minced

1 teaspoon finely grated fresh ginger

1 tablespoon soy sauce

Tear the kale leaves from the tough ribs, wash and drain them thoroughly, and chop them coarsely. Discard the ribs.

Place the sesame seeds in a small skillet over medium heat; stir constantly for a minute or two to toast them. Take the skillet off the heat as soon as the seeds begin to color because they burn quickly.

Heat the oil in a large skillet or wok over medium heat; add the shallot, garlic, scallions, and ginger and cook, stirring, for about 1 minute. Add the kale and cook, tossing, for 3 or 4 minutes, until just softened—the leaves should retain some shape.

Remove the pan from the heat and toss the kale with the soy sauce, then sprinkle with sesame seeds and serve.

KALE

Kale elicits passionate responses. It is embraced by those who have come to understand how to coax luscious flavors from its fibrous leaves, revered by those who treasure its enormous nutritional value, and scorned by those who have simply received one CSA week of kale too many.

I love kale because it is good for me and because it tastes great. But ours is a romance that took years to take root (no pun intended!). From time to time, I cooked it, usually as "Swamp Soup"—a thick rich chicken stock with lots of shredded kale and other murky ingredients. Or I braised it with potatoes, onions, garlic, and curry. After these and other flirtations, I learned to love kale itself, even raw in a salad.

When Farmer Bob and I discussed our first crop plan, my only request was that we plant very very little kale. Fortunately, he ignored my request. Now, when I walk the fields at Katchkie Farm on a busy day, I pinch leaves off the plants for my impromptu snack. At our Greenmarket stand, the kale has the most dedicated group of followers and is often the first vegetable to sell out.

Kale is one of the healthiest plants on the planet, a powerhouse of beta-carotene, vitamins K and C, magnesium, a handful of minerals, and a good source of fiber. Kale is a relative of cabbage, broccoli, and Brussels sprouts—the very healthful cruciferous family.

Kale's nutrients, along with its color and texture, are optimal when cooked quickly. Steam it just enough to tenderize it or eat it raw; cut into very thin shreds, it can be added to a salad (see page 74) or slaw. Or chop it up and toss it into stew; vegetable, bean, or lentil soup; or minestrone for a few minutes at the end of cooking. Toss kale with browned garlic, pasta, and ricotta salata or feta cheese, or with white beans, braised onions, and whole-wheat pasta.

Plain and curly-leafed kale are the most familiar types, but another, variously known as dinosaur kale, Tuscan kale, Lacinato, or cavolo nero, is now being widely cultivated and can be found in supermarkets. This type has long narrow leaves with a bubbly texture and a deep, nearly black, green color. As most of the names imply, this kale has an Italian background; it has been cultivated for at least two hundred years, but kale itself goes back even longer, to ancient Greek and Roman times.

Less common but worth looking for in farmers' markets is a spiky, purple-green type that may appear in early autumn under various names, including Russian kale. This kale is quite tender and is good raw in salads or wilted. And then there is the ornamental kale that looks like a giant blossom and comes in a range of colors from purple to pale greenish white. It makes a pretty decoration in fall but is also edible if it hasn't been treated with chemicals, so look for it at a food market rather than a florist's shop if you mean to eat it, and check before you do.

Kale grows fast, a characteristic that made it a recommended vegetable for victory gardens during World War II. It is among the first crops in early spring and the last as the growing season ends.

4. Kale Salad

I have a friend whose daughter makes a kale salad that has become a family favorite. "It's never quite the same each time," she told me. "Use any kind of kale, thinly shredded; dress it simply—good olive oil and red wine vinegar, not too much—and make it an hour or so ahead of time to let it soften a bit. Lemon juice also is nice. Toasted pine nuts or walnuts, Parmigiano-Reggiano, lightly sautéed pancetta or good smoky bacon, or turkey are all options to add. When I use walnuts I use walnut oil; it's lovely with the kale. Even dried cranberries or cherries can be added if you like that sort of thing. Salt and pepper to taste, of course, sea salt preferred."

5. Kale Crisps

This is a sensational idea, and a treat for kids that might surprise them. Preheat the oven to 400 degrees. Tear the leaves from the ribs, wash and dry them, then brush them lightly with olive oil and arrange them, in single layers, on baking sheets. Bake the leaves until they are crisp, 5 to 7 minutes, then sprinkle with salt—sea salt if you have it. You may need to make more than you imagine to keep up with the demand.

6. Spanakopita

Spinach is invariably a big annual crop at Katchkie, which leads directly to making these savory Greek pastries. It's fun and quite easy, one of those projects that falls somewhere between cooking and craft, which means it has great appeal for children. They can do the squeezing and mixing, but the construction of the triangles is the most fun. Let them brush on the oil and then fold the filled pastries, flag-style, and place them on the baking sheets. If you are cooking with several children, have everything ready, then line up a few sheets of pastry and let them proceed. (Turn this into a competition at your own peril.) You can have enough brushes to go around if you buy inexpensive one-inch-wide ones at a paint store. The reward, needless to say, is a delicious, nutritious treat.

What is particularly fun about cooking spinach with kids is that spinach is the symbolic green vegetable of disdain. Initially, none of the children admits to loving spinach, let alone a willingness to try it. So we start the cooking process anyhow and by the time the spanakopita come out of the oven, we have a room full of spinach-loving Popeyes! They cannot get enough. And we like to tell the children that "spanakopita" comes from the Greek words for "spinach" and "pie"; the word for "pie" is *pitta,* which is like "pita" and even a little like "pizza," at least on the ear. SERVES 4 TO 8

2 pounds fresh spinach

¼ cup olive oil, plus more for brushing

1 medium onion, finely chopped

½ pound feta cheese, crumbled

Coarsely ground black pepper

24 phyllo sheets, whole-wheat if possible (see Note)

Wash and rinse the spinach well. In a large skillet over medium heat cook the spinach, in batches if necessary, until just wilted. Transfer the spinach to a large colander, refresh under cold water, and set aside to drain well.

Return the skillet to the heat and pour in the oil; add the onion and sauté slowly over medium heat until golden but not browned, 10 to 15 minutes. Transfer the onion to a large mixing bowl and let cool.

Squeeze the excess water out of the spinach. Chop the spinach and add it, along with the feta cheese, to the onion, and mix everything to combine well; season with pepper to taste.

Preheat the oven to 400 degrees. Line one or two baking sheets with parchment paper.

Place a sheet of phyllo dough on a work surface and brush it lightly with oil; cut it in half, lengthwise, and fold each piece in half; brush the top of the folded sheets lightly with oil. Arrange about 1 rounded tablespoon of spinach filling at the bottom corner (see illustration). Pick up the corner of the phyllo and fold it over the filling to the opposite side, to form a triangle, brushing lightly with oil as you fold. Continue lifting and folding from one side to the other all the way to the end, as you would a flag, tucking in any leftover bits and ending up with a tidy filled triangle. Brush the top with a bit of olive oil and place the triangle on the baking sheet. Repeat with the remaining phyllo and filling.

Bake until golden crisp, 15 to 20 minutes.

The spinach water is actually quite delicious. Save it by squeezing the spinach over a bowl and use it for a refreshing and nutritious drink, on its own or added to another juice, like carrot or tomato. But make sure you have washed the leaves very well—the delicious liquid won't taste so nice if it contains grit or dirt! If in doubt, strain it through cheese-cloth. Or save the cooking water from spinach and other greens and add it to vegetable stock.

Phyllo dough is now easily found in supermarkets, almost always frozen. Be sure to defrost the sheets fully according to the package directions, usually overnight, before you use them. The sheets dry quickly, so unfold them one at a time, keeping the thawed ones in the refrigerator as you work. Even better, if you live near a Greek or Middle Eastern bakery, you can buy freshly made phyllo daily.

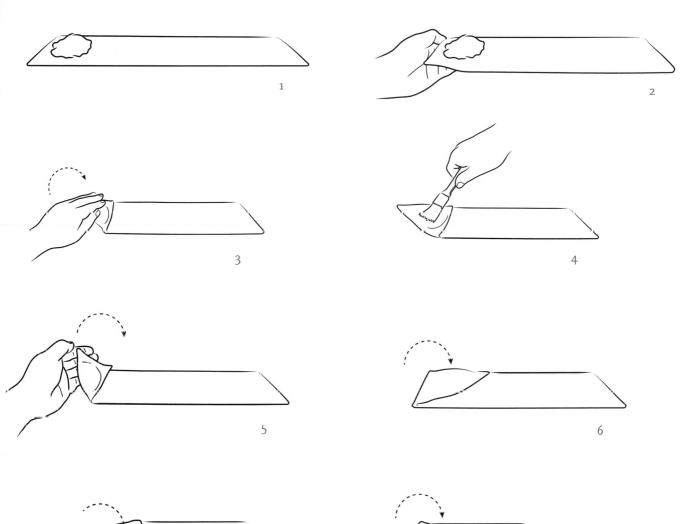

1

2

3

4

5

6

7

8

9

10

11

7. Braised Red Cabbage

This is a perfect, basic method for one of winter's most appealing and versatile dishes. Braised cabbage is a traditional accompaniment to pork—alongside a roast or chops, or with cooked sausages like bratwurst, kielbasa, or knockwurst buried underneath it. Braised cabbage is also a satisfying counterpoint to rich birds like duck and goose. Applesauce (page 318) makes a fine companion to menus with red cabbage.   SERVES 6 TO 8

½ pound slab bacon or
    smoked turkey (optional),
    diced
1 pound (2 or 3 medium) red
    or yellow onions, chopped
1 large (1½ to 2 pounds)
    red cabbage, cored and
    shredded
2 green apples, such as
    Granny Smith, cored and
    chopped
1 cup red wine
1 cup red wine vinegar
1 cup sugar
⅔ cup red currant jelly
1 tablespoon salt
1 cinnamon stick
3 whole cloves
6 juniper berries
2 bay leaves
Freshly ground pepper
2 tablespoons cornstarch, if
    needed

Cook the bacon in a large Dutch oven over medium heat, stirring from time to time, until it is crisp and has given up most of its fat.

Pour off all but about 2 tablespoons of fat from the pan and add the onions. Cook until softened but not brown.

Add cabbage, apples, the wine, vinegar, sugar, jelly, salt, cinnamon, cloves, juniper berries, and bay leaves. Season with pepper. Cover the pot and braise the cabbage for 45 minutes, or until tender, stirring from time to time. Most of the liquid should be absorbed, but if it is not, dissolve the cornstarch in 2 tablespoons water and stir some of it into the cabbage, adding more if necessary. Cook, stirring, until the cabbage reaches a desired consistency.

CABBAGE

Cabbage can be preserved and kept for a long time. In olden times, when there were very few fresh vegetables to eat during the winter, cabbage was made into sauerkraut, a kind of pickle, that can be kept for months. Today, of course, we think of sauerkraut mostly as something to put on top of hot dogs.

Cabbage is a pretty easy crop to grow in a home garden. It can be harvested anytime after the heads form. For highest yield, cut the cabbage heads when they are solid (firm to hand pressure) but before they crack or split.

Korean kimchi is another kind of preserved cabbage and it is becoming so popular here that you can find it in just about every supermarket. For kimchi, the cabbage is usually sliced thicker than for sauerkraut and is combined with onions, chiles, garlic, and sometimes ginger—it is delicious but can be quite spicy. (And it is good on hot dogs!)

Kimchi is eaten with nearly every meal in Korea and is so important in the diet that a special kimchi was developed for the first Korean astronaut to take into space. And I've been told that Koreans say "kimchi" instead of "cheese" when they have their pictures taken.

See page 323 for a kimchi recipe.

8. Roasted Vegetables

Roasting is one of my favorite ways to cook almost any vegetable. It is not only simple and fast; the results are always delicious, as roasting brings out the deep flavors of each veggie. Years ago, when I first started to roast cauliflower, my guests were simply astounded and begged for the recipe. In truth, roasting vegetables requires few rules and just a little imagination.

Asparagus, green beans, sliced peppers (all colors), broccoli, Jerusalem artichokes, turnips, fennel, zucchini, tomatoes, corn kernels, scallions, celeriac, carrots, cauliflower, and parsnips: all these are perfect candidates for roasting. Keep in mind that most veggies will shrink as they give up water during this process, so don't make florets of broccoli or cauliflower too small; include peeled broccoli stems sliced into disks. You can cut the zucchini on a bias, in disks, or into batons. Carrots and parsnips make good partners, cut into similar sizes as well, or left whole if they are "baby" varieties. Similarly, baby fennel can be roasted, trimmed but whole, while mature fennel bulbs are best trimmed and sliced either horizontally or vertically.

Corn kernels cut off the cob (save those cobs for your soup stockpot!) are delicious roasted, good on their own or mixed into a salad with diced red peppers and scallions or, of course, tomatoes. Chopped green beans or cooked beans are good additions. Make a selection based on what's in season or what looks appealing at the market.

You can roast several vegetables together, taking care to cut and group them by similar characteristics like size and density, so that they will cook uniformly. For instance, asparagus spears are great to pair with string beans because they are similar in size and retain their distinctive tastes.

To roast mushrooms, leave them whole or slice or chop them, depending on how you plan to use them—chop them for risotto (page 250), for instance.

I start with a hot oven, cranking it up to 400 degrees and then dropping it down to 375 when the vegetables go in. Toss the veggies with a bit of olive oil, spread them out on a sheet pan, and sprinkle with kosher salt or your favorite sea salt. Watch carefully and as they brown on one side, gently turn them over with a spatula. It will take between 20 and 40 minutes for the vegetables to brown, depending on what you are roasting. Chopped onions or garlic can be added halfway through the cooking; don't add them sooner or they will burn. Just as the vegetables come out of the oven, throw on whatever herb or spice makes sense, such as chopped mint on zucchini, red chile flakes on broccoli, sage or rosemary on mushrooms, cumin or curry powder on root vegetables, and chili powder on corn.

Katchkie Favorites

9. Oven-Roasted Tomatoes

Plum tomatoes are ideal for roasting, but any tomato variety is a candidate; I suggest that each batch be of uniform size. When we have lots and lots of tomatoes at the farm, I roast big quantities as a way to preserve them.

Preheat your oven to 350 degrees and have a baking sheet ready—or sheets, depending on how many tomatoes you are dealing with. Choose a sheet with low sides to keep the tomatoes from sliding off.

Slice the tomatoes in half, stem to bottom, then toss them in a bowl with olive oil, salt, pepper, dried basil, and parsley. Lay the tomatoes, skin down, on the baking sheet. Drizzle very lightly with balsamic vinegar.

Place the sheet in the oven and bake the tomatoes for an hour, more or less, depending on the degree of dryness you are after—still a bit juicy or drier and more chewy. So watch as the tomatoes shrink and give up their moisture. Sometimes I let them go until they're practically crisp by keeping them in a warm oven at 250 degrees for several hours. Store the tomatoes in an airtight container for several weeks; if very crisp, they can be kept at room temperature, otherwise, keep them in the refrigerator.

A dehydrator is also useful for drying tomatoes.

YOUNG GARLIC

Immature garlic and garlic fresh out of the ground are nearly different species from the faithful workhorse we always have in our kitchens. "Green" or new garlic looks like a chubby scallion at the end of a grassy green top; it has a sweet taste, but is by no means insipid. Cut a bulb crosswise and you will see a few silky outer skins circling undeveloped but quite distinct segments just beginning to shape up as individual cloves; altogether, this slice will look like a little wheel, quite white and juicy. Since any child over three is familiar with garlic, this can be an interesting demonstration in how the plants we eat "grow up."

At the next stage, the characteristic cloves will have developed, but the skin around them will still be soft and moist, not yet papery, and the cloves uniformly white and juicy. It is quite common to see freshly pulled garlic at farm stands and greenmarkets, often still on long stalks.

The other garlic kin to look for is the garlic scape, which now is even showing up in supermarkets, at least briefly in spring. The scape is the immature flower that farmers used to remove and discard to encourage larger bulb growth—until they discovered that people would pay for them. Scapes are terrific with asparagus, green beans, and potatoes, and in soups and omelets. I like to use them in a pesto or to puree them with oil to make a rub for chicken or fish. They would also be great on a Whole Wheat Pizza (page 336). Rows of garlic in the field with their scapes dangling in a gentle breeze remind me of modern dancers.

Garlic is hardy and easy to grow by planting the cloves before the first frost in cold climates, even in pots if they are deep enough. Keep in mind that larger cloves yield larger heads. This is an excellent crop for even tiny farmers, because it is so easy to push the cloves into the dirt, and then, in spring, they can harvest their garlic and see for themselves the magical growing cycle.

10. Brussels Sprouts with Butternut Squash and Apples

I like an all-inclusive side dish like this one. As well as being a splendid combination of autumn crops, it goes with lots of main courses, chicken and duck to lamb and beef, and even substantial fish entrees, like roasted striped bass or salmon. This combination can be varied with pomegranate or pumpkin seeds, toasted walnuts or pine nuts, or bacon, all of which add some crunch along with their flavors. Needless to say, I always choose a type of Hudson Valley apple that will hold up during roasting, like a Baldwin, Cortland, or Rome (see page 319 for varieties). SERVES 6

2 cups Brussels sprouts, trimmed and halved or quartered, depending on their size

2 cups peeled and cubed butternut squash

2 large apples, roughly cubed (about 2 cups)

1 shallot, diced

2 tablespoons olive oil

Salt and freshly ground pepper

1 tablespoon maple syrup

Preheat the oven to 375 degrees.

Toss the Brussels sprouts, squash, apples, shallot, and olive oil in a large, shallow baking dish. Season with salt and pepper to taste. Place the dish in the oven and bake until the vegetables and apples are wrinkled and slightly brown and the edges of the squash are beginning to crisp, 45 minutes to 1 hour, tossing and stirring from time to time. Remove the vegetables from the oven; toss with maple syrup before serving.

BRUSSELS SPROUTS

Brussels sprouts are not baby cabbages, not even miniatures, but they are part of the same family—crucifers—that also includes kohlrabi, collards, kale, and broccoli. In other words, they are very good for you, full of vitamins A and C, folic acid, and plenty of fiber. They go way back in time, to the Romans, but the ancestors of the "modern" thirteenth-century Brussels sprout are, unsurprisingly, Belgian and were brought to Louisiana by French settlers. Serious cultivation in the United States began in the 1940s in California, where the growing conditions are ideal. Small farmers bring some locally grown Brussels sprouts to market these days, but big California growers still dominate the market: about 80 percent of all Brussels sprouts grown are later frozen.

One of my favorite methods for cooking Brussels sprouts is to trim the bottom, cut the core out (the way you do for cabbage), and then separate the leaves (discarding any tough, yellowed, or bruised outer ones). The leaves can then be sautéed or stir-fried in a bit of oil, with garlic or shallots. (You want to avoid overcooking, so if the leaves seem tough, add a couple tablespoons of water or stock and cover and shake the skillet for a minute or two to hasten softening.) This has become the must-have vegetable at a friend's Thanksgiving dinner; she finishes it with walnut oil and toasted walnut pieces. Olive oil and toasted pine nuts also are good. Or you can slice the sprouts thinly, crosswise, and cook them in a similar fashion.

If you buy loose Brussels sprouts or those still on the stem, you may come home with a mixed bag of sizes, which I've come to regard as an opportunity. Wash and trim the heads and set them on a sheet, along with loose leaves, to roast as above. As they cook, the large leaves will crisp, the small ones will cook through and take on a nutty roasted flavor, while what remains of the larger bulbs will retain a softer interior. It makes for a nicely textured dish. If you do come upon sprouts on the stem, show them to your kids; until the proliferation of farmers' markets, almost no one knew where or how Brussels sprouts grow—the larger ones are at the top, with teeny ones lower down. This is also true for artichokes.

Finally, however you cook Brussels sprouts, don't overdo it. After six or seven minutes of cooking a compound is released that gives off a sulfurous aroma. The sprouts lose flavor, color, and texture when this happens. This gassy smell was why a lot of people of my generation grew up hating Brussels sprouts, all because our mothers sometimes cooked them to death. Take care, and your children will never need to go through the kind of "Brussels sprouts re-education process" their parents did.

11. Potato and Brussels Sprout Gratin

My friend Alexandra—Alex—Guarnaschelli shared this great and substantial side dish with me. I feel a particular connection to Alex because we share a college alma mater, Barnard, and now both work in the food hospitality business; she is the executive chef at Butter and The Darby and also has a passion for teaching cooking skills to children, including her own young daughter. Alex was one of the pioneer chefs who shopped the Greenmarket for their restaurants' daily menus.

This would be good with any meat or poultry—lamb, turkey, and duck in particular.

SERVES 8

1 tablespoon unsalted butter

2 garlic cloves, minced

4 medium Yukon Gold potatoes (about 3 pounds), peeled and thinly sliced

Kosher salt and freshly ground white pepper

2 cups heavy cream

2 cups whole milk

Pinch of freshly grated nutmeg

1 cup grated Parmigiano Reggiano

¾ cup grated Gruyère

1½ pounds Brussels sprouts

2 tablespoons extra-virgin olive oil

2 teaspoons sugar

Pinch of paprika

½ cup fresh bread crumbs

¼ cup ground, toasted almonds

Preheat the oven to 350 degrees.

Grease the bottom and sides of a 12-inch gratin dish or other, similar-size ovenproof dish with the butter. Distribute the minced garlic over the bottom of the dish.

Put the potato slices in a large pan and season them liberally with salt and pepper. Pour in the cream and milk and add the nutmeg. Mix to blend, taking care not to break the potatoes.

Place the pan over low heat, bring the liquid just to a simmer, and simmer gently for 10 minutes. Make sure the potatoes don't stick, but take care not to stir too frequently so as not to break them up as they cook. Remove the pan from the heat and stir in ½ cup of the Parmigiano-Reggiano and ½ cup of the Gruyère. Taste and adjust the seasoning.

While the potatoes are cooking, trim, wash, and dry the Brussels sprouts and cut them crosswise into very thin slices.

Heat the olive oil in a large skillet. When the oil begins to smoke lightly, add the Brussels sprout slices and season them with salt, pepper, and the sugar. Sauté the sprouts, stirring, for 1 to 2 minutes, just until they begin to wilt. Drain off any excess fat, sprinkle with paprika, and set the Brussels sprouts aside.

Place about one-third of the potatoes on the bottom of the gratin dish. Top with half the Brussels sprouts and sprinkle sparsely with some of the remaining Parmigiano and Gruyère, leaving enough cheese for the top layer. Repeat the process, then top with the remaining potatoes. Carefully pour any remaining liquid from the potatoes over the gratin and top with any remaining cheese.

Place the gratin dish in the center of the oven and bake until it is tender when pierced with the tip of a small knife, 40 to 45 minutes. Combine the bread crumbs and the ground almonds; top the gratin with the mixture and bake for 10 more minutes. Set the gratin aside for about 20 minutes before serving.

The dish can be made in advance up to the point of baking and kept at room temperature for a few hours. If you refrigerate it, bring it back to room temperature before you put it in the oven.

The potatoes and Brussels sprouts can easily be sliced with a good sharp knife. Or the potatoes can be sliced with the slicing disk of a food processor or with a mandoline, but you'll need a knife for the Brussels sprouts. The mandoline—not to be confused with a mandolin—is a good piece of equipment to add to your collection for slicing and making julienned vegetables. Affordable mandolines are available in most cookware shops and online.

PEAS AND PEA SHOOTS AND SPROUTS

As far as I am concerned, the best way to prepare fresh spring peas is to gently sauté them in a bit of butter and chicken broth and sea salt, and perhaps a light sprinkle of minced parsley or chives. You don't want to do anything to alter their elegant taste. Or put fresh peas to a similar simple use in Fresh Spring Pea Soup (page 53).

Shoots and sprouts each have the delicate but distinctive flavor of fresh peas—kids love peas and that shoots and sprouts deliver the same taste. I've wandered the Katchkie fields with little kids, munching pea shoots as we go; if we aren't careful, we could wipe out the entire pea crop. The shoots are the vines or tendrils of pea plants. Long revered in Chinese cooking—sometimes taking a starring role near the end of a banquet—they are getting around and you may find them in a Chinatown near you or at farmers' markets when peas are in season. Pea shoots should be barely cooked, if at all, gently steamed or sautéed or added to a soup just before serving; raw, they are lovely and elegant in a green or seafood salad or with cold salmon or chicken or combined with peas prepared as above.

Pea sprouts, like other sprouts, come from the pea seed itself and are used similarly—raw, in salads or sandwiches, as a garnish, or in a stir-fry.

In the market, look for shoots with a consistent deep green color and no sign of yellow; sprouts should have green tops, no yellow, and crisp white stems. Avoid either if they seem to be wilting. Use them within a day or two.

12. Roasted Jerusalem Artichokes and Cipollini

Cipollini onions are delicious when roasted as they are here. They also are terrific when braised as a side dish and finished with a bit of balsamic vinegar or in stews—substitute them for the usual pearl onions in a *boeuf bourguignonne* or *coq au vin.* Either method of cooking brings out the sweetness of these distinctive onions.

Years ago Italian Americans who longed for cipollini had to settle for imported ones in vinegar that come in jars. More recently, fresh cipollini began to be imported and now there is a significant domestic crop; you can find cipollini in farmers' markets and supermarkets, usually packaged. Besides the usual pale tan, these onions also come in a rosy red; they are interchangeable and attractive when cooked together.   SERVES 4

½ pound Jerusalem artichokes, peeled and cut into 1-inch pieces

10 cipollini onions, cut into quarters

1 tablespoon olive oil

2 garlic cloves, minced

2 tablespoons white balsamic vinegar

2 tablespoons minced flat-leaf parsley

Salt and freshly ground pepper

Preheat the oven to 450 degrees.

Toss the Jerusalem artichokes and cipollini onions with the olive oil in a roasting pan. Reduce the heat to 400 degrees. Scatter the garlic on top and roast in the oven until tender, about 20 minutes, tossing at least once about halfway through; the Jerusalem artichokes should be tender and the onions nicely browned. Transfer the vegetables to a serving dish, toss them with the vinegar and parsley, and season with salt and pepper to taste.

The Language of Cooking: *Cipollini*

In Italian, *cipollini* simply means "little onions," but the name also refers to a particular small, flat variety, usually pale yellow or gold in color. "Ini" at the end of an Italian word almost always means a small version of something or other. If you tell this to a child, he invariably will ask, "What if it's big?" That would usually be "oni."

JERUSALEM ARTICHOKES

First, they are not from Jerusalem or any nearby place. Second, though they are distantly related (by way of the daisy), they are not a kind of artichoke, in spite of a hint in the taste. Jerusalem artichokes—also widely known as sunchokes—are North American natives, perennial tubers that grow under tall plants topped by flowers that look very much like daisies. The story goes that to Italian immigrants they also resembled sunflowers, *girasole* in Italian, which sounded enough like Jerusalem to other people for the name to stick.

Jerusalem artichokes can be roasted like potatoes, combined with other vegetables (see Roasted Vegetables, page 80), or sliced and sautéed.

13. Asparagus with Roasted Red Peppers

Serve this brightly flavored and pretty dish at room temperature for lunch or brunch alongside a frittata or other egg dish, or as a side to just about anything at dinner. SERVES 4

15 medium asparagus stalks

Sea salt

2 red bell peppers, roasted and peeled (see page 114)

1 garlic clove, slivered

2 tablespoons chopped flat-leaf parsley

1 tablespoon sherry vinegar, or more if needed

Good-quality extra-virgin olive oil

Freshly ground pepper

Set a pot or deep skillet of water to boil.

Trim the ends of the asparagus, usually about an inch. Peel the asparagus from just under the tip to the end, taking care not to apply too much pressure or the stalks will break.

Gather the asparagus together in a bundle, all pointing the same way, then tie them together, not too tightly, with kitchen twine or a rubber band.

Add a big pinch of salt to the boiling water. Drop in the asparagus and cook until tender, 2 to 4 minutes, depending on the thickness of the stalks. Cut off a slice and take a bite to see if it is tender. It's the only way to judge. Using tongs, remove the asparagus, drain them in a colander, and refresh them under cold water; carefully place the asparagus on paper towels to absorb excess water, and remove the string.

Cut the peppers into thin slices and toss them with the garlic, parsley, and sherry vinegar; season with salt and pepper to taste.

Place the asparagus on a serving platter; drizzle the oil on top and sprinkle with salt and pepper to taste. Arrange the roasted peppers over the asparagus.

14. My Family's Favorite Everyday Potatoes

When the fingerlings first appear in the Greenmarket I never fail to make this herby roasted potato dish. Other sorts of small potatoes will do—small Yukon Golds or new red- or white-skinned potatoes—but fingerlings are the ones that will become the most deliciously creamy in the hot oven.

Preheat the oven to 500 degrees and place a baking sheet or large cast-iron skillet inside so that it is hot when the potatoes hit it.

For four to six people, toss about 2 pounds of small potatoes in a bowl with about 3 tablespoons of olive oil, the leaves from 2 sprigs of rosemary, a few sprigs of thyme, 6 unpeeled garlic cloves, a big pinch of coarse salt, and a few grindings of pepper. Put everything into the hot pan, reduce the heat to 425 degrees, and roast for about 20 minutes, until the potatoes are crisp outside and tender within; toss once or twice. The garlic flesh will be soft and can be pushed out of the cloves and served with the potatoes.

In place of the whole unpeeled garlic, you can use peeled and roughly chopped garlic, but wait to add it until about halfway through the roasting time or it will burn and become bitter. Sage can be included in the herb mix or substituted for one or the other, and chopped parsley can be tossed on when the potatoes emerge from the oven.

15. Our Favorite Smashed Potatoes

We've also become nearly addicted to smashed potatoes. Again, most varieties will do, but waxier types like Yukon Golds, French La Rattes, and fingerlings, along with creamy German Butterballs, are particularly good. Boil them up, unpeeled, until just tender, then drain them. A trick I use to dry boiled potatoes before a next step is to drop them back into the pot and shake them around over a medium-high flame for a few minutes—you can hear them squeaking as they give up moisture.

Crank the oven up to 400 degrees. Smash the potatoes roughly with a masher to flatten them enough to burst the skin; you will end up with a kind of potato cushion. Pour some oil into a heavy skillet—cast iron is great—dump in the potatoes, and spread them out. Bake until the potatoes acquire as crisp a top as you like, 20 minutes or so, turning them over a couple of times. Onions, garlic, parsley, chives, and thyme are all good to add, along with an additional drizzle of olive oil to finish.

POTATOES

What is great about potatoes is that, above all, everyone loves them; they are an excellent storage root vegetable, and they are bountiful even in winter at farmers' markets. On the deadest winter Saturday, I can go to the Union Square Greenmarket and choose from several types of potatoes. It is comforting to find such variety!

Cooking potatoes with children is fun when you can offer different colors and shapes.

Not so long ago just two types of potatoes were commonly available: starchy russets, also known as Idaho (even when grown somewhere else), Burbank, or simply "baking potatoes," or the waxier "all-purpose" potatoes. The selection today is pretty splendid, though the basic potato types prevail. It is good to know which are best for which purposes, but it also is good to learn that there is a fair amount of wiggle room, that potatoes are extremely versatile.

The medium-waxy Yukon Gold is a good example, a fine all-purpose potato—the larger Yukons are good to mash or to use in gratins; the little ones are delightful roasted whole, or simply boiled and finished with butter or olive oil and whatever fresh herbs are at hand.

Fingerlings are named for their elongated and somewhat knobby shape, and often are only about the size of an average human finger, though they can be larger. You will mostly find buff-colored fingerlings, but there are orange and purple varieties as well.

The fingerling is an old variety that has been brought back into cultivation and become so popular that big growers are now supplying them to supermarkets. But newly dug local fingerlings are the tastiest, so look for them at farmers' markets or specialty produce shops. The fingerling also falls into both camps: small ones are good roasted, as above, but larger fingerlings can be mashed; I usually leave their thin skins on when I do either.

Regionally, you will find even more types. The German Butterball has become a favorite; if it sounds as if it might be good whipped, it is, smooth, creamy, with a slight nuttiness to its taste. This is an exquisite, medium-size, round potato with a thin, golden-tan skin.

I am also seeing more of the French La Ratte, an elegant fingerling variety, and the Russian Banana, even in supermarkets; both also are creamy-fleshed and good to mash.

Waxy potatoes, because they are less starchy, are the ones you want for potato salad or boiling, as they will be firmer after cooking. Red-skinned potatoes and potatoes simply labeled "all-purpose" are reliable waxy types.

New Potatoes: This term can be a little confusing. Any potato, whether in the baking or starchy category, is "new" if it is harvested before its starch is fully developed; new potatoes are thin-skinned and, because of their lack of starch, can be juicy when sliced. New potatoes are small, but not all small potatoes are new. Unlike mature potatoes, these are not meant to be stored; treat them as a fresh vegetable and cook them within a week.

There are tiny potatoes referred to as "nubbins" by the farmers in upstate New York and nearby Connecticut near us—they are so small they fall between the prongs of the harvester. These are the size of the tip of your finger, and have a light, clean taste. They should just be washed well and then thrown into a skillet with some oil or butter to cook in minutes.

Potatoes are very high in most vitamins except A; they have no fat and deliver about the same number of calories as an apple of comparable size—150 for a medium one. Nevertheless, the diet-conscious remain averse to potatoes. I think that's because potatoes are often the innocent vehicles for fat, in the form of butter, cheese, oil, or sour cream. Nevertheless, a baked potato dressed with about a tablespoon of olive oil is still relatively low in calories and terrifically healthful.

16. Basil Mashed Potatoes

This is the version of mashed potatoes I make when the herb garden yields a bumper crop of basil, which is practically through the entire growing season. These mashed potatoes are rich and buttery and a pretty pale green color. The pestolike puree could also be tossed with pasta or used to dress green beans.   SERVES 4 TO 6

1 small head garlic

5 tablespoons extra-virgin olive oil, plus extra for the garlic

2 pounds (5 or 6) Idaho potatoes, peeled and cut into 1-inch chunks

Salt

1 cup heavy cream

6 tablespoons unsalted butter, at room temperature

1 teaspoon pine nuts

1 cup basil leaves, roughly chopped, plus more, cut into chiffonade (page 163), for garnish

Salt and cracked black pepper

Preheat the oven to 400 degrees.

Rub the garlic head with olive oil. Wrap the head in foil and bake for 45 minutes. Remove and let cool.

While the garlic is roasting, place the potatoes in a large pot with cold water to cover and 2 tablespoons salt and bring to a boil. Reduce the heat to medium and cook until the potatoes are very tender, about 15 minutes. Pour the cream into a small pan and set it over medium heat to warm; do not let it boil. Drain the potatoes well and return them to the pot. Add the cream and butter and push the mixture through a ricer or blend with a hand mixer, just until smooth. If you use a mixer, take care not to overwhip or the potatoes will become gummy.

When the garlic is cool enough to handle, squeeze the flesh from each clove into a blender or mini food processor. Add the oil, pine nuts, and basil leaves and puree until smooth, adding a few additional drops of oil if necessary to make a thick puree.

Fold the basil puree into the whipped potatoes until fully incorporated. Season generously with salt and pepper, top with the basil chiffonade, and serve immediately.

17. Potato Latkes

True to form for any beloved foods that evolve from traditions hundreds of years old, the latke has as many recipes as there are people who make it. And then there is the store-bought version that paradoxically becomes the standard bearer. No wonder people are amazed when they try an authentic homemade latke. I grew up with the commercial variety and found my inner latke only when my children were in preschool; then I volunteered annually to be the mom who came into the classroom during Hanukkah to shred and fry. There is nothing like a fresh latke straight out of the pan!

Use russet potatoes, peeled and shredded. Here I will horrify many purists by saying that I always shred my potatoes in my food processor, using the shredding disk, and have rarely hand grated them. And let me also confess that half a package of onion soup mix produces very delicious latkes; mix it in with the potatoes, flour, and egg and skip the onions and salt.

The following is a pretty basic recipe for enough latkes for four people. It can easily be increased proportionately, but I've never known a reason to make fewer. And I've never understood eating latkes without applesauce or sour cream—or both!   SERVES 4

---

1 medium onion, chopped

Olive oil and canola oil

4 russet potatoes, peeled and shredded (by hand on the coarse side of a box grater or in a food processor, using the shredding disk)

3 tablespoons of flour, matzo meal, or potato starch

3 eggs

Salt and freshly ground pepper

Applesauce (page 318), to serve

Sour cream, to serve

Sauté the onion in about 2 tablespoons olive oil until soft and lightly colored, but not browned. Set the onion aside to cool.

Mix the potatoes, onions, flour, and eggs together in a large bowl and season with salt and pepper to taste. Then turn them into a colander set over a large bowl. Drape a damp dishtowel over the colander. When it seems that very little liquid is draining from the potatoes, after about 15 minutes, carefully pour off the water, leaving the starch that has collected at the bottom of the bowl; mix the starch back into the potatoes—this starch will help hold the latkes together as they cook.

Place a large skillet over medium-high heat and pour in equal amounts of the olive and canola oil to a depth of about 1 inch. (If I'm making a large batch, which I usually do, I use two pans.) The oil is hot enough when a tiny bit of the latke mixture sizzles when you drop it in.

I make small latkes, 3 to 4 inches across, scooping up a large tablespoon of batter into my palm and flattening it out before sliding it into the pan. I like the mixture to be wet, so I don't squeeze out the excess moisture. The edges of the latke are very ragged and make me think of multiclawed crabs! It takes only a few minutes for the latkes to brown. Then I gently flip them. As they come out of the pan, I move them onto a cookie sheet lined with paper towels. Sometimes I have to hide the pan in the oven, safe from marauding snackers!

Then it's off to the table to enjoy them with sour cream or applesauce while the latkes are nice and hot!

A latke doesn't have to be made from potatoes. I make an excellent vegetable pancake using four large carrots, peeled and shredded, and one medium zucchini, shredded. A parsnip can replace one of the carrots. You need only 2 eggs for this and ¾ cup of flour, due to the extra moisture in the zucchini.

A Late-Night Memory

One spring evening, I was reading a stack of bedtime stories to Sam and Sylvia, who were seven and five at the time. The final book was *A Song for Lena* by Hilary Horder Hippely, a beautiful tale about apples, strudel, baking, and sharing. That got us on the subject of applesauce, which led to latkes, an unplanned take on *If You Give a Mouse a Cookie.* Within moments, they were pleading with me for a bedtime reprieve so we could go to the kitchen and whip up a pile of latkes. It was late, it was a school night, but it was one of the magical moments when saying yes had infinite possibilities and off we marched into the kitchen to cook. A few hours later, with full bellies and big smiles, they climbed into bed and fell off to sleep. I never regretted it for a moment.

Needless to say, the memories of that adventure are priceless.

Latkes at the Winter Market

Latkes are in the larger tradition of potato pancakes that more or less follows the line of potato cultivation, especially through Europe. Germany, Austria, Poland, Russia, Ireland, and Sweden all have their versions—the Swiss *rosti,* for instance, which is made without eggs or flour.

The latke—the Yiddish word—is a traditional Jewish Hanukkah dish; the oil for cooking them is a reminder of the miracle of the oil that lasted for eight days to light the Second Temple in ancient Israel. We make them around the winter holidays at the New Amsterdam Market in Manhattan before it closes for the season. These latkes are truly a seasonal and local dish, the perfect snack on a snow-covered market day. I must say my latke booth is a big draw: each year, we sell out before the market closes, and it's fun to hear nostalgic comments ("These remind me of my mom's") or to introduce them to someone who has never had a latke. In a good year, I will make close to one thousand latkes at my little booth!

As I make my way through the pounds of shredded potatoes, I pause to either add more oil to the pan as needed, or if it gets very dark and smoky, to wipe it out and start fresh with new oil.

18. Sweet Potatoes with Rosemary and Shallots

Sweet potatoes are not really potatoes; they come from a different family and are more closely related to the morning glory than to the white potato. If you ever see a sweet potato vine in flower, you will notice a resemblance. SERVES 4

Leaves from 1 sprig rosemary

2 medium shallots

2 garlic cloves

2 tablespoons olive oil

Salt and freshly ground
   pepper

4 medium sweet potatoes,
   washed, each cut into 6 to
   8 wedges

Preheat the oven to 400 degrees.

Chop the rosemary leaves with the shallots and garlic. Pour the oil into a medium bowl, add the rosemary, shallots, and garlic, and whisk to combine well; season generously with salt and pepper. Add the sweet potatoes and toss to coat them well.

Place a large piece of heavy-duty foil on a work surface, then cover it with an equal-sized piece of parchment paper. Place the sweet potatoes on one side of the paper, then fold the other half over. Crimp the edges of the paper together to make a package; bring the foil over to wrap the package.

Place the package on a baking sheet and then put it in the oven for 30 to 40 minutes, or until the potatoes are tender—insert a cake tester through the foil to test; it will penetrate easily if the potatoes are cooked through. Take care when you open the package, as there will be a lot of steam built up inside.

19. Pureed Sweet Potatoes with Smoked Chile and Maple Syrup

This dish makes me think of a fall dinner, Thanksgiving above all. I use New York State maple syrup or break into the jugs I haul down from my road trips to Maine. Whatever the provenance, use the pure stuff: real maple syrup is more expensive than maple-flavored syrup but it is less sweet and far more intense and satisfying. In the end, you will use less of the pricey syrup. SERVES 4

1½ pounds (3 or 4) sweet potatoes
½ cup plus 3 tablespoons heavy cream
1 teaspoon chipotle powder
2 tablespoons pure maple syrup
1 teaspoon grated orange zest
2 tablespoons unsalted butter, at room temperature
Kosher salt and freshly ground white pepper

Preheat the oven to 350 degrees.

Wash and scrub the potatoes as necessary, but leave them a bit damp (see below). Put the potatoes on a baking sheet and bake until tender when tested with a cake tester or a fork, about 1 hour. Remove the potatoes from the oven and let them cool enough to handle, 10 to 15 minutes; peel and discard the skin. Put the potatoes in a food processor fitted with the steel blade.

Meanwhile, pour the cream into a 2-quart pot, stir in the chipotle powder, maple syrup, and orange zest, and set the pot over medium heat. Bring just to a simmer and cook for 5 minutes; remove the pot from the heat.

Stir the cream mixture, pour it over the potatoes, and add the butter. Puree the potato mixture until smooth. Season with salt and pepper to taste. Keep covered and warm until ready to serve.

> Leaving the potatoes a bit damp lets them first steam inside their skins and then, after the moisture evaporates, begin to bake. As the flesh dries it becomes smoother and more intensely flavored. This technique also prevents the potato skin from burning during long cooking.

Maple Syrup Memories

For several years, we tapped trees for maple syrup in Putnam County, New York, with our neighbors, the Cummings. We watched the trees as their leaves turned in autumn to identify the sugar maples, and then tied red strings around their trunks. We waited for the ideal moment, late in March, when the days began to warm, for the sugar stored in the roots to start to rise: it was time to tap the trees, hanging plastic bags from the spouts. Hauling the bags through the snowy woods to giant waiting pots was only the beginning. We cooked the sap down for hours and marveled at how much yielded so little (forty gallons of liquid for one gallon of syrup!). But the golden syrup we were left with was the most delicious liquid ever. Just like fruits and vegetables consumed immediately after harvest, fresh homemade maple syrup is a completely unique flavor sensation. It is a lot of work, but worth the reward. I have never since bought imitation maple-flavored syrup.

Even if you never have the opportunity to tap maple trees for syrup, your children will be fascinated to know where their syrup comes from and how it's done—you do not simply drill a hole in a tree, stick a spout in, and get something to pour over pancakes. Canadian and American Indians had figured out how to gather and process maple syrup long before the first colonists arrived, and they passed the techniques on to the Europeans. As arduous as the process is, it caught on and became a significant part of Colonial life; what began as a household activity grew into an industry. The people who make maple syrup today are following a tradition that goes back to those early days. Modern methods of extraction, like plastic pipes, have increased the yield and decreased the time it takes to reduce the liquid to syrup.

20. Baked Sweet Potato Fries

These aren't fries, exactly—they get crisped in the oven—but kids love them so much you could serve them at a party. The recipe can easily be doubled or varied.   SERVES 6

2 large sweet potatoes, peeled
  or scrubbed well, cut into
  ½-inch-thick sticks
1 to 2 tablespoons olive oil
½ cup grated Parmigiano-
  Reggiano
Kosher salt and freshly
  ground pepper

Preheat the oven to 450 degrees.

In a large mixing bowl, toss together the sweet potato sticks and olive oil. Sprinkle with the cheese and season with salt and pepper to taste.

Line a baking sheet with parchment paper and scatter the potato sticks evenly in a single layer. Bake until golden and crisp, about 30 minutes total, turning them halfway through.

> The seasonings can be varied: herbs such as rosemary and thyme are good, as are various spices—curry or chili powder or cumin; minced garlic can be added, but near the end of the roasting time or it will burn and be bitter.

21. Lyonnaise Beets

Almost always, "Lyonnaise" in the title of a dish means with onions. Lyon is an important French industrial city, but the surrounding area is also rich with food and known for excellent potatoes and onions. Lyonnaise potatoes may be the more famous dish, but this version with beets is a strong challenger.

If they are available, mix red and yellow beets or use Chioggias for a pretty result.

SERVES 8

2 pounds medium red beets
¼ cup olive oil
Salt and freshly ground white pepper
4 red or yellow onions, thinly sliced
2 tablespoons chopped garlic
½ cup butter
1 tablespoon finely minced parsley, plus whole leaves (optional)

Preheat the oven to 400 degrees. Wash, trim, and dry the beets. Drizzle the beets with a bit of the olive oil, season with pinches of salt and a few grindings of pepper, then wrap them tightly in heavy-duty foil.

Place the wrapped beets on a cookie sheet and roast until just tender when tested with a cake tester or sharp knife, 45 minutes to 1 hour. Take care not to overcook the beets at this stage, as they will be baked again in the final step. Do not turn off the oven.

While the beets are roasting, heat a large cast-iron or other oven-proof skillet over medium-high heat. Pour in the remaining olive oil; add the onions and sauté them slowly until they are lightly colored, 8 to 10 minutes. Stir in the garlic and continue sautéing until the onions are deep brown, but not burned, and the garlic is soft. Transfer the onions and garlic to a bowl.

When the beets are ready, carefully open the foil to allow the steam to escape. When the beets are cool enough to handle, remove the skins and slice the beets ¼ inch thick.

Return the skillet to the stove over low heat. Add the butter; when it is melted, place one-third of the beets in the bottom of the skillet and season with salt and pepper. Cover the beets with half the onions, cover the onions with another third of the beets, top with the remaining onions, and finish with a final layer of beets, seasoned with salt and pepper.

Place the pan in the oven and bake for 10 to 12 minutes, or until the beets are browned on top. Remove from the oven and use a spatula to carefully transfer the beets—they should hold together in a disk, but never mind if they don't; you can push everything together on your serving platter. Sprinkle with the minced parsley and whole leaves and serve.

You can make a quick version by dicing the beets and onions. Sauté the beets over medium heat in about ¼ cup olive oil, or a combination of olive and canola. Cook until the beets begin to brown on one side, then add the onions and salt and pepper to taste; cook, stirring occasionally, until the beets are tender and the onions soft but not browned. Sprinkle generously with the parsley.

Corn: An American Love Story

In addition to "as American as apple pie" we could easily say "as American as corn on the cob." So passionate are we about it that we long for the season's first crop to present itself. In many parts of the country, this happens, appropriately, around the Fourth of July. Corn has always been with us, but the romance was slow to start. To be blunt, the earliest Americans ate corn because there was little else; along with beans, corn saved the Massachusetts Bay Colony from the starvation that had nearly wiped out the Jamestown Settlement. Those Colonial Americans ate their corn in the form of porridge or mush once they'd learned techniques for growing, drying, and grinding corn from the Indians. Early Americans also roasted cobs on their hearths and boiled it for as long as 30 or 40 minutes, a horrifyingly long time by today's standards, but those early cooks were dealing with a tough high-starch variety, quite unlike today's sweet and tender corn. In time, many corn dishes were created, including iconic American ones like corn bread and corn pone, Indian pudding, creamy corn puddings, and succotash.

By the nineteenth century, corn was firmly established on the national menu, a dish as democratic as any. On Manhattan's Lower East Side, coal-roasted corn from sidewalk vendors sustained poor immigrants while uptown hostesses fretted over etiquette—how could corn on the cob be eaten with dignity at dinner parties? But I think there is something joyous about corn, and eating it with our hands is part of that, especially for children and for the child lingering in most grown-ups. We break the rules when we eat with our hands, but it is permitted, even encouraged, with corn—it's fun, liberating, a touch revolutionary; it connects us to our earliest time.

Corn on the cob, buttered and salted and eaten out of hand, may just be our national vegetable.

22. My Favorite Corn on the Cob

I've noticed that people can be quite particular about how they cook—and eat—corn, and there even seem to be regional styles. If I am grilling chicken, fish, or meat, I grill the corn as well. It is a true summertime treat, and with a salad or plate of tomatoes, it's a perfect dinner—with no cleanup.

I am fussy about freshness: corn should be eaten the day it is picked. I have a friend who knows the picking schedule at her local farm stand and heads out as late as possible before dinner to pick it up. I've also heard of families who grow their own corn; the children are sent out to grab stalks—and return on the run—but not before the water is boiling. With the proliferation of farmers' markets and Greenmarkets in our cities, even urbanites can manage to have same-day corn. You can extend freshness if you keep corn in the refrigerator or a cool place, in its husks, until you do cook it; this slows the conversion of sugar to starch, which begins almost immediately after picking.

Speaking of which, a lot of today's corn is quite high in sugar—sometimes, I think, too high; the sweetness can overwhelm the clear taste of the corn itself. Corn is one of the most easily hybridized vegetables, and has been bred to please our national sweet tooth. But, as with heirloom tomatoes and apples and heritage farm animals, a movement is just beginning to reestablish early varieties of corn. Stay tuned.

Bring a large pot of water to a fast boil. Slip in 8 ears of shucked corn, return to a boil, and cook for 3 to 5 minutes, depending upon the freshness of the corn and preferred doneness. Remove the corn from the pot and place on a serving platter. Serve with butter or with the Herb Butter below.

PICKING CORN

There are those who have nothing but scorn for cooking corn at all, which is impractical unless you can eat it fresh from the field while it is juicy and tender. I've done this with my children while driving along country roads in summer. We stop at stands with "just picked" bushels and hunt for young ears—slender ones with small kernels and soft silk—shuck them on the spot, and eat them raw. When the kids were young, some of their friends thought I was a little crazy, until they tried it themselves. Comparing the flavors of raw and cooked corn is instructive; each cob has different qualities—add salt or seasoned butter to reveal even more complexity!

Shucking corn is a great chore for children. It takes muscles and discipline to pull off the fine silk. It can be a rewarding task when done as a team. Then, off to the compost pile with the silks and husks.

HERB BUTTER FOR CORN ON THE COB

Unless you're a purist, corn takes nicely to flavored butters. In the Southwest, chili and cumin, along with lime zest, may go into the butter; oregano and lemon zest can vary this theme. Or try gentler notes like mint, parsley, thyme—lemon thyme is especially nice. Follow the method here, playing with seasonings as you like.

Put 4 tablespoons of unsalted butter in a small bowl and let it soften.

Finely chop a combination of washed herb leaves—chives, tarragon, chervil, parsley, or whatever you choose—to end up with about 2 tablespoons. Combine the herbs well with the butter, along with a pinch of salt (sea salt is nice for this).

Transfer the butter to a small dish, such as a ramekin, to pass at the table.

23. Corn Pudding Soufflé

This dish must appear at least once a summer at my house, perhaps in late August when we see the end is in sight and want to celebrate with a flourish. Its richness makes it a perfect accompaniment for a simple roasted fish or grilled meat.   SERVES 6 TO 8

3 cups fresh corn kernels
   (from 5 or 6 cobs)
6 tablespoons unsalted butter,
   plus more to coat the dish
2 tablespoons sugar
2 tablespoons flour
½ cup heavy cream
4 large eggs, beaten
1½ teaspoons baking powder
1 teaspoon salt
1 cup grated Parmigiano-
   Reggiano

Preheat the oven to 350 degrees.

Spread the corn kernels on a lightly oiled baking sheet and roast them until golden brown, about 15 minutes, turning once or twice. Set the corn aside.

Heat the butter and sugar together in a saucepan over medium heat until the butter is melted, then add the flour and stir until combined; cook the mixture, known as a roux, over low heat for 5 minutes while stirring, but do not let it brown. Remove the pan from the heat and gradually stir in the cream, then add the eggs, baking powder, and salt; stir in the corn.

Butter a shallow 2-quart gratin or baking dish and pour in the corn mixture. Place the gratin in a baking pan and add hot water to the pan to within an inch or two of the top of the gratin dish. Bake the pudding for 45 minutes; when done it should remain slightly wobbly in the center.

Preheat the broiler while the pudding is in the oven. Sprinkle the cheese over the pudding, then set it under the broiler for about 5 minutes, or until the cheese is melted and golden brown. If the broiler is in the same oven, turn it up after 40 minutes and then sprinkle the cheese over the pudding.

24. Grain-Stuffed Peppers

Here is a perfect vegetarian main dish or side. I particularly like to serve these peppers with a nice big green salad or sautéed leafy greens; they also are good with cheese or egg dishes at brunch. Plan on one to two per person, depending on the size of the peppers and what else is on the plates.   SERVES 4 TO 8

Olive oil
½ cup diced green bell
　pepper
½ cup diced tomato
½ cup diced celery
3 garlic cloves, minced
2 cups cooked quinoa (page
　255), at room temperature
2 cups cooked farro (page
　260), at room temperature
1½ cups cooked lentils
1½ quarts vegetable stock,
　homemade (page 38) or
　good-quality store bought
Salt and freshly ground
　pepper
¼ cup roughly chopped
　cilantro
8 large green or red bell
　peppers
2 to 3 cups tomato sauce,
　warmed

Pour about 2 tablespoons olive oil into a large skillet or sauté pan over medium-high heat. Add the diced pepper, tomato, celery, and garlic and sauté until just tender, not browned.

Add the quinoa, farro, and lentils and gradually add stock until the mixture begins to absorb it and appears to "tighten up"; you may not need all the stock. Season generously with salt and pepper and add the cilantro.

Preheat the oven to 375 degrees.

Remove the tops from the peppers and carefully cut away the ribs and seeds. Rub the outside of the peppers with olive oil and season the inside with salt and pepper. Fill the peppers with the mixture and place them in an ovenproof dish just large enough to hold them snugly. Tuck the tops between the peppers. Cover with aluminum foil and bake for 30 minutes, or until the peppers are soft and tender but not collapsing. Remove the foil and continue to cook until the filling is browned and crisp, about 15 minutes. Serve immediately with the tomato sauce spooned around the peppers; the tops can be set on the peppers or served alongside.

Equal amounts of cooked wild rice or cooked red or green lentils can be substituted for one or the other of the grains or used together.

PEPPERS

Columbus stumbled upon chile peppers as he explored for black pepper, which is how the plants got named. The plants are not in any way related, but confusing them is not uncommon. In any case, chiles had been cultivated in Mexico for thousands of years, but after the discovery of the New World, they quickly caught on in China, Thailand, India, Africa, and Hungary—imagine those cuisines without chiles! They went the long way around to North America, arriving later with European colonists.

So, where to begin? Peppers are such a big category, with two distinct basic types, that, short of a book of their own, a comprehensive guide is impossible. Here, then, is a basic guide, in two parts: sweet and hot.

SWEET PEPPERS

Bell Peppers   These dominate among the sweet peppers and come in a variety of colors, beginning with the familiar bright green. That green just indicates the point at which the pepper was plucked; most other colors are signs of maturity—a green pepper can turn lilac, red, or the rich deep purple of an eggplant. Along with their color, peppers develop deeper and sweeter flavor.

Bell peppers are mostly four-lobed, but can vary a little in shape; common types like Big Bertha are rather elongated, while others, still bell-like, are shorter and boxier. The skin of a pepper may be slightly rough or silky-smooth.

Thanks to hybridization, the choice at farmers' markets and even supermarkets has exploded in recent years. Chocolate Beauty, which begins green, is an example of a pepper that develops a deep flavor along with gorgeous brown skin. Dark purple and nearly black varieties like Mavras and Purple Beauty have thick walls that make them ideal for stuffing and baking.

Unfortunately, learning the distinctions among everyday peppers at a supermarket will be a matter of trial and error, as they are rarely well labeled. You may have better luck at a farmers' market, where a staggering assortment may come along with a knowledgeable guide—the person who grew them.

Long-Shaped Peppers   These include the cubanelle, banana, sweet Italian, and other types often simply referred to as "frying" peppers. They are elongated, even horn-shaped, with walls that may be quite thin and supple, good for sautéing or pan frying, or thick and crunchy, in which case they also are good to grill.

Other Sweet Peppers   You may come across peppers that look hot but are not. One of my favorite names is Fooled You Jalapeño, a tasty little pepper that looks like the familiar jalapeño but is not hot; it is good for salsas when you want a hint of chile flavor without the heat. Others in this category are paprika, cultivated mostly as the familiar spice, but it sometimes appears fresh; the peperoncino is delicious pickled.

And then there are the lovely little shisito (Japanese) and Padrón (Spanish) peppers that seemed to pop up suddenly a couple of years ago and quickly became very popular. They are similar to each other, small and sweet with barely a hint of heat, although the occasional Padrón can surprise you. (My editor refers to this as Pepper Russian Roulette.) I like to throw a bunch of either type into a very hot cast-iron skillet barely coated with olive oil and toss them for a minute or two to scorch their skins. Sprinkle with salt; this is a classic tapas dish, so serve them whole as appetizers.

Holland Peppers   These bright and shiny imported hothouse peppers are almost impossibly perfect and pretty, not to mention expensive. And, with the energy needed for their cultivation and transport, they are "green" in color only, as well as red, yellow, and orange. I don't find them as flavorful as local peppers in season, but in the dead of winter they are a reasonable alternative. Roasting them brings out flavor, and they tend to be sturdy, good for stuffing.

HOW TO ROAST PEPPERS

Place the peppers on a stovetop or charcoal grill, broiler, or directly on the burners on your stove, turning them until the outsides are blackened. Put the peppers in a bowl, cover them with a towel, and let them sit until cool enough to handle. The skins should slip off quite easily, but you needn't fret if you don't get every bit; slice the peppers open to remove the seeds.

An alternative method is to put the blackened peppers into a plastic or paper bag, seal it, put it into the refrigerator, and peel them when they are cool enough.

HOT PEPPERS

Mildly hot peppers include the jalapeño, which is by far the most common hot pepper in this country, no doubt because even young children easily tolerate it. The degree of heat depends on a jalapeño's strain and origin; they can be so mild that I recommend buying more than your recipe calls for to be sure to get the level of spiciness you anticipate.

The Fresno is similar to the jalapeño, and similarly found green (though lighter) or bright red.

The dark red Anaheim is the pepper you see braided or formed into wreaths as decoration, especially in the Southwest. Grown in California and New Mexico, the Mexican variety is slightly hotter than the Californian, but in either case, like the jalapeño, the Anaheim can range from barely to mildly hot. The Anaheim goes by other names, by the way, New Mexico chile and long green or red chile among them.

Another chile is called Poblano in its shiny dark green state, and Ancho when it matures and turns red (and becomes hotter); Ancho is used dried as well. This is a really delicious rich-flavored pepper that is increasingly available. The flesh can be roasted and peeled, the same way as bell peppers, to enhance other dishes; it also is thick-walled enough to stuff.

Cherry peppers, which are also known as pimentos, are red, round, sweet, and mildly spicy. They are often pickled or brined; use them as appetizers or add some, sliced, to sautéed frying peppers along with some of their juice.

HOTTER PEPPERS

The habanero chile may appear as green, yellow, pink, or red, and is tiny, about the size of your fingertip. It is a powerhouse, however, among the hottest peppers commonly found and used in cooking.

The serrano also is quite spicy, though it resembles the jalapeño both in size, about two inches long, and in its green color, so choose carefully.

The Thai pepper, another teeny variety, is less than 1 inch to about 1½ inches long. It is very hot but not uncommonly used, especially in Southeast Asian dishes. The Thai pepper also goes by the name bird's eye.

Other hot varieties include the cayenne and the Tabasco, names more familiar for their other uses, as the spicy powder and as the ubiquitous condiment, and the Scotch bonnet, similar to the habanero. The ghost pepper is said to be the hottest in the world; one seed is enough to burn your mouth.

HOW TO HANDLE A CHILE

The spiciness of any kind of chile can vary and many of the hot peppers you prepare will be of the milder sort, but all should be treated with respect. To avoid stings and worse to your fingers, try using thin food handler's gloves, and be vigilant: do not touch your face or eyes, or other people, or anything else, edible or not, as you work with these peppers.

To judge the hotness of a chile, slice a bit of the flesh away from the rib and taste it. Too little heat can be as disappointing in the finished dish as too much; it's all a matter of taste. For more heat, include some of the rib, where it resides (not in the seeds as is widely believed). And be on the alert—hot peppers can sometimes insinuate themselves onto sweet ones growing nearby, so you may be surprised by some uncommon heat in a sweet pepper. This can happen even when sweet and hot peppers are tossed together in a bag.

There is an actual scientific way to measure the heat of a chile, the Scoville scale, invented by an American pharmacist a century ago. The scale can measure pepper heat into the millions of units, but the ones we think are seriously hot—habaneros, Scotch bonnet, Thai (bird's eye)—fall far below, topping out in the 50,000 to 350,000 range.

The Scoville scale, available on the Internet, can be interesting to children; it is simple and can let them see where the peppers they know fall, compared with the truly evil ones, which will register far above anything they—or you—are likely to taste. The Scoville also provides a simple lesson in how to read a scale.

TASTING PEPPERS

The way cooking changes food is interesting to children. So, if you are preparing peppers, demonstrate the differences between raw and cooked ones: the taste, the texture, and so on. Let them tell you what they experience. Tell them also that most red peppers were once green; compare those tastes too and see how much sweeter the red pepper is, and how the green one is a touch tart. If you grow them, you all can watch the green ones gradually turn red on the vine as they ripen. Red peppers, by the way, are more nutritious than green ones—the vitamins, minerals, and antioxidants, including lots more carotene—all develop as the peppers ripen.

25. Mushroom-Hazelnut Stuffing

My friend Dan Barber is the owner-chef of the three-star Blue Hill restaurant in New York's Greenwich Village and a second Blue Hill at Stone Barns in Pocantico Hills, about thirty miles outside the city. Dan has been in the forefront of the sustainable farming movement as a writer and as a culinary leader. There are times I am not sure which of his tools is more powerful—his pen or his knife.

Dan and I first came to know each other in an unusual, bittersweet way. His stepmother, Phyllis, and I were saying Kaddish at our neighborhood synagogue during the same year, I for Sylvia, Phyllis for her mother. Over the weeks and months, we became friends; when she learned my profession, she told me she had a son in the culinary field and asked if I knew Dan Barber. Of course I did! Even then, Dan was a rock star for me. Phyllis arranged my introduction to one of the most talented, yet down to earth, chef-activists I have ever met. Dan's work with educating children, chefs, agricultural interns, and adults at Stone Barns inspires all of us to do more ourselves to connect our communities to our farms.

As well as the obvious turkey, this dressing is a great accompaniment to duck or roasted chicken or pork.   SERVES 8

12 tablespoons (1½ sticks) butter

4 small shallots, finely chopped

3 garlic cloves, minced

1 cup chopped onion

3 teaspoons thyme leaves

1 pound portobello, shiitake, or a combination of wild mushrooms, stems removed, cut into ½-inch chunks

½ cup white wine

1 cup chicken stock, homemade (page 38) or good-quality store bought

Preheat the oven to 350 degrees.

Melt 10 tablespoons of the butter in a large skillet over medium heat; add the shallots, garlic, and onion and let sweat until translucent. Add 1 teaspoon of the thyme and the mushrooms. Cook, stirring, until the mushrooms are lightly browned. Add the wine and cook over medium-high heat until the liquid is nearly evaporated. Add the stock and continue to cook until it nearly evaporates. Season the mixture well with salt and pepper and transfer it to a large bowl.

Butter a 9-x-13-inch baking pan or 3-quart casserole with the remaining 2 tablespoons butter.

Add the bread, parsley, sage, hazelnuts, and the remaining 2 teaspoons thyme to the mushroom mixture and mix everything well.

Combine the eggs, cream, and hazelnut oil, if using, and stir into the stuffing until well mixed. Season with 1 teaspoon salt and ½ tea-

Sea salt and freshly ground
  white pepper
8 cups cubed day-old bread,
  crusts removed
¼ cup chopped flat-leaf
  parsley leaves
3 sage leaves, chopped
¾ cup hazelnuts, halved and
  lightly toasted
3 extra-large eggs, beaten
2 cups heavy cream
1 teaspoon hazelnut oil
  (optional)

spoon pepper. Spread the stuffing in the pan, cover with foil, and bake for 45 minutes. Remove foil and bake for another 30 minutes, until the top is golden brown.

STUFFED MUSHROOMS

The stuffings for Fried Squash Blossoms (page 124) are equally good for mushrooms. Choose large caps of white cultivated or portobello mushrooms, wipe them clean, and fill them generously, mounding the tops. Place the mushrooms on a cookie sheet or in an ovenproof dish (I like to use something I can take to the table) and bake at 375 degrees, until the tops are browned and the mushrooms are tender, about 10 minutes.

MUSHROOMS

Until not so long ago, the white cultivated mushroom—the button—was the only fresh one available. It may come as a shock to know that before that, fresh mushrooms of any sort were even scarcer, a quandary when the Julia Child generation began whipping up *boeuf bourguignonne* and *coq au vin.* The ubiquitous slippery little canned mushrooms would not do.

The selection of mushrooms routinely found in any supermarket has steadily increased, while specialty food shops and farmers' markets have pushed the options even further. Mushrooms are low in calories and high in vitamin D and minerals, but never mind that; I love mushrooms for their taste, so complex, earthy but delicate, even the most intense of them.

Most mushrooms can be treated lightly, sautéed with shallots or garlic in butter or olive oil, maybe with thyme, and finished with a shower of fresh parsley. I also like to roast or grill mushrooms, which brings out lots of flavor and crisps them up a bit. Mushrooms are elegant in soup and risotto; over pasta or polenta, they make an easy but special everyday dinner. A well-made omelet folded over fresh sautéed mushrooms defines luxurious simplicity.

Cremini are now nearly as common as the white button mushroom and can be substituted for a deeper flavor. Another, the portobello, a grown-up cremini, is particularly good grilled or roasted to eliminate some of its moisture and concentrate its flavor. Shiitake are also versatile, though more delicate, and excellent in a stir-fry, a simple soup, with sautéed chicken or fish, or in a lightly dressed salad.

Other, more exotic, mushrooms are the hen-of-the-woods, also known as the maitake, rich and clean tasting, and the oyster, with its sea-creature looks, pale ivory color, and velvety texture. The cèpe (in France), or porcini (in Italy), is one of the kings of the mushroom world and can be the star of a meal, great pan-broiled with a tiny bit of garlic or grilled and drizzled with olive oil.

I also adore the pretty little trumpet-shaped chanterelles and morels, so meaty and fragrant, that appear in spring in most places.

As for dried mushrooms, I've come to regard them as an essential pantry item. The ones I have been using lately seem to be less gritty than in the past, but some careful preparation is still called for. Give the mushrooms a rinse to remove excess grit. Then soak the mushrooms in just enough water—tepid, not hot—to cover (unless your recipe calls for a specific amount). The soaking time needed can vary, depending on the mushrooms' type, size, and condition; it may be as little as 20 minutes or as long as 40; the mushrooms are ready to use when the pieces are fully pliable, without hard, still-dry parts.

When ready, carefully remove the mushrooms from the water, rinse them again, and set them aside. Strain the soaking water through a strainer lined with cheesecloth and save it, if not for the dish at hand, for another, like mushroom soup.

Just a tablespoon or so of chopped reconstituted dried mushrooms and some of the soaking liquid can emphasize the flavor of fresh mushrooms; add them to the pan near the end of cooking and let the liquid soak in and evaporate. Or add a chopped slice or two and the liquid to a stew or soup. Another trick is to pulverize a piece or two of dried mushroom in a coffee or spice grinder and sprinkle it into your dish.

Dried mushrooms may seem expensive—an ounce of good-quality porcinis or chanterelles can cost around $15—but they are light in weight and very small amounts can bring lots of flavor to a dish. And, depending on the type, an ounce will yield around a half pound when reconstituted. Think of dried mushrooms more as a flavoring ingredient, like a spice, than a component.

26. Eggplant Caponata

This recipe produces what seems like a lot of caponata. But then we start using it and bringing it to friends, and suddenly it doesn't seem like so much. In any case, I need to do something with my eggplant crop and, frankly, making a lot of caponata is hardly more bother than making less. Furthermore, caponata keeps well and is a good addition to any meal, a light lunch with cheese or on the dinner table with grilled meats or fish—it is even delicious with eggs. It freezes well, too. I use both yellow and red bell peppers to add color, but just one variety or the other will do. MAKES ABOUT 3 QUARTS; 1 QUART SERVES 4 TO 6

¾ cup golden raisins

Olive oil

3 medium eggplants, washed but not peeled, diced

Salt and freshly ground pepper

2 medium onions, diced (about 3 cups)

¾ cup peeled and diced celery

2 tablespoons minced garlic

2 teaspoons fresh thyme leaves

1 tablespoon chopped fresh rosemary leaves

1–2 yellow bell peppers, roasted (page 114), peeled, and diced

1–2 red bell peppers, roasted (page 114), peeled, and diced

¾ cup capers in vinegar, drained and roughly chopped

¾ cup red wine vinegar

¼ cup sugar

2 cups peeled, seeded, and roughly chopped tomatoes

½ cup chopped parsley

Put the raisins in a medium bowl and cover with lukewarm water to soften. Set aside until needed.

Pour enough oil into a large sauté pan or skillet to cover the bottom generously and place the pan over medium-high heat. When the oil is hot, add the eggplant and sauté, until tender, adding oil as needed; you may need to do this in batches. Transfer the eggplant to a bowl, season with salt and pepper, and set it aside to cool.

Pour additional oil into the pan and add the onions, celery, and garlic, then the thyme, rosemary, and salt and pepper to taste and cook, stirring from time to time, until tender.

Add the peppers, capers, vinegar, sugar, and tomatoes; drain the raisins and add. Cook until slightly thickened. Adjust the seasoning as necessary with additional vinegar and sugar to achieve a pleasing balance of sweet to acid, and season with salt and pepper to taste.

Let the pepper mixture cool to room temperature, then fold in the eggplant.

Fold in the chopped parsley before serving. Caponata can be served warm, but never cold. I think the flavors are at their best at room temperature.

27. *Berenjenas al Escabeche* (Marinated Eggplants)

This is a recipe from my dearest friend, Dodi Meyer, who grew up in Argentina. Dodi lives in New York now and is a pediatrician; healthy eating is a cornerstone of her practice. She is also on the board of the Sylvia Center and her expertise has grounded our work.

Dodi's memories include the home of friends, where Saturday lunches around a beautifully set table were as much long visits as meals. Over two or three hours many platters of traditional food came forth, including this one. In Argentina a meal is not a meal unless meat, beef in particular, is one of the main courses. *Berenjenas al Escabeche* is served to "wet" the meat and enhance its flavor.

The *berenjenas* should be prepared a few days ahead to allow the eggplant to absorb the marinating flavors. Typical of home cooks and the dishes they make from memory, Dodi did not send along much in the way of specific quantities, but her basic guidance is all you need for this home-style dish.   SERVES 6 TO 8

2 medium eggplants

Kosher salt

1 quart distilled white
   vinegar

Olive oil

Paprika

Leaves from 2 or 3 sprigs
   oregano

2 garlic cloves, thinly sliced

3 to 4 bay leaves

Cut the eggplants in thin lengthwise slices, about ½ inch. Put them in a strainer and sprinkle them generously with kosher salt. Let the eggplant stand for an hour or so.

Rinse the slices and place them on paper towels. Bring the vinegar to a low boil in a saucepan or deep skillet. Put the eggplant slices, a few at a time, into the vinegar for 2 to 3 minutes, just long enough to soften them. Remove the slices with a slotted spoon to a strainer.

Place a few slices of eggplant into a clean 1-quart Mason jar. Dribble a tablespoon or two of olive oil over the slices, then sprinkle with paprika and add a few leaves of oregano and a slice or two of garlic. Continue this layering, ending with a slice or two of eggplant. Place the bay leaves on top.

Close the jar and let it stand at room temperature for a few days before serving, or store longer in the refrigerator.

28. Baked Stuffed Zucchini Boats

These are among the most favorite dishes the children make at the Sylvia Center. They are fun to make, and we've found that giving dishes interesting names, like "boats," captures the attention of young people. They help to make the boats; the little ones remove the seeds with small spoons. Then they mix everything together for the filling—yes, with clean fingers. You can use other herbs, along with or in place of the parsley; basil or chives would be nice.

SERVES 4 TO 8

Salt

8 young zucchini, washed

2 tablespoons olive oil, plus extra to drizzle

1 medium onion, finely chopped

¼ teaspoon freshly grated nutmeg

Freshly ground pepper

2 eggs

1 cup grated Parmigiano-Reggiano

1 cup fresh bread crumbs

½ cup chopped flat-leaf parsley

Preheat the oven to 375 degrees. Bring a large pot of water to a boil; add a big pinch of salt.

Meanwhile, cut the zucchini in half lengthwise. Remove as many of the larger seeds as possible. Scoop out and reserve the flesh, being careful not to break through the skin.

Roughly chop the zucchini flesh. Heat the oil in a skillet over medium heat, then add the onion and zucchini flesh and sauté until soft but not browned, about 5 minutes. Add the nutmeg and season with salt and pepper to taste. Remove the pan from the heat.

Blanch the zucchini shells in the boiling water for 2 minutes and refresh them under cold water, taking care to keep them intact.

Beat the eggs in a medium bowl and stir in the zucchini mixture; mix in the cheese, bread crumbs, and parsley. Divide this filling among the boats, place them on a baking sheet, and drizzle them with olive oil. Bake for 15 to 20 minutes, until golden brown.

29. Fried Squash Blossoms

Squash blossoms appear at the best time of year, when the cold has gone away and summer is just coming in. My favorite way to cook them is to quickly pan-fry them in olive oil with garlic and then toss them with angel hair pasta and grated Pecorino Romano cheese. Deep-fried squash blossoms is a traditional and much loved preparation that I do for special occasions, sometimes stuffed Italian-style with a bit of mozzarella or fresh ricotta. The options for stuffings are nearly limitless; I've included three below.

If you grow zucchini, as many home farmers do, you can pick blossoms without squandering your crop by choosing just males, since only the females develop fruit. The male blossoms are longer and thinner than the females, which are round and closer to the leaves; you can see the fruit beginning to develop inside the flower. Conversely, harvesting the females will control the squash population, which sometimes can be a blessing—zucchini can be very prolific.

SERVES 4

3 cups flour, plus more for
   dredging
1 teaspoon baking powder
1 egg, lightly beaten
2 cups seltzer or beer
Oil such as canola, for frying
Salt and freshly ground
   pepper
8 to 12 squash blossoms,
   depending on their size

GOAT CHEESE STUFFING
1 tablespoon chopped
   rosemary leaves
¾ cup fresh goat cheese
4 tablespoons (2 ounces)
   cream cheese
2 tablespoons panko (see
   page 218)

Sift the flour and baking powder together into a large bowl and make a well in the center. Pour the egg and the seltzer into the well, and, using a fork, slowly combine the ingredients, working from the sides to the center. Do not overmix; let the batter rest for one hour.

Pour the oil into a deep pot or electric fryer to about 3 inches deep and heat it to 325 degrees.

Spread some of the batter on a sheet of wax paper and season it with salt and pepper. Dredge the squash blossoms in the seasoned flour, shake off the excess, then dip them into the batter and place them on a plate. Carefully add the blossoms to the hot oil, two or three at a time, and fry them until golden brown. Quickly remove the blossoms from the oil, sprinkle with salt, and serve immediately.

You can stuff the squash blossoms before frying them to enhance the flavor.

Mix the bread-crumb ingredients for the stuffing together (follow my suggestions or create your own). Spoon them into a pastry bag. Carefully squeeze the filling into the blossoms, then follow the directions for frying above.

SAUSAGE STUFFING

2 sweet Italian sausages,
  casings removed

1 hot Italian sausage, casing
  removed

2 eggs

1 cup grated Parmigiano-
  Reggiano

ITALIAN BREAD CRUMB
  STUFFING

2 cups packaged Italian bread
  crumbs

1 teaspoon chopped garlic

2 teaspoons thyme

2 teaspoons chopped oregano

2 teaspoons chopped basil

½ cup white wine

½ cup grated Parmigiano-
  Reggiano

30. Butternut Squash Bread Pudding

If home cooking is to a large degree circumstantial, bread pudding is one of the best examples, a nifty merger of bread going stale and a cook's ingenuity. Savory bread puddings have not been as much in the home cook's collections as sweet versions, but I think they should be. Some, like this one, can be all that's needed in the way of a sturdy side dish. I like to use brioche or challah for this to intensify the egg-custard effect, but don't hesitate to make it with whatever you have.   SERVES 8

2 tablespoons unsalted butter, melted

2 medium butternut squash (about 1½ pounds each)

2 tablespoons extra-virgin olive oil

Salt

Pinch of freshly grated nutmeg

Pinch of cinnamon

2 tablespoons pure maple syrup

3 cups half-and-half

6 large eggs, beaten

½ cup grated Parmigiano-Reggiano

Freshly ground pepper

1 loaf of brioche, challah, or good-quality white bread, crusts trimmed and bread cut into ½-inch cubes (8 cups)

Preheat the oven to 400 degrees. Brush a shallow, 3-quart baking dish with a bit of the melted butter.

Cut the squash in half lengthwise, remove the seeds, and peel the skin. Thinly slice the bulbous lower parts of the squash into crescents and arrange them in a single layer on a rimmed baking sheet. Cut the necks of the squash into ½-inch cubes and spread them on another baking sheet.

Mix the remaining butter and olive oil together, then lightly brush it on the squash crescents. Season with salt. Drizzle any remaining butter and oil over the diced squash, sprinkle with the nutmeg and cinnamon, and season with salt to taste. Roast the squash for about 10 minutes, turning once, until softened and lightly browned in spots. Drizzle both pans of squash with the maple syrup and roast for 5 minutes longer. Let cool.

Whisk the half-and-half with the eggs in a large bowl; whisk in the cheese and a pinch each of salt and pepper. Add the bread and squash cubes; toss gently. Spoon the mixture into the dish and arrange the squash crescents on top. Bake for 1 hour, until the top of the pudding is golden in spots and the center is just firm. Let cool for 15 minutes before serving.

WINTER SQUASHES

As much as I love them, I am always a little ambivalent when the winter squashes make their seasonal appearance. The pumpkins are first, showing up at farmers' markets, shoving their way among the late tomatoes and corn, letting you know that summer is not endless, and that socks and sweaters are not far behind. But once I decide to embrace the inevitable, I fall in love again with these tasty and versatile vegetables. They differ extravagantly in shape, size, and color, but the differences in taste and texture are subtler; these squashes often can step gracefully into one another's recipes. Their thicker skins keep the winter squashes fresher far longer than summer's thin-skinned and more watery zucchini and yellow squash—and I think they are ultimately more interesting. In the old days, winter squashes were among the mainstays of the cold-weather larder, kept for the duration along with potatoes and onions.

Many kinds of winter squashes are becoming more widely distributed, even to supermarkets. I suspect part of the reason is the growing aware-ness of their nutritional benefits: they are low in carbohydrates and fat, and deliver healthful amounts of minerals including calcium, iron, magnesium, potassium, and zinc, and vitamins C, B_5, and B_6.

The dark green round kabocha squash is one of my favorites; it has lots of beta-carotene and a deep, sweet flavor. Turbans and hubbards are so interesting to look at that they can do double duty as table decorations. The pretty delicata squash seemed to appear suddenly as the new thing a few years ago. It is, in fact, an heirloom variety developed in the late nineteenth century. Somehow, the delicata fell out of favor—it has a thinner skin than other winter squashes, and perhaps was impractical to ship. It is now back and quite widely available. The skin is edible, so just scrub it, then cut the squash down the middle or into chunks. Or add it to a potato puree or to a vegetable soup for extra flavor, body, and nutrition.

Easy to prepare, winter squashes take well to roasting, steaming, and sautéing, and they are good in soup (see pages 50–52). Even vegetable-resistant children will eat these squashes—just roast chunks with a tiny bit of brown sugar and butter. Pureed, they are a good early food for babies.

The other popular varieties are acorn, butternut, and banana, all of which take well to any preparation.

Pumpkins are practically a subcategory of their own, and some are more or less interchangeable. Sweet dumplings, jack-o'-lanterns, and little orange and white pumpkins can be steamed whole and served with butter or olive oil and herbs or stuffed. But check that they haven't been waxed, as these are often sold as seasonal decorations. Sugar pumpkins and pie pumpkins are the ones to choose for pie.

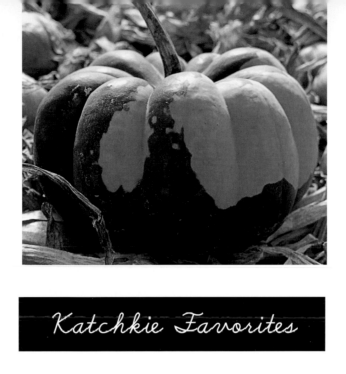

Katchkie Favorites

31. Roasted Squash Seeds

I don't roast just pumpkin seeds. The seeds of any winter squash are candidates. This is a good project for kids; they can pull off most of the strings, but don't worry if the seeds are not pristinely prepped. It's best to roast a single type and size together, but then you can store mixed batches in jars for snacking or sprinkling over roasted squash. Toss the seeds onto a baking sheet, drizzle with olive oil, spread them out, sprinkle with coarse salt—sea salt if you have it—and roast at 350 degrees for about 15 minutes, depending on the size of the seeds and your own taste, stirring once or twice. Sometimes I add cumin or chili powder toward the end.

32. Fava Beans with Scallions and Mint

Prepping fava beans can be tedious for grown-ups, but, like shelling peas, fun for kids. Once you have boiled the beans and let them cool down, children can help to get the favas out of the pods and then peel away the inner skin. If incentives are needed, and you have more than one helper at hand, make this a contest—whoever gets to fifty first is the champion. Have the kids make piles of ten for a multiplication lesson. SERVES 4

Salt

About 4 pounds shelled fresh fava bean pods

2 tablespoons olive oil

1 garlic clove, minced

1 pound scallions, quartered if small, diced if large, including tender part of green tops

Sea salt and freshly ground pepper

½ cup roughly chopped mint

Bring 5 quarts water to a boil in a large pot and prepare an ice water bath. Add a large pinch of salt to the boiling water, and then dump in the fava beans. Boil for 2 minutes, or until just tender. Drain and immediately plunge the beans into the ice water. This bath will stop the beans from cooking further and will help hold their bright green color. Drain the beans when they are completely cooled.

Tear a small opening in the thin opaque skin surrounding the beans, then gently squeeze them out.

Warm the oil in a skillet over medium heat; add the garlic and scallions and cook, stirring, until just tender, about 4 minutes. Add the beans and cook to just heat them through, then season with salt and pepper to taste. Toss in the mint and serve immediately.

33. Chickpea Ragout with Roasted Vegetables and Cumin

This makes for a terrific one-dish vegetarian main course with a sturdy whole-grain bread or quinoa on the side. It's also a good all-in-one side to grilled or roasted fish or meat, perfect for a casual buffet supper. It can be prepared in advance up to the point of topping with the yogurt sauce, and served warm or at room temperature.   SERVES 6 TO 8

3 tablespoons vegetable oil

1 cup finely chopped onion

1 tablespoon finely chopped garlic

1 tablespoon peeled and grated fresh ginger

2 teaspoons cumin seeds

2 tablespoons ground coriander

1 medium zucchini, cut into ½-inch pieces

1 red bell pepper, cored, seeded, and cut into ½-inch pieces

1 carrot, peeled and cut into ¼-inch pieces

1 eggplant, cut into ¼-inch pieces

Coarse salt and freshly ground pepper

3 cups cooked chickpeas (see page 308) or one 32-ounce can, drained and rinsed

1½ cups chopped tomatoes (about 2 or 3 medium)

2 tablespoons tomato paste

½ cup plain yogurt

½ cup chopped cucumber

½ cup chopped scallion, including 2 inches of green

½ cup chopped cilantro

1 tablespoon chopped hot green chiles, or to taste

Heat the oil in a large pot or Dutch oven over medium-high heat. Add the onion, garlic, ginger, cumin, and coriander and cook, stirring often, just until the onion is light brown, about 8 minutes. Add the zucchini, pepper, carrot, and eggplant, and season with salt and pepper to taste. Cook the vegetables until they are quite soft, stirring occasionally, 5 to 7 minutes.

Mix together the chickpeas, tomatoes, and tomato paste in a large bowl. Add the chickpeas and tomatoes to the vegetables. Pour in just enough water to cover and bring just to a boil. Lower the heat and simmer, covered, for 10 to 15 minutes, or until the flavors are blended and the sauce is very thick; stir from time to time and add water as needed.

While the ragout is cooking, mix together the yogurt, cucumber, scallion, cilantro, and hot green chiles. Serve the ragout topped with the yogurt sauce.

34. Vegetarian Chili

To me, chili is mostly about informal gatherings. A successful version delivers spicy flavors and interesting texture. I think the portobello mushrooms here add enough meaty richness along with nicely balanced healthful ingredients. This is good on its own or as a side to broiled or grilled meats.   SERVES 4 TO 6

2 tablespoons vegetable oil

1½ cups chopped onions

3 carrots, chopped (1 cup)

1 red bell pepper, chopped (1 cup)

2 tablespoons minced garlic

2 or 3 serrano peppers (depending on taste), seeded and minced

1 medium zucchini, diced

3 ears corn, kernels removed (2 cups)

1 cup sliced okra (optional; use frozen if it's out of season)

1½ pounds (about 5 large) portobello mushrooms, stemmed, wiped clean, and cubed

2 tablespoons chili powder

1 tablespoon ground cumin

Heat the oil in a large, heavy pot over medium-high heat. Add the onions, carrots, bell pepper, garlic, and serrano peppers, and cook, stirring, until soft, about 3 minutes. Add the zucchini, corn, okra, and mushrooms and cook, stirring, until the vegetables are soft, give off their liquid, and begin to brown, about 6 minutes.

Add the chili powder, cumin, coriander, salt, and cayenne, and cook, stirring, until fragrant, about 30 seconds. Add the tomatoes and stir well. Add the beans, tomato sauce, and vegetable stock, stir well, and bring just to a boil. Reduce the heat to medium-low and simmer, stirring occasionally, for about 20 minutes.

Remove the chili from the heat and stir in the cilantro. Taste and adjust the seasoning.

To serve, ladle the chili into individual bowls and top each serving with a dollop of sour cream, a spoonful of avocado, and a sprinkling of scallions.

1 tablespoon ground
   coriander

2 teaspoons salt

½ teaspoon cayenne pepper

4 large tomatoes, peeled,
   seeded, and chopped

3 cups cooked or canned
   black beans, rinsed and
   drained

One 15-ounce can tomato
   sauce

1 cup vegetable stock,
   homemade (page 38) or
   good-quality store bought

¼ cup chopped cilantro
   leaves

Sour cream, diced avocado,
   chopped scallions, for
   serving

35. Vegan Fall Lentil Stew

This is a good model for constructing a vegetarian meal or a sturdy side dish by using beans or legumes along with greens and root vegetables. Such dishes are wholesome and satisfying and subject to whatever herbs or spices appeal to you.   SERVES 4

1 teaspoon vegetable oil

2 garlic cloves, minced

1 medium onion, diced

1 carrot, sliced into ¼-inch rounds

1 rutabaga, diced

1 medium all-purpose potato, diced

3 cups vegetable stock, homemade (page 38) or good-quality store bought

1 cup red wine

1 cup dried green lentils

1 teaspoon chopped fresh thyme

1 teaspoon chopped fresh rosemary

2 bay leaves

Salt and freshly ground pepper

1 pound spinach, roughly chopped

1 tablespoon fresh lemon juice

Heat the vegetable oil in a large, heavy pot or Dutch oven over medium heat, then stir in the garlic, onion, carrot, rutabaga, and potato; continue to stir until the onions are translucent, 5 to 7 minutes.

Add the stock, wine, lentils, thyme, rosemary, bay leaves, a big pinch of salt, and several grindings of pepper. Bring just to a boil, then reduce the heat, cover, and simmer until the lentils are soft, about 45 minutes.

Remove and discard the bay leaves. Stir in the chopped spinach and cook until just wilted; add additional stock if you want to loosen the mixture. Add the lemon juice just before serving, and season to taste with salt and pepper.

36. Black-Eyed Pea Salad

The Senegalese chef and cookbook author Pierre Thiam gave me this recipe. Members of Pierre's family are wonderful cooks, and he was influenced especially by his mother and one of his uncles, who brought Vietnamese flavors into the family repertoire. Thiam spent many hours of his childhood absorbed in his mother's copy of *Larousse Gastronomique.* Pierre lives in Brooklyn now, and this is one of the dishes that reminds him of home. Senegal has an interesting cuisine; as a colony of France, it was influenced by French food, and subsequently by the food of Vietnam when the French—and many Senegalese—fought there. Both Pierre and his uncle were unusual in a culture where, even today, few men cook.   SERVES 4

2 limes

1 cup olive oil

Salt and freshly ground
    pepper

3½ cups cooked black-eyed
    peas or two 15.5-ounce
    cans, drained and rinsed

1 tomato, roughly chopped

1 unwaxed cucumber, seeded
    and diced

1 red bell pepper, seeded and
    diced

1 bunch scallions, white
    and 1 inch of green parts,
    chopped

Leaves from ½ bunch fresh
    flat-leaf parsley, roughly
    chopped

Whole leaves of Bibb or
    Boston lettuce, washed

Squeeze the limes into a small bowl, then slowly whisk in the olive oil; season with salt and pepper.

Toss the black-eyed peas, tomato, cucumber, bell pepper, scallions, and parsley in a serving bowl. Pour the dressing over the salad, folding to combine well. Let the salad marinate for about 1 hour; adjust the seasonings as necessary and spoon into the lettuce leaves to serve.

BLACK-EYED PEAS

Black-eyed peas are not really peas, but a kind of bean that is native to India and Africa. From the West Indies, black-eyed peas made their way to the southern United States, most likely on slave ships and possibly as early as the 1600s. By the time of the American Revolution, they were firmly established as a part of cooking in the South, where it is a tradition to eat black-eyed peas with vinegar, greens, and some sort of pork on New Year's Day. The swelling of the beans as they cook is taken as a sign of prosperity.

Black-eyed peas are highly nutritious, rich in calcium, folate, and vitamin A, among other nutrients.

37. *Porotos Granados* (Fresh Beans, Pumpkin, and Corn)

This recipe comes from Nina Simmons, the education director of the Sylvia Center. Nina was an early volunteer at the Sylvia Center and now is our best chef instructor. For this dish, Nina encourages using fresh beans when they are around; look for large, pregnant-looking pods, which will have mature beans inside. In the market, these are known as shelling beans.

This dish connects Nina to her childhood and her family. As she told me, "A field of bright orange pumpkins brings out the kid in all of us. But while children think, 'Jack-o'-lanterns,' I think, '*Porotos Granados!*' That's a traditional Chilean harvest dish my mother used to make. It's basically a version of a 'three sisters' recipe [see page 138] that uses freshly shelled cranberry beans. I have yet to meet anyone who doesn't swoon over this." SERVES 4

2 pounds fresh cranberry
   bean pods, or ½ pound
   dried beans
3 tablespoons olive oil
1 medium onion, diced
1 quart chicken stock,
   homemade (page 38) or
   good-quality store bought
6 ears corn
1 small pumpkin or medium
   butternut squash, peeled
   and cut into large dice
   (saving the seeds to roast,
   see page 129, and eat while
   you work)
1 cup julienned basil
Salt and freshly ground
   pepper
2 jalapeños, minced
   (optional)

If using dried beans, soak them overnight and then drain them. If using fresh beans, rinse them well.

Heat the oil in a large soup pot over medium heat; add the onion and sauté until translucent.

Add the beans, along with the stock, to the pot. Bring to a boil, then simmer, covered, until the beans are just tender but not cooked through, about 10 minutes for fresh beans, or 40 minutes for dried. You may need to add water as you cook the dried beans.

While the beans are cooking, cut the kernels off 3 of the corncobs and set them aside. Grate the three remaining ears into a separate bowl.

When the beans are ready, add the pumpkin and continue to cook until it is tender, about 10 minutes. Add the corn kernels to the pot and cook for 3 minutes, then add the grated corn and cook for a final 2 minutes.

Add the basil and salt and pepper to taste. Sprinkle with the minced jalapeño, if using, and serve.

The Story of the Three Sisters

Ask your children and their friends if they know what a "three sisters" garden is, then tell them this sweet story.

A three sisters garden is an ancient method of growing corn, beans, and squash all together, usually in a rounded mound of soil, often refered to as a hill. Some American Indians planted their crops this way.

Corn is the oldest sister. She stands tall in the center.

Squash is the next sister. She grows over the mound, protecting her sisters from weeds and shading the soil from the sun with her leaves, keeping it cool and moist.

Beans are the third sister. She climbs through the squash and then up the corn to bind everything together as she reaches for the sun.

If your children like to draw, and most do, see if they'd like to illustrate the story of the three sisters.

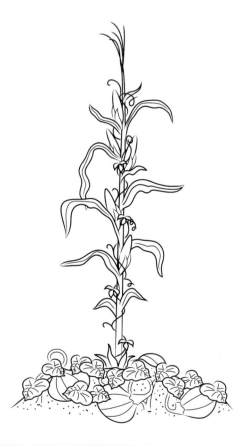

A Visit to a Farmers' Market

If a busy farmers' market can excite us grown-ups, imagine what it's like for children. From ancient times, the market was at the heart of a community, the place where people met and shared news, gossip, and recipes. Today's urban markets are no different. Markets are an exquisite form of entertainment, a kind of theater full of characters, color, and delicious smells, none of which is lost on kids.

You may be able to scout out what's available at your local farmers' market online. In New York the extensive Greenmarket system can be checked at grownyc.org/greenmarket—the locations, the days for each one, the vendors' schedules, and what's at their stalls. Another, localharvest.org, can guide you to markets in many American cities; I use it whenever I travel to see what's happening and where.

At the Sylvia Center we know the transformative effect on children when they see where their food comes from. Farmers' markets, and, outside of cities and towns, roadside stands, have the same effect. The food is immediate, and the person who grew it is often right there, inevitably eager to talk about it. In her book *Local Flavors,* Deborah Madison wrote that at some markets modest little events like apple tastings for children take place and that in Santa Monica, California, a kids' salad bar of mostly organic fruits and vegetables went, in a short time, from being completely ignored to incredibly popular.

A supermarket may not offer quite the same excitement, but it can have a similar effect. Children are naturally curious. Stay on the perimeter, avoiding the aisles of packaged and processed foods and cartoon characters pitching products at the eye level of three-year-olds. Produce has its own appeal, and some parents are chagrined to learn that their kids gravitate to foods they hadn't thought the children were ready for. The daughter of a friend of mine began pilfering raspberries and tree fruit at eighteen months; to avoid culpability, my friend routinely turned in empty berry boxes, cores, and pits at checkout.

The point is to simply and casually expose kids to real food. Whatever attracts them can easily lead to tasting—buy the thing, take it home, serve it, and the chances are they will eat it.

Playing with Food

At the Sylvia Center we have many activities that are both fun and instructive.

Plant a Seed

We make little pots from newspaper by wrapping a sheet—a tabloid is just the right length, folded to about five inches deep—around a wine bottle and tucking it into the space at the bottom. Remove the bottle, fill the formed "pot" with moist soil, and plant one seed, flower or veggie. You can tie the paper in place with a bit of twine, but it will begin to hold its shape anyway as the paper absorbs moisture. If you don't tie it, you can put the paper pot right into the ground. Either way, the children get to watch their plants grow.

Veggie Taste Test

We have magnets of various vegetables and put chopped samples of each under their match—cucumbers under cucumbers, beets under beets and so on. The kids have duplicate magnets that they use to vote for their favorites. As the day progresses, you would be amazed to see how interested they are to see what veggie wins the popularity contest. Interestingly, the favorites have been beets, carrots, sugar snap peas, and kohlrabi. Because the samples are so tiny, we also have the entire vegetables as well as the various seeds on hand so they can get a sense of the growing process.

Make a Snack

The children build a little sandwich on a cracker, a classic combination like basil, tomatoes, and mozzarella, for instance. Then we talk about what's new to them, what they might change, and the seasonality of the ingredients.

Herb Taste Test

We set out samples of some common herbs, such as mint, sage, parsley, oregano, and basil, and ask the children how they might use them. With a little guidance, they begin to understand why mint tastes good in iced tea or lemonade, oregano on pizza, sage in the stuffing they have at Thanksgiving, and the ever-popular basil with tomatoes.

A Greens Tasting

Late in the growing season we put out bits of chard, spinach, kale, mizuna, and mustard greens and compare their characteristics. This is an especially effective way to introduce greens, a category that kids sometimes need to be coaxed toward.

Poultry and Meat

1. Grilled Chicken Breasts
2. Mama Romano's Lemon Chicken
3. Bertha's Chicken
4. Moroccan Chicken with Preserved Lemon and Olives
5. Norma Jean's Fried Chicken
6. Grandma Debby Neumark's Honey-Dijon Chicken
7. Roasted Chicken with Herbs
8. Roasted Chicken with Basil and Caramelized Shallots
9. Oven-Roasted Wild Heritage Turkey with Cornbread and Andouille Sausage Dressing
10. Grilled Tamarind Turkey Burgers
11. Roast Breast of Duck with Pears
12. Orange-Scented Duck Breast with Daikon Salad and Pureed Sweet Potatoes
13. Tuscan Pot Roast
14. Hearty Winter Beef Stew
15. Braised Beef Short Ribs with Star Anise, Orange Zest, and Ginger
16. Thai Beef and Ginger Salad
17. Katchkie Farm Meatloaf
18. Chipotle-Honey Barbecued Baby Back Ribs
19. Garlic-Studded Leg of Lamb with a Rosemary Crust
20. Butterflied and Roasted Leg of Lamb with Cumin Rub and Mint Pesto
21. Leg of Lamb with a Chile-Citrus Rub

Chicken is endlessly versatile and pretty easy to prepare. It is flexible, forgiving, universally loved, and not very expensive. Lots of people who don't eat red meat will eat chicken; it appeals to children and is the perfect companion to whatever is growing seasonally. Chicken lends itself to global flavors and has inspired countless "Chicken Recipes/365 Ways" collections, thanks to its good nature. In its simplest form—roasted—it defines Sunday dinners. In soup form, it is the stuff of childhood memories and the world's most reliable cure for symptoms of the common cold.

As a child, I remember how my grannies relished the feet, neck, and gizzard ("pupick") that came with their fresh chickens; these treasures were not to be wasted and always were used to enrich their soup. I know it is hard to believe, but I was well into my teens when I discovered that people had strong preferences for dark or light meat. We just loved it all and never distinguished between the two!

I've also included here a handful of recipes for duck. In the last decade or so it has become easy to buy first-class boned duck breasts that lend themselves to preparations as easy and quick to execute as those for steak. Duck has a rich flavor of its own and adapts as easily to modern notions of seasoning—Asian, for instance—as it does to classic preparations.

Other meats—beef, lamb, pork—take well to various cooking methods such as grilling, roasting, and braising, which in turn lend themselves to an endless world of flavors and combinations with other ingredients.

At Katchkie Farm we are close to many small sustainable farms where grass-fed meat is being raised humanely without antibiotics or hormones. There are sheep farms where not only is meat raised and cheese made but simply gorgeous wool is produced and naturally dyed—and all of it to be found at farm stands and Greenmarkets throughout New York City. This is a national movement, of course, that began more than thirty years ago. And meat from animals such as bison and buffalo is beginning to return to the American diet. There are a growing number of producers in this field now, which is important if more wholesome locally grown meat is going to be available and affordable to more people.

The movement to raise heritage breeds also has expanded impressively. Like heirloom fruits and vegetables, a lot of these products may seem new, but we are mostly going back to an earlier time, when great variety was unexceptional.

1. Grilled Chicken Breasts

Boneless chicken breasts are fast food for home cooks, as well as being healthful and subject to endless interpretation. Brillat-Savarin put it perfectly: "Poultry is for the cook what canvas is for the painter."

Here is my basic method for preparing boneless chicken breasts on a gas or charcoal grill, or even under your broiler, along with enough variations that you could serve these weekly without risking monotony. In these preparations, the chicken marinates for as little as 30 minutes, and cooks in around 10, which gives you time to prepare the rest of the meal while your very young staff sets the table. Besides convenience for you and the comfort of the familiar for your kids, these chicken recipes will provide a gentle introduction to a variety of new flavors.

I used chicken breasts for these recipes because everyone seems to like them, but boneless thighs, which are also widely available, can be used as well. They are meatier and often less expensive; the cooking time will be just a couple minutes longer. These marinades are just as suitable for cut-up whole chickens, though you will need to adjust the cooking times when you grill or broil them. Roughly double the amount of marinade for a 3- to 3½-pound chicken. Cut-up whole chickens can be marinated for longer, even overnight.

The quantities here are enough for four full servings, or more if small people will be at the table. The chicken breasts are great for sandwiches or as part of a lunchtime salad plate; in those cases, you probably will have enough for six.   SERVES 4

---

1 batch marinade of your
   choice (see suggestions
   following this recipe)
4 skinless, boneless chicken
   breasts, trimmed of excess
   fat
Salt

Prepare your marinade in a glass or ceramic (nonreactive) pan that will accommodate the chicken breasts snugly. Or do what I do and put everything, including the chicken, into a plastic bag with a zipper; turn to coat the chicken well on both sides and refrigerate for at least 30 minutes or up to 4 hours.

Heat a stovetop grill, grill pan, or gas grill to high heat, or prepare a charcoal fire in a covered grill, placing coals on one side only (see page 173). Remove the breasts from the marinade and season them with salt.

If you are using a stovetop grill, a grill pan, or a gas grill, place the chicken on it and cook for 2 to 3 minutes, or until you see good grill marks. Flip the breasts and turn the heat to low; cover with aluminum foil and continue to cook until the juices run clear; the internal temperature should be 165 degrees.

If you are cooking over charcoal in a kettle grill, grill the breasts for 2 to 3 minutes on each side over the fire, then move them to the cooler side, cover the grill, and finish as above for a few minutes longer, taking care not to overcook. Otherwise, move the breasts to the cooler side and cover with foil, as above.

If a grill is not available, you can use a griddle pan or a heavy skillet on a burner. The advantage here will be that you will have the cooking juices to dribble over the cooked breasts.

Let the breasts rest for 5 minutes before serving.

THE MARINADES

Lemon-Pepper Marinade

Zest from 1 lemon
¼ cup fresh lemon juice
1 small shallot, minced
¼ cup olive oil
Salt
½ tablespoon coarsely ground pepper

Whisk the ingredients together.

Herb Marinade

1 heaping tablespoon each chopped thyme, rosemary, and flat-leaf
    parsley
2 tablespoons olive oil
2 tablespoons Dijon mustard
Salt and freshly ground pepper

Whisk the herbs together with the other ingredients, and season
with salt and pepper.

Cumin-Marjoram Marinade

1 tablespoon chopped fresh marjoram or oregano
1 tablespoon ground cumin
1 small shallot, minced
¼ cup olive oil
Salt and freshly ground pepper

Whisk the ingredients together.

Red Chile Pepper and Citrus Marinade

¼ cup plus 1 tablespoon olive oil
4 garlic cloves, minced
1 teaspoon red chile flakes
2 tablespoons grated lemon zest
2 tablespoons grated orange zest
2 tablespoons fresh lemon juice
2 tablespoons fresh orange juice

Salt and freshly ground pepper

2 tablespoons chopped fresh flat-leaf parsley

Heat 1 tablespoon of the olive oil in a small sauté pan; add the garlic and chile flakes and gently cook until fragrant. Transfer the flavored oil to a medium bowl. Stir in half the lemon and orange zest, lemon juice, orange juice, the remaining ¼ cup olive oil, a pinch of salt, and a few grindings of pepper.

Prepare the chicken according to the basic recipe. Mix the remaining lemon and orange zest with the parsley and sprinkle the mixture over the chicken before serving.

Lemon, Rosemary, and Roasted-Garlic Marinade

1 whole head garlic

¼ cup plus 1 tablespoon olive oil

Salt and freshly ground pepper

1 tablespoon grated lemon zest

¼ cup fresh lemon juice

1 tablespoon chopped fresh rosemary

1 tablespoon Dijon mustard

1 small shallot, chopped

Preheat the oven to 400 degrees.

Cut the garlic head just under the very top but do not peel it. Coat the garlic with 1 tablespoon of the olive oil and season with salt and pepper. Wrap the head tightly in aluminum foil and roast it in the oven until soft when tested with a cake tester or the tip of a very sharp knife, about 1 hour. (The garlic can be prepared hours, or even a day, in advance.)

Unwrap the garlic and let it cool until it can be handled, then squeeze the flesh from the cloves into a small mixing bowl. Add the lemon zest, lemon juice, rosemary, mustard, shallot, the remaining ¼ cup olive oil, and a pinch of salt and pepper and whisk until smooth.

2. Mama Romano's Lemon Chicken

Mama Romano is the mother of Michael Romano, the executive chef and partner of Union Square Cafe, one of New York's perennially favorite restaurants. Michael is one of the most passionate people I know when it comes to connecting children, healthful food, and cooking. Years ago, he would take groups of children to the Union Square Greenmarket on Saturday mornings, then back to the restaurant to cook up a meal from what they'd gathered. Now he's involved, along with Michael Anthony of Gramercy Tavern, in Wellness in the Schools, which was organized to help prepare healthful food for children in public schools.

Mama Romano's chicken is simple and wholesome, typical of Italian home cooking, and universally appealing, even to renowned chefs like Michael.   SERVES 4

One 3½-pound chicken, cut into 10 pieces (cut the 2 breast pieces in half), rinsed and patted dry

1 teaspoon kosher salt

¼ teaspoon freshly ground pepper

Flour, for dredging

2 tablespoons olive oil

3 cups thinly sliced red or yellow onions

1½ teaspoons thinly sliced garlic

8 sprigs thyme

2 lemons

1½ cups chicken stock, homemade (page 38) or good-quality store bought

Season the chicken with ½ teaspoon of the salt and ⅛ teaspoon of the pepper and set it aside at cool room temperature for 1 hour.

Preheat the oven to 400 degrees.

Dredge the chicken in flour.

Heat 1 tablespoon of the oil in a 10-inch ovenproof skillet or Dutch oven over medium high heat. Sauté the chicken pieces, a few at a time, until a rich golden brown all over; set them aside on a platter as they are done.

Discard the fat from the skillet and add the remaining 1 tablespoon oil. Add the onions, garlic, and remaining salt and pepper and cook over medium heat for 25 minutes, stirring occasionally, until the onions are very soft and lightly browned; do not let them burn. Remove the pan from the heat.

Spread the thyme sprigs over the onions and garlic. Arrange the chicken pieces side by side over the onions. Squeeze 1 of the lemons through a strainer onto the chicken. Pour the stock into the pan.

Cut the remaining lemon into 10 slices and remove the seeds. Place 1 slice on each piece of chicken. Return the pan to the heat and bring the stock just to a simmer. Cover the pan and place it in the oven.

After 15 minutes, baste the chicken with the liquid in the pan. Continue cooking, uncovered, for an additional 35 to 40 minutes, basting every 10 minutes. When done, the chicken and lemon slices will be nicely browned. Let the chicken rest for 5 minutes, than transfer to a deep serving platter.

3. Bertha's Chicken

When I asked Steve Hertzling for a family-style recipe for my book, he sent in this one from his mother-in-law, Bertha. Steve and I worked together for years, and now he is with D'Artagnan, a company that raises everything from first-rate poultry to truffles and wild mushrooms for professional as well as home cooks. Steve has a deep understanding of high-quality ingredients. Bertha and her husband emigrated from Poland to Belgium to Uruguay to the United States, but her cooking remained solidly Middle European.

According to Steve, Bertha cooked from scratch and from memory and instinct, even when making cookies and cakes. Steve had this to say about Bertha's chicken: "From all my years working as a professional chef I've never had a roast chicken as succulent and satisfying as Bertha's. The preparation defies the logic of most chefs' experience and training. The chicken roasts, or actually braises, for at least two and a half hours. The result is a very moist and tender bird. This is a one-pot meal with the potatoes and vegetables that cook along with the chicken. The best pan to use for this preparation is a roasting pan with a cover—the ones available at most hardware stores work the best." SERVES 4

2 tablespoons paprika,
   Spanish preferred
1 tablespoon kosher salt
¼ teaspoon freshly ground
   white pepper
3 tablespoons vegetable oil
¼ cup water
One 3½-pound free-range or
   organic chicken, rinsed and
   patted dry
2 large onions, quartered
2 pounds Idaho potatoes,
   peeled and quartered
1 pound carrots, peeled and
   cut into 2-inch pieces
1 cup apple juice or cider

Preheat the oven to 350 degrees.

Mix together the paprika, salt, pepper, 1 tablespoon of the oil, and the water to make a paste. Rub this paste all over the chicken, inside and out. Place two pieces of the onion inside the chicken cavity. Scatter the potatoes, carrots, and the remaining onion in a large roasting pan with a cover, drizzle with the remaining 2 tablespoons oil, and toss to coat the vegetables; season to taste with additional salt and pepper.

Push the vegetables to the sides of the pan and place the chicken, breast side up, in the center of the pan. Pour in the apple juice, cover the pan, and bake for 2 hours. Remove the lid and let the skin crisp for 30 to 45 minutes.

Cut the chicken into serving pieces and place it on a platter surrounded by the vegetables, or pass the vegetables in a separate dish. Serve the pan juices in a gravy boat on the side.

4. Moroccan Chicken with Preserved Lemon and Olives

Preserved lemons are one of the ingredients that draw me to a dish. I just love them. This chicken dish from Bahija Cherkaoui, an event chef at Great Performances, is really easy—the chicken is not even sautéed before braising—and very delicious. Serve it with couscous to soak up the wonderful sauce.   SERVES 4

One 3- to 3½-pound chicken, cut into 8 pieces

¼ cup olive oil

2 large white onions, chopped

¼ cup chopped cilantro, plus more to garnish

¼ cup chopped flat-leaf parsley

2 or 3 garlic cloves, minced

1 teaspoon ground ginger

1 teaspoon freshly ground white pepper, plus more if needed

1 teaspoon ground turmeric

½ teaspoon saffron threads

1 or 2 preserved lemons, depending on size, homemade (page 306) or store bought, plus more for garnish, if desired

1 cup green olives (see Note)

Salt

Rinse the chicken under cold water and set it aside.

Combine all the remaining ingredients, with the exception of the preserved lemon, olives, and salt, in a Dutch oven or deep sauté pan large enough to hold the chicken pieces in one layer. Add the chicken to the pan and pour in enough water to cover about halfway, 1 to 2 cups.

Bring the water to a simmer over high heat, reduce the heat to medium, cover, and cook the chicken for 30 minutes. Uncover and continue to cook until the chicken is quite tender, about 10 more minutes.

Meanwhile, roughly chop the olives. Cut the preserved lemon into four pieces and cut away and discard the flesh.

Add the olives and preserved lemon to the pan and simmer for about 5 more minutes. Taste and add salt and white pepper to taste. Transfer the chicken to a serving platter and pour the sauce over, placing the olives, pieces of lemon, and cilantro leaves on top.

Olives are easiest to eat when pitted. But this is an unfussy dish, so you might just alert your guests if you do leave in the pits.

5. Norma Jean's Fried Chicken

People who grow up with good fried chicken long for it always, and it always evokes memories. Fried chicken is a family dish, almost by definition, often nostalgically referred to as "my mother's" or "my great-aunt's." And when these accomplished home cooks talk about fried chicken—the pan, the seasonings, the fat of choice—they come away reassured that theirs is the best way.

In any such argument I yield to my friend Norma Jean Darden, a Harlem legend, the proprietor of Miss Mamie's Spoonbread Too and a keeper of family food traditions. Like many African American families, hers drifted from the South in several directions, her branch to New Jersey. Norma Jean's father was a doctor who devoted Sundays to preparing what she refers to as a "well-laden table" of roasted meats, sweet potatoes, greens—Swiss chard, collard greens, beet tops—lots of sides, and a couple of desserts. The Fourth of July meant suckling pig, but for most other gatherings, fried chicken could be expected.   SERVES 4

One 3-pound chicken, cut
  into 8 pieces
1 cup flour
1 teaspoon paprika
1 teaspoon dry mustard
¾ teaspoon freshly grated
  nutmeg
½ teaspoon garlic powder
Pinch of cayenne pepper
½ teaspoon salt
¼ teaspoon freshly ground
  pepper
One 3-pound can vegetable
  shortening, for frying

Rinse the chicken in lukewarm water and set it aside.

Place the dry ingredients in a brown paper or plastic bag and shake to combine.

Melt the shortening in a Dutch oven or a large, heavy skillet; cast iron is ideal.

Wipe the chicken of excess water, leaving a bit of moisture. Drop the chicken, a few pieces at a time, into the bag of flour mixture, shaking to coat well.

Test the fat—when a drop of water sizzles as it hits, the fat is hot enough. Carefully add the chicken a few pieces at a time and cook until it is golden brown all over, about 15 minutes. Adjust the heat as necessary; it should be hot enough to cook the chicken through without burning. Transfer the pieces to paper towels to drain before serving.

The garlic powder may come as a surprise to modern cooks, myself included, who are so focused on fresh ingredients, but it is a reflection of a much earlier time, when even the best home cooks used such spices, often to excellent results. You can omit it, but don't try to substitute fresh minced garlic, which will burn. Or you might substitute the new kind of dried garlic that comes in a grinder like peppercorns.

Wash the chicken in lemon juice before dredging to freshen its flavor.

To reuse the shortening, let it cool to room temperature, pour it through a fine strainer, then store in the refrigerator. You can do this a couple of times, reusing the shortening until you can detect the flavor of previous batches, especially if you've fried up some fish.

6. Grandma Debby Neumark's Honey-Dijon Chicken

I grew up in a family where if six of us were at dinner, there would be food for twelve. You never knew who might stop by, and nothing would be worse than not having enough. My mom—Grandma Debby to her sixteen grandchildren—only liked cooking for company. Then she was inspired to experiment with ingredients for a more receptive audience than her own family. Though she never indulged in baking while we were growing up, as soon as the last child was out of the house, she took cooking classes and learned how to make desserts galore.

Grandma Debby remembers that Sylvia always enjoyed chicken soup. This dish incorporates the principal elements of a good soup—chicken and vegetables—with Provençal seasonings to make a substantial main course for our whole family, a large group. And this kind of make-ahead dish gives Mom time to decorate the chandelier that hangs over the dining room table and to be with us.   SERVES 4 TO 6

2 pounds boneless chicken
   breasts, not pounded
4 large red potatoes,
   quartered
1 medium butternut squash,
   peeled, seeded, and cubed
   (2 cups)
3 leeks, white parts and
   about 1 inch of green,
   well washed, and roughly
   chopped
2 garlic cloves, chopped
Handful of dried cranberries
1 cup chicken stock,
   homemade (page 38) or
   good-quality store bought
¼ cup honey
3 tablespoons Dijon mustard
2 teaspoons herbes de
   Provence
1 bay leaf

Place the chicken on the bottom of a 6-quart slow cooker.

Add the potatoes, squash, leeks, garlic, and cranberries, layering each ingredient over the chicken. Whisk together the stock, honey, mustard, and herbs and pour the mixture into the cooker. Place the bay leaf on top and cover.

Cook on low for 6 to 7 hours, until the chicken is tender.

Chicken thighs can be combined with the breasts or substituted.

A slow cooker is a versatile piece of equipment, and, with the recommended adjustments, can be used for many recipes. If you do not have a slow cooker, this can be made in a heavy 6-quart covered casserole or Dutch oven. Brown the chicken in a bit of olive oil, and proceed as above. Bring the stock just to a simmer and place the casserole in a preheated 350-degree oven until the vegetables are tender when pierced with a fork, 1 to 1¼ hours.

HERBES DE PROVENCE

Herbes de Provence is as much a marketing idea—and a relatively recent one at that—as an authentic ingredient of the cooking of the French region. The herbs usually included in the blend are dried thyme, basil, savory, fennel, and lavender. These and other herbs, including rosemary, are certainly familiar ones in Provençal cooking, but standardized mixes started to appear only about forty years ago, sometimes packed in charming little terra-cotta pots. In any case, herbes de Provence is a good and useful blend to have on hand to flavor stewed dishes like this one or to add to a marinade; I especially like it for lamb.

7. Roasted Chicken with Herbs

If frying is one of my favorite methods for preparing chicken, roasting is the other. It is easy enough for everyday meals if you factor in the roasting time, but it still always feels a little festive. A roasted chicken is perfect in any weather, hot or cold. On warm days, I put one in the oven early in the day and then serve it at room temperature with summery sides like tomato, beet, or potato salads, and, needless to say, corn. If you have lunch guests, Salade Monique (page 22) and some good bread are all you need to add. In any case, chicken ready for sandwiches or salad is never in the "tyranny of the leftovers" category—and don't forget to stockpile the carcass for homemade stock (see page 38).

This is my basic method (variations follow), and it produces a juicy bird with crisp skin. Work out your own combination of herbs or increase the amount of chicken stock or substitute water if you prefer to omit the wine. I've found the skin stays crisper if I don't baste the chicken as it roasts, so I don't suggest it here.

Roasted or mashed potatoes are an essential side.   SERVES 4 TO 6

One 4- to 5-pound roasting
  chicken, rinsed and patted
  dry
1 teaspoon kosher salt
½ teaspoon freshly ground
  pepper
2 tablespoons unsalted butter,
  at room temperature, or
  olive oil
½ cup sliced carrots
½ cup sliced celery
½ cup sliced onion
4 sprigs thyme, plus 1
  tablespoon chopped thyme
2 sprigs rosemary, plus
  1 tablespoon chopped
  rosemary

The day before or at least 8 hours ahead of when you want to roast the chicken, season it inside and out with the salt and pepper. Cover the bird loosely with foil or plastic wrap and refrigerate.

Preheat the oven to 425 degrees. Truss the chicken, tying its legs together with kitchen twine. Rub the butter all over the chicken.

Put the carrots, celery, onion, and thyme and rosemary sprigs into a roasting pan with a rack. Place the chicken on the rack and set it into the pan; roast the chicken for 30 minutes. Reduce the heat to 350 degrees and roast for another 35 to 40 minutes, or until skin is nicely browned.

To check for doneness, place a meat thermometer in the thickest part of the thigh, being careful not to pierce through to the cavity or strike a bone; the chicken is done at 165 degrees. If you don't have a thermometer, tilt the chicken forward on the rack so that juices run from the cavity; the chicken is done if the juices that run out are clear, with no trace of pink. Return the chicken to the oven if necessary for 5 to 10 minutes. (Keep in mind that the chicken will continue to cook a bit after it is removed from the oven.)

2 cups chicken stock,
   homemade (page 38) or
   good-quality store bought
1 cup white wine
3 tablespoons Dijon mustard
2 tablespoons chopped
   tarragon
2 tablespoons roughly cut
   chives

Transfer the chicken to a platter and let it rest in a warm spot for 15 minutes.

While the chicken is resting, remove the rack from the pan and pour off the excess fat but not the vegetables and herbs. Place the pan over medium-high heat and pour in the chicken stock and wine, as well as any juices that have accumulated around the chicken. Cook the pan juices while stirring and scraping up any browned bits with a wooden spoon, for 4 to 5 minutes, or until they are slightly thickened. Strain the sauce into a bowl, pressing down to exude all the juices and flavors. Whisk the mustard into the juices to incorporate it well, then stir in the chopped thyme, rosemary, tarragon, and the chives.

Carve the chicken and serve it with the sauce.

8. Roasted Chicken with Basil and Caramelized Shallots

You might also enjoy roasting a chicken this way. The method is the same as for Roasted Chicken with Herbs (page 160) but the accompanying flavors vary. Caramelized shallots are wonderful with chicken.   SERVES 4 TO 6

One 4-to-5-pound roasting chicken, rinsed and patted dry

6 tablespoons (¾ stick) unsalted butter or olive oil, or a combination

2 pounds shallots (about 16 large shallots), cut in half lengthwise

3 tablespoons sugar

3 tablespoons red wine vinegar

½ teaspoon kosher salt

¼ teaspoon freshly ground pepper

Leaves from 1 bunch fresh basil, cut in chiffonade (below)

While the chicken is roasting, melt the butter in a 12-inch ovenproof sauté pan. Add the shallots and sugar, and toss to coat. Cook over medium heat for 10 minutes, tossing occasionally, until the shallots start to brown. Take care that they do not burn, and adjust the heat accordingly. Add the vinegar, salt, and pepper and toss well. Place the sauté pan in the oven and roast the shallots for 15 to 30 minutes, depending on their size, until they are tender.

Complete the Roasted Chicken recipe but do not use the herbs in the sauce. Serve the carved chicken with the shallots and the basil.

The Language of Cooking: *Chiffonade*

"Chiffonade" comes from the French word *chiffon,* for "rag," or "shred." So chiffonade is something made into rags, though that sounds a little less appealing than the effect we are looking for to finish and flavor dishes. In any case, the leaves of a vegetable or herb, such as basil, are stacked, neatly rolled tip to stem, and then cut across with a sharp knife to produce lovely ribbons. Let the children do the stacking and rolling; and don't make the final cuts too far in advance or your ribbons may discolor. Spinach is another leaf that takes nicely to this technique; chiffonade is a pretty but unfussy way to garnish dishes.

AIR-DRIED CHICKENS

Lots of chefs, and now home cooks, are letting their chickens sit, uncovered, for a time in the refrigerator before cooking. An hour is good, overnight is better. This dries up excess moisture and results in a crisp, tasty skin, especially for roasted chicken. Rinse and pat dry your chicken—whole or in parts—and place it on a platter in the refrigerator; on a rack is even better. Some experts also recommend that you resist the urge to baste the bird while it is cooking, because that also hydrates it. There are "air-dried" chickens now on the market from small, specialized breeders, but chickens from most of the big producers typically hold more moisture than others.

HERITAGE TURKEYS

Heritage turkeys are the descendants of the original American turkeys. It may not be true that the Pilgrims served turkey at the first Thanksgiving, but this was the turkey the earliest settlers encountered. Heritage turkeys are beautiful, with lots of showy plumage, but they are prized above all for their rich taste. Heritage birds take longer to reach market weight than the familiar White Breasted Tom that has dominated the American market for a half century. This deliberate raising method results in deeper flavor, juiciness, and crisp skin. It is also costlier, which is reflected in the prices, but greater demand may help as time goes on.

As with "heirloom" when applied to apples or tomatoes, "heritage" refers to more than one breed. I love the names: Standard Bronze, Bourbon Red, Narragansett, Jersey Buff, Slate, Black Spanish, White Holland, Royal Palm, White Midget, and Beltsville Small White, among others.

You can find heritage turkeys through Heritage Foods USA online.

9. Oven-Roasted Wild Heritage Turkey with Cornbread and Andouille Sausage Dressing

My friend Erik Blauberg is a chef, consultant, and all-around culinary expert. Erik has long been a fellow champion of the farm-to-table movement in the Hudson Valley and is an enthusiast for local products, including heritage meats. I love the simplicity yet richness of his style, evident in this dish. SERVES 6 TO 8

One 8-pound Heritage (wild) turkey
¼ cup olive oil
Coarse sea salt and freshly ground pepper
Leaves from 6 sage sprigs, finely chopped
Leaves from 6 thyme sprigs, finely chopped
Leaves from 3 rosemary sprigs, finely chopped

FOR THE DRESSING

2 tablespoons olive oil
1 cup diced onion (about 1 large)
1 cup seeded and diced red bell pepper (about 1 large)
1 cup peeled and diced celery
1 cup diced andouille sausage
4 cups crumbled cornbread
1 cup thinly sliced scallions, including about 2 inches green part
2 cups chicken stock, homemade (page 38) or good-quality store bought
Sea salt and freshly ground white pepper
Butter, for greasing the pan

Preheat the oven to 375 degrees.

Wash the turkey inside and out with cool water. Drain the turkey and pat dry with paper towels. Brush the turkey with the olive oil; lightly coat the outside and inside of the bird with salt and pepper and the sage, thyme, and rosemary.

Put the seasoned turkey in a roasting pan and place it in the oven. When the skin turns golden brown—after 35 minutes or so—lower the oven temperature to 350 degrees. (Total cooking time will be 2 to 2½ hours.) After about two hours, check for doneness using a meat thermometer—the internal temperature of the thickest part of the thigh should be 165 degrees. Pierce the thigh; the juices should run clear, not pink. Remove the turkey from the oven and let it sit at room temperature for 20 minutes before carving so that it can absorb its own natural juices.

While the turkey is roasting, prepare the dressing. Heat the oil in a large sauté pan or skillet over low heat. Add the onion, bell pepper, and celery and cook slowly for 3 minutes; add the sausage and cook for 1 minute longer, or until the vegetables are soft but not browned. Remove the pan from the heat and let the mixture cool to room temperature.

Toss the vegetable mixture, cornbread, scallions, and chicken stock in a mixing bowl and season with salt and pepper to taste. Butter a shallow pan or gratin dish, spread the stuffing in it, and cover it with aluminum foil. Place the pan in the oven and cook for about 20 minutes. Remove the foil and cook for an additional 5 minutes, or until the top is golden brown. Serve immediately with the carved turkey.

10. Grilled Tamarind Turkey Burgers

Most children today have been exposed to a greater range of flavors than we were when we were very young, and their tastes are more developed, even for spicy foods. I cannot count the number of times I meet children who can rattle off their favorite sushi! So there's no worry that the warm but not too spicy Southeast Asian seasonings in these turkey burgers won't appeal to young palates.

Ground turkey, like boneless chicken breasts, is receptive to a wide range of flavorings, making it another option for good, tasty, quick, and affordable meals. This recipe can be halved, but the mixture freezes well, so, unless the turkey has already been frozen, you may want to make it all and freeze some of the burgers. MAKES 8 PATTIES

FOR THE GLAZE

2 tablespoons canola oil

1 tablespoon minced fresh ginger

1 teaspoon peeled and minced garlic

½ cup tamarind concentrate (see page 168)

½ cup honey

2 tablespoons Sriracha (see page 168)

¼ cup water

2 tablespoons fresh lime juice

FOR THE BURGERS

Cooking spray or vegetable oil

½ cup mayonnaise

1 tablespoon peeled and minced fresh ginger

For the glaze, heat the oil in a heavy medium saucepan over medium-high heat. Add the ginger and garlic and sauté for 2 minutes. Add the tamarind concentrate, honey, Sriracha, and water and bring to a boil. Reduce the heat and simmer the mixture until it is thick enough to coat the back of a spoon and reduced to about 1 cup, stirring often, about 8 minutes.

Let the glaze cool completely, then mix in the lime juice.

Prepare a charcoal fire or gas grill to medium heat or place a grill pan over medium-high heat and coat it with cooking spray or oil. A nonstick or cast-iron pan is also fine for cooking these.

For the burgers, mix together the mayonnaise, ginger, salt, pepper, cumin, jalapeño, cilantro, and 4 teaspoons of the glaze in a large bowl, then mix in the scallions. Add the ground turkey and mix it well but loosely with the mayonnaise mixture; do not overwork. Shape the turkey into eight ½-inch-thick patties (or smaller ones for little people).

Grill the rolls, cut side down, until golden, about 2 minutes; transfer them to a serving platter. Grill the burgers until cooked through

2 teaspoons salt

1 teaspoon freshly ground pepper

1 teaspoon ground cumin

1 jalapeño with seeds, minced

2 teaspoons chopped fresh cilantro

½ cup thinly sliced scallions, white and about 1 inch of green parts

2½ pounds ground turkey, ½ white, ½ dark meat

Hamburger or other rolls

Garnishes of your choice: sliced tomatoes, onions, cucumbers, pickles, etc.

and a thermometer inserted into the center registers 160 degrees, about 8 minutes on each side. Brush each burger with the remaining glaze and serve with garnishes, and a spread of your choice for the buns—I like mayonnaise spiked with a drop or two of Sriracha.

TAMARIND

The tamarind tree thrives in frost-free climates, leafy and lovely, with pod-like fruit (strictly speaking a legume). The fruit is made into a paste and is widely used throughout Southeast Asia, India, Africa, and, thanks to Portuguese colonists, in Mexico. Tamarind brings a pleasant sour taste to dishes as diverse as chutneys, drinks, and sweets. It is easy to find tamarind concentrate as well as paste in Asian and Indian food stores, specialty food shops, and online; it is inexpensive and keeps naturally for a long time. I recommend the concentrate, which is ready to use, whereas the paste has seeds that you will need to remove.

Americans may be surprised to learn that the tamarind grows in our country; if you've been to Hawaii or South Florida—where it yields a big commercial crop—you've seen the tamarind tree, though you might not have known it.

SRIRACHA

Suddenly this Thai chili sauce is nearly as ubiquitous as ketchup, and for some of us, far more addictive. The main ingredient is roasted hot chiles that are blended with vinegar, sugar, and garlic to produce a typical Thai contrast of hot-sweet-sour tastes. Sriracha delivers more than just heat and is more interesting than many other hot sauces. You will find Sriracha on grocery shelves under many labels, including some from big brands, a true sign of its popularity.

11. Roast Breast of Duck with Pears

A great change in the last ten years or so is the wide availability of boneless duck breasts; you can find them even in a decent supermarket. If you do need to have a whole duck butchered to get the breasts, the legs can be roasted and the carcass used to make a sauce or rich stock. This is an easy dish, but special enough for entertaining. Basil Mashed Potatoes (page 98) are good on the side, a nice contrast to the warm spices in the sauce.   SERVES 4

2 Long Island duck breasts, halved to yield four 6-ounce pieces, skin on

¼ cup mirin (see page 171)

4 scallions, white and light green parts only, finely chopped

1½ teaspoons cinnamon

⅛ teaspoon ground ginger

1 whole star anise

Salt and freshly ground pepper

1 tablespoon fresh lemon juice

½ teaspoon fine sea salt

2 firm Bosc pears, peeled

2 tablespoons olive oil

2 tablespoons unsalted butter

1 tablespoon superfine sugar

To prepare the duck breasts, identify the piece of flesh attached to the underside of the duck breast (the tenderloin). Remove it (add it to your cache of trimmings for stock) and trim away the excess fat, leaving just a thin layer. (Keep your duck fat in a small container in your freezer; it's great for roasting potatoes and root vegetables.)

Combine the mirin, scallions, ½ teaspoon of the cinnamon, the ginger, star anise, a big pinch of salt, and a few grindings of pepper in a bowl. Add the duck breasts and let them marinate in the refrigerator, covered with plastic wrap, overnight or for at least 8 hours, turning the breasts a few times.

Bring 4 cups of water to a boil in a 2-quart saucepan. Add the lemon juice, the remaining 1 teaspoon cinnamon, and the sea salt. Reduce the heat to medium-low and add the pears, standing up, partially covered. Simmer the pears until just tender, about 15 minutes, then, using a slotted spoon, transfer them to a rack set over a plate or baking sheet. Let the pears drain and cool to room temperature.

Preheat the oven to 375 degrees. Remove the duck from the marinade and pat it dry. Pour the oil into an ovenproof medium sauté pan over medium heat. Place the breasts skin-side down and cook for about 6 minutes. Flip the breasts, place the pan in the oven, and roast for 4 more minutes; the meat should be medium rare. Remove the duck from the pan.

Slice each pear in half lengthwise and remove the core, using a melon baller or small spoon. While the duck is cooking, melt the butter in a heavy skillet over medium-high heat. Stir in the sugar, then add the pears and coat them with the mixture. Cook the pears, turning them once, until they are caramelized, 5 to 6 minutes per side. Remove the pears from the pan.

Slice the breasts and arrange them and the pears on four individual plates or a platter.

MIRIN

Mirin is a sweet rice wine from Japan; you could substitute another sweet wine like sweet sherry. You also could add a tablespoon or so of sugar to ¼ cup rice vinegar in this recipe. However, mirin for cooking is easy to come by, inexpensive, and will keep indefinitely in your pantry.

12. Orange-Scented Duck Breast with Daikon Salad and Pureed Sweet Potatoes

This is a successful if unpredictable combination of flavors—rich, fresh, sweet, spicy. Follow the methods for preparing, marinating, and roasting in the recipe for Roast Breast of Duck with Pears (page 169), substituting the ingredients here.   SERVES 4

2 Long Island duck breasts, halved to yield four 6-ounce pieces, skin on

1 cup balsamic vinegar

2 blood (or navel) oranges, zest of 1, juice of both

1 lemon, zested and squeezed to yield ¼ cup juice

1 garlic clove, very thinly sliced

½ cup honey

2 teaspoons chopped fresh rosemary

1 teaspoon freshly ground pepper, or to taste

6 ounces chicken stock, homemade (page 38) or good-quality store bought

1 tablespoon butter

Salt

Daikon Salad (page 15)

Pureed Sweet Potatoes with Smoked Chile and Maple Syrup (page 103)

Combine the vinegar, orange zest and juice, lemon zest and juice, garlic, honey, rosemary, and 1 teaspoon pepper and marinate the duck as on page 169. After removing the duck from the marinade, strain and reserve the marinade.

Roast the duck as as on page 169 and remove from pan. Pour off the excess fat from the pan; pour in ½ cup of the strained marinade and cook over medium heat until reduced by half, about 1 minute. Add the chicken stock, bring just to a simmer, and whisk in the butter; season to taste with salt and pepper. Place the breasts on a platter or individual plates and spoon the pan sauce on top. Serve with the Daikon Salad and Pureed Sweet Potatoes.

How to Grill Like a Chef

When I asked one of our Great Performances chefs to give my readers a guide to grilling meat, he looked at me in surprise. "Doesn't everyone know how to grill?" he asked. My answer: "Not really." Grilling is simple, which is why many men who never go near a stove gallop eagerly to an outdoor grill. But there are things to know in order to get results like the pros do.

DIRECT GRILLING, over live hot coals or on a stovetop or gas grill, is by far the favorite method of home cooks; it's best for foods that require moderate heat and cook relatively quickly: steaks, chops, cutlets, and burgers; fish steaks or thick fillets; skewered combinations; and vegetables. It comes as a surprise to many that the characteristic steakhouse grill marks are more than decoration. Those marks result when the meat is given a quarter-turn about midway through the cooking time. The purpose is to equalize the heat coming from the grids themselves and to prevent burning. Do this when you grill, using tongs rather than stabbing the meat with a fork and losing juices.

INDIRECT COVERED GRILLING is for large whole fish, chicken (and is a wonderful treatment for a small turkey), ribs, and meat roasts—anything that requires more than 30 minutes of cooking time. (It also works for chicken breasts and keeps them moist; see page 147.) In effect, this method is just like roasting in an oven—the heat surrounds the food, but it takes on a light smoky flavor without becoming overwhelmed by it. Indirect grilling is done in a kettle-type charcoal grill that has a cover or a covered gas grill; the food is not placed over the heat. Bank the coals along the sides of the kettle, keeping the center clear. If you want to catch the drippings, place a pan in the center. Once the fire is ready, place whatever you are cooking in the center of the grid, over the pan if you are using one, and cover the grill. Lift the cover only to baste, check for doneness, or to add coals.

If you are using a gas grill, turn on the outside flames only and cook with the lid closed.

Marinating

Opinions about marinating meat for the grill vary. I think it depends on the dish at hand, but generally a short time is sufficient for most foods. There are exceptions, including some of the recipes in this chapter. In any case, it is a good idea to remove most of a marinade before cooking in order to avoid flare-ups that can leave a burned and bitter flavor on meat. Marinades are good, however, for indirect cooking when no flame or charcoal is near the meat.

A good basic marinade combines acid, oil, sugar, and flavoring. Here are examples of each category; combine them to your taste, in quantities that make sense for the amount of meat you are preparing:

Acid . . . lemon juice, vinegar, wine
Oil . . . olive oil, vegetable oil
Sugar . . . white or brown sugar, molasses, honey
Flavoring . . . mustard, Worcestershire sauce, onions, garlic; herbs such as rosemary, sage, thyme, mint; salt and pepper

For a quick marinade use an emulsified vinaigrette, a balsamic dressing, or French dressing; even an hour or two will be enough for tasty results. Always remove the meat from the refrigerator long enough to reach a cool room temperature before cooking.

A top-quality steak needs little to enhance it and is best left more or less alone. The famous *bistecca alla Fiorentina,* for instance, involves nothing more than brushing a porterhouse steak with good olive oil and letting it sit for a few hours before salting and grilling.

A dry rub is another excellent way to marinate meat for the grill, especially over direct heat. This one is a favorite of mine, good for beef, pork, lamb, and even chicken, and it can serve as a guide for other variations.

1 tablespoon salt
1 teaspoon cumin
1 teaspoon paprika
1 minced garlic clove
¼ teaspoon ground coriander
1 teaspoon dried marjoram
¼ teaspoon red chile flakes
1 teaspoon cracked pepper

Combine all the ingredients and use liberally on meat prior to grilling.

The Salt Rule

Whatever you are grilling, dust it with sea salt or kosher salt just as you are throwing it on the grill.

13. Tuscan Pot Roast

M ark Strausman is one of the most energetic of the chefs who give time and talent to the local sustainable food organizations in our region. Mark is the executive chef of the Fred's restaurants in Barneys New York stores, but his heart is in his local products and produce, and in the meals he prepares for his teenage sons. "The most important thing to remember, and to teach your children, is to be moderate, and that food is a pleasure," Mark says. Mark and I became friends through his support for regional farmers. His culinary passion for great-tasting meals along with his paternal zeal for introducing kids to healthful, fresh, and appealing food provide us with lots to talk about. I love the way he infuses everything he does with intensity and originality.

This dish is a typical example of Mark's robust home cooking. Like all simple food, it relies mainly on good ingredients and careful preparation; once assembled, only time and patience are needed for perfect results. Mark is a nice Jewish boy from Queens who I suspect was Italian in a past life; he suggests serving this with a Rosso di Montalcino, "which is like a baby Brunello, an everyday table wine, but with a touch of greatness." SERVES 6 TO 8

One 5- to 6-pound beef brisket, trimmed of excess fat
Kosher salt and freshly ground pepper
2 tablespoons olive oil
2 carrots, peeled and diced
2 celery stalks, peeled and diced
1 onion, diced
3 garlic cloves, minced
3 chicken livers, membranes removed and cut into ½-inch pieces (optional)
1 bottle (750 ml) dry red wine

Set a rack in the middle of the oven; preheat the oven to 325 degrees. Season the brisket with salt and pepper and set it aside.

Heat the olive oil in a 7- to 8-quart Dutch oven with a tight-fitting lid over medium-high heat. Add the brisket and brown it well on both sides, about 10 minutes. Transfer the meat to a platter.

Add the carrots, celery, onion, and garlic to the pot, reduce the heat to medium, and cook, scraping up any browned bits, until all the vegetables are almost soft and the onion is golden but not browned, about 5 minutes. Add the chicken livers, if using, and cook, stirring, until they begin to firm, about 2 minutes. Add the wine, stock, tomatoes, bay leaf, and rosemary. Return the brisket, along with any juices, to the pot, raise the heat to medium-high, and bring to a simmer.

Cover the pot and place it in the oven. Cook, turning the meat once, until it is fork-tender, 3 to 3½ hours. Transfer the brisket to a cutting board and lightly cover it with aluminum foil to rest for 15 minutes.

3 cups chicken stock,
   homemade (page 38) or
   good-quality store bought
1 cup canned Italian plum
   tomatoes, preferably San
   Marzano, lightly crushed
1 bay leaf, fresh if available
3 tablespoons chopped
   rosemary
2 tablespoons chopped
   flat-leaf parsley

Meanwhile, spoon off the accumulated fat from the surface of the sauce. Using an immersion blender, puree the sauce right in the pot. Or transfer the sauce to a blender or food processor to puree, then return it to the pot. Season with salt and pepper, and stir in the parsley.

Slice the meat and serve with the warm sauce on the side. Alternatively, slice the meat, return it to the pot, and refrigerate overnight. Remove any solidified fat from the surface of the sauce and reheat, covered, in a 300-degree oven until piping hot.

14. Hearty Winter Beef Stew

This is a dish that can be tailored to reflect what you find in the winter vegetable market. Sometimes I add more veggies and a little more stock accordingly. It is a one-plate meal and tastes even better the next day.   SERVES 4 TO 6

1¼ pounds boneless beef chuck roast, cut into 1-inch pieces

¼ cup vegetable oil

6 large garlic cloves, minced

8 cups beef stock, homemade or good-quality store bought

2 tablespoons tomato paste

1 tablespoon thyme

1 tablespoon Worcestershire sauce

2 bay leaves

2 tablespoons butter or olive oil

2 russet potatoes, peeled and cut into ½-inch dice

1 large onion, chopped

½ pound butternut squash, peeled and cut into ½-inch dice

2 parsnips, peeled and cut into ½-inch dice

2 or 3 carrots, peeled and cut into ½-inch dice

2 tablespoons chopped flat-leaf parsley

Pat the meat dry. Pour the oil into a large, heavy pot or Dutch oven—enameled cast iron is perfect—over medium-high heat. Add the beef and brown it on all sides, working in batches to avoid crowding the pan; remove the beef as it browns. Add the garlic to the pan and sauté for 1 minute. Add beef stock, tomato paste, thyme, Worcestershire sauce, and bay leaves and stir to combine.

Return the meat to the pot and bring the mixture just to a boil. Reduce the heat to medium-low, then cover and simmer for 1 hour, stirring occasionally.

Meanwhile, melt the butter in another large pot over medium heat. Add the potatoes, onion, butternut squash, parsnips, and carrots and sauté until golden brown, about 20 minutes. Transfer the vegetables to the beef pot. Simmer, uncovered, until the vegetables and beef are very tender, about 40 minutes. Discard the bay leaves. Tilt the pan and spoon off as much fat as possible from the surface; transfer the stew to serving bowls or a deep platter, sprinkle with the parsley, and serve.

Like soup, stew is infinitely variable. You can turn this one into a lamb stew by exchanging the meat and using lamb stock if you have it for all or some of the beef stock. The vegetables can include other winter root vegetables, such as turnips, rutabagas, and sweet potatoes, and other varieties of local potatoes. Mushrooms, including reconstituted dried ones (see page 119), are always good in stews; add them during the final 20 minutes of cooking. It often surprises people to learn that lamb and anchovies have a great affinity for each other and frequently turn up in French and Italian lamb dishes. Add a few or a tablespoon or so of anchovy paste toward the end of cooking the stew—even people who don't like anchovies or think they don't will like this. Alternatively, toss in a handful of dried cherries or currants for a touch of sweetness.

15. Braised Beef Short Ribs with Star Anise, Orange Zest, and Ginger

Short ribs are a perennial favorite, both at home and in the event world. There is something comforting yet festive about them—the simplicity combined with the luxury of slow braising, not to mention the rich, beefy taste. Wherever we serve them, the plates come back spotless!

Here, a standard braising method for short ribs is married to warm Southeast Asian flavors, making a familiar dish less predictable. This is a gentle way to expand young palates. Needless to say, rice, noodles, or potatoes are good accompaniments; you could extend the Asian theme by serving rice noodles or cellophane noodles.   SERVES 6 TO 8

3 pounds beef short ribs

Salt and freshly ground
   pepper

2 tablespoons vegetable oil

1 carrot, peeled and diced

1 red or yellow onion, diced

1 stalk celery, peeled and
   diced

1 tablespoon peeled and
   grated fresh ginger

1 tablespoon tomato paste

2 cups red wine

2 cups beef stock, homemade
   or good-quality store
   bought

1 piece star anise

3 strips orange zest

2 bay leaves

Preheat the oven to 300 degrees.

Pat the short ribs dry of any excess moisture and season them well with salt and pepper. Heat the oil in a wide, heavy-bottomed stainless-steel or enameled saucepan over medium-high heat. When the oil is hot but not yet smoking, add the ribs a few at a time and brown them evenly on all sides. As the ribs brown, remove them.

Add the carrot, onion, celery, and ginger to the pan and sauté, just until they begin to soften and brown, about 5 minutes. Stir in the tomato paste. Reduce the heat to medium, add the red wine, and stir, scraping up any browned bits from the bottom of the pan; reduce the wine by half. Stir in the beef stock, star anise, orange zest, and bay leaves.

Return the short ribs to the pan, reduce the heat to a simmer, cover the pan, and place it on the middle rack of the oven. Cook until the beef is fork tender, turning once or twice, about 3 hours.

Transfer the beef to a serving dish. Spoon the accumulated fat from the surface of the sauce. Strain the sauce into a saucepan over medium-high heat. Reduce to thicken the sauce as desired, then ladle it over the short ribs and serve.

16. Thai Beef and Ginger Salad

This recipe demonstrates the effortless way our food changes, thanks to immigrants who bring their traditions with them. Fortunately for all of us, the ingredients follow. The ones for this dish can all be gotten in a supermarket. This can be served as an appetizer, as part of a dinner consisting of several other dishes, or over noodles to make for a more substantial dish. SERVES 4

8 ounces skirt or flank steak

1 tablespoon olive oil

Salt and freshly ground pepper

6 cups torn mixed salad greens

1 cup torn herb leaves, such as mint, cilantro, Thai basil, or a combination

¼ cup minced red onion

1 medium cucumber, seeded and diced

2 red bell peppers, seeded and julienned

2 carrots, peeled and julienned

1 jicama, peeled and julienned

2 small hot red chiles, with seeds, minced, or to taste (page 115)

Juice of 2 limes

1 tablespoon peeled and minced fresh ginger

1 tablespoon dark sesame oil

1 tablespoon fish sauce

2 tablespoons soy sauce

½ teaspoon sugar

1 bunch scallions, white parts only, thinly sliced

Cilantro and crushed, unsalted roasted peanuts, for garnish

Rub the steak with the olive oil and season it with salt and pepper. Sear the steak in a large, heavy skillet over medium-high heat until nicely crusted, flip, and cook until medium rare, about 6 minutes altogether. Let cool to room temperature.

Toss the salad greens with the herbs, onion, cucumber, red peppers, carrots, and jicama. Whisk the chiles, lime juice, ginger, sesame oil, fish sauce, soy sauce, and sugar together in a bowl; the dressing will be thin.

Toss half the dressing with the greens mixture, then transfer the salad to a platter. Slice the beef thinly, reserving any juice; whisk the juice into the remaining dressing. Lay the slices of beef over the salad and drizzle with the remaining dressing. Garnish with the sliced scallions, cilantro, and crushed peanuts.

17. Katchkie Farm Meatloaf

This is a simple meatloaf that may even remind you of your mother's—great for Sunday night supper and, of course, sandwiches. On a summer day, after a long morning outside at the farm, it's the perfect hearty sandwich, in a crusty roll with sliced tomatoes, a handful of lettuce, and a generous swipe of mustard. Needless to say, we use our own Katchkie Farm Ketchup in this recipe, but others will do; look for specialty brands that are low in sugar and preservatives.

I sometimes make mini-meatloaves by baking the mixture in muffin pans. Other dishes lend themselves to miniaturizing—such as lasagna, mac and cheese, and quiche. Fit the ingredients into muffin or cupcake pans and cut the cooking time about in half—in the case of meatloaf, about 20 minutes—but check for doneness depending on the size of your pans. Kids seem to like the novelty of individual portions. SERVES 6 TO 8

Oil for greasing the pan
2 pounds lean ground beef
   or ground turkey, or a
   combination
2 teaspoons salt
¼ teaspoon freshly ground
   pepper
2 eggs, lightly beaten
½ cup fresh bread crumbs
½ cup milk
1 teaspoon Worcestershire
   sauce
¼ cup finely chopped onion
¼ teaspoon dried thyme,
   crumbled
¼ teaspoon dried rosemary,
   crumbled
¼ cup Katchkie Farm
   Ketchup (page 311) or
   store bought

Preheat the oven to 350 degrees. Lightly oil a 9-×-5-×-3-inch (or similarly proportioned) loaf pan.

Place all the ingredients, except the ketchup, in a large mixing bowl and knead until combined; do not overmix. Fold in half the ketchup. Pack the mixture into the loaf pan. Top with the remaining ketchup, place in the oven, and bake for 1 hour or until cooked through.

Let the meatloaf rest in the pan for about 10 minutes before turning it out onto a serving platter.

18. Chipotle-Honey Barbecued Baby Back Ribs

Any corn dish is perfect with this, including Sweet Corn, Fava Bean, and Shiitake Salad (page 31). SERVES 4 TO 6

¼ cup minced canned
   chipotle chiles in adobo
½ cup honey
½ cup ketchup
2 tablespoons peeled and
   minced fresh ginger
¼ cup dry mustard
3 tablespoons salt
2 teaspoons freshly ground
   pepper
2 racks pork baby back ribs
   (2½ pounds each)
Vegetable oil, for grill grates

Preheat the oven to 250 degrees.

Combine the chiles, honey, ketchup, ginger, mustard, salt, and pepper in a blender or small food processor and blend until smooth.

Place a double layer of foil large enough to wrap the ribs on a large rimmed baking sheet. Place the ribs on the foil and rub them all over with three-quarters of the chipotle mixture; reserve the rest. Wrap the ribs tightly in the foil and place the sheet in the oven.

Bake the ribs until they are fork-tender when pierced, about 3 hours. When the ribs are nearly done, prepare a charcoal fire or heat a grill to medium-high. Lightly oil the grates. Remove the ribs from the foil and let the excess drippings run off. Brush the ribs with the remaining chipotle mixture and grill them until lightly charred, 2 to 3 minutes per side.

Separate the ribs by cutting between the bones and serve.

CHIPOTLE-HONEY BARBECUED BABY BACK RIBS   183

PORK

In years past, pork was routinely well-cooked and often over-cooked in order to eliminate trichinosis; back then, home cooks had a legitimate concern about the parasite. Today, the infection has virtually disappeared in the developed world, but in any case, pork needs to be cooked only to 137 degrees to overcome the danger, lower than some guidelines suggest. Or test to see that the juices in cooked pork are running clear, not bloody (a hint of pink at the center of the flesh is ideal though). Always remember that food continues to cook after it is removed from the heat.

As if concerns about trichinosis weren't enough, pork was subjected to other injustices. Factory-farmed pork pretty much monopolized the market and pork was bred to be so lean that it was also dry and bland; the "other white meat" was as dull as it sounded. The rich taste and succulent nature of pork was a thing of the past.

Today, a demand for better pork, along with the interest in more humane breeding methods—which also have less impact on the environment—has brought more delicious pork to the market. Like heirloom apples and tomatoes, this means a return to heritage breeds, such as Berkshire, an English strain (also known by its Japanese name, Kurobuta); Duroc, once the most popular American pig; and Red Wattle. The meat from these animals can have various taste characteristics—clean and crisp to deep and herbaceous, making them suitable for a wide range of preparations. The meat from heritage breeds even looks better, with flesh that ranges from creamy in color to parts that are soft taupe. Distinctive varieties of pork can be found at specialty food shops and butchers and by mail order.

As for us at Katchkie, every spring we get piglets for the farm. We feed them well on our vegetables—tomatoes, zucchini, and cucumbers—and the visiting children bring them scraps after the cooking sessions. This is always a highlight of a Sylvia Center outing. When vegetable burritos are on the lunch menu, the piggies get any extra ones. They like them enough that I've been known to buy some for them at the local diner.

The question always gets asked: What do you do with these pigs? For some kids, the idea that the animals become bacon, ham, sausage, and other mouthwatering meals puts smiles on their faces. For others, it opens the way to eating more vegetables. Either way, knowing where their food comes from will forever change the way they look at their plates. And they learn the importance of raising animals humanely.

19. Garlic-Studded Leg of Lamb with a Rosemary Crust

Years ago, leg of lamb was the dish my sister Miriam and I chose when we wanted something different for a family Passover dinner in Israel. We visited the butcher and came away with a medium-sized leg of lamb—and a sense of adventure, because, for some reason, lamb was rarely served at home. Home cooks back then seemed to have the notion that lamb needed to be cooked through, not rare or even medium, so it was often overcooked, which destroyed its delicate flavor and succulence. So lots of people of my generation grew up not liking lamb. Miriam and I developed a simple dish that lends itself to a variety of preparations, good for festive or casual family meals and easy to prepare. In spring nothing is better with lamb than asparagus; in cold months Potato and Brussels Sprout Gratin (page 87) is a good choice. SERVES 6 TO 8

One 7-pound leg of lamb, trimmed of excess fat

3 tablespoons olive oil

¼ cup minced garlic (about 4 large cloves)

¼ cup minced rosemary, plus a sprig

¼ cup Dijon mustard

Salt and freshly ground pepper

About 1½ cups beef stock, homemade or good-quality store bought

½ cup port

Preheat the oven to 400 degrees.

Cut 16 slits about ¾ inch deep in the lamb on all sides. Combine the olive oil and garlic and push the mixture into each slit (a tiny spoon and a chopstick are good for this). Combine the minced rosemary and mustard and rub it all over; season well with salt and pepper.

Place the roast on the rack of a broiler pan or roasting pan. Insert a meat thermometer into the thickest part of the lamb, taking care not to touch bone. Place the pan in the oven and roast the leg for about 1½ hours, or until the thermometer registers 140 degrees for medium-rare or 155 degrees for medium; keep in mind that the meat will continue to cook as it rests, increasing the internal temperature by about 5 degrees.

Remove the lamb, cover it loosely with foil, and let it stand in a warm spot for 15 minutes.

Spoon off as much accumulated fat as possible from the pan drippings, scrape up any browned bits with a rubber spatula, and pour the drippings into a small saucepan. Add the stock, port, and the sprig of rosemary to the pan; bring to a low boil and reduce by half, about 7 minutes. Strain the sauce, discard the rosemary, and season to taste with salt and pepper. Cut the lamb into slices and place them on a platter; ladle a bit of sauce on top and pass the rest at the table.

20. Butterflied and Roasted Leg of Lamb with Cumin Rub and Mint Pesto

Until about twenty years ago, I don't think many people were cooking lamb this way. It really is a great method that seems less challenging for the cook and that produces good, juicy results. The nature of the butterflied leg is that it has thicker and thinner areas, which means you can satisfy those who prefer rare or more cooked slices.

Assertive marinades like the ones here are wonderfully tuned to lamb's richness. But some of the traditional flavorings, like the tried-and-true combination of rosemary, garlic, lemon, olive oil, and Dijon mustard, are foolproof as well. The lamb can also be cooked in a covered charcoal or gas grill, first with the cover open, then with it closed. SERVES 6 TO 8

¼ cup olive oil

8 garlic cloves, minced

2½ teaspoons salt

1 teaspoon freshly ground
    pepper

3 tablespoons ground cumin

2 tablespoons dried oregano

One 5-pound leg of lamb,
    boned and butterflied

FOR THE MINT PESTO

½ cup toasted pine nuts

3 garlic cloves

2 tablespoons grated
    Parmigiano-Reggiano

½ teaspoon salt

½ teaspoon freshly ground
    pepper

1½ cups (packed) mint leaves

½ cup (packed) flat-leaf
    parsley leaves

2 tablespoons fresh lemon
    juice

⅓ cup extra-virgin olive oil

Whisk the oil, garlic, salt, pepper, cumin, and oregano together. Spread the mixture on both sides of the lamb and let it sit for 1 hour at cool room temperature, or about 20 minutes if your kitchen is very warm.

Preheat the broiler and adjust the oven rack to the upper or middle position. Line a roasting pan with heavy-duty foil and set a wire rack in it.

Place the lamb on the wire rack and set it under the broiler. Broil the lamb, moving the pan as necessary to brown it evenly, about 8 minutes. Turn the lamb to the second side and continue to broil until it is well browned, about 8 minutes longer. Remove the lamb and let it rest for 10 minutes in the pan.

Meanwhile, lower the oven temperature to 325 degrees. Place the lamb in the oven and roast it for 40 minutes to 1 hour, or until a thermometer placed in the thickest portion registers 140 degrees for medium-rare. Remove the lamb, cover it loosely with foil, and let it stand in a warm spot for 15 minutes before slicing.

Meanwhile, prepare the pesto. Combine the pine nuts, garlic, Parmigiano-Reggiano, salt, and pepper in a food processor; pulse the mixture until it is smooth. Add the mint, parsley, and lemon juice; process until smooth, stopping occasionally to scrape down the sides of the bowl with a spatula. With the machine running, gradually add the oil through the feed tube and process again until smooth and creamy and serve with the lamb.

21. Leg of Lamb with a Chile-Citrus Rub

Follow the methods for preparing and cooking the lamb in the recipe for Butterflied and Roasted Leg of Lamb with Cumin Rub and Mint Pesto (facing page), using the ingredients here. SERVES 6 TO 8

3 stalks lemongrass

One 2-inch piece fresh ginger, peeled and roughly chopped

5 garlic cloves, roughly chopped

6 fresh lime leaves (optional)

1 tablespoon cumin

3 tablespoons chile powder

Zest and juice of 2 lemons

Zest and juice of 1 orange

One 5-pound leg of lamb, boned and butterflied

Salt and freshly ground pepper

3 tablespoons chopped mint

1 cup plain yogurt

Remove the tough outer leaves of the lemongrass. Place the stalks on their sides and press down with your palm on the side of a heavy knife, then slice the stalks in half lengthwise. Cut the stalks into large pieces and mash them with the ginger, garlic, lime leaves, if using, cumin, chile powder, the zest and juice of 1 lemon, and the orange zest and juice with a large mortar and pestle or pulse them in a mini food processor to a rough paste. Coat the lamb all over with the paste and sprinkle it with a few pinches of salt and several grindings of pepper. Proceed as in main recipe.

Stir the chopped mint and the remaining lemon zest into the yogurt and add the remaining lemon juice and salt and pepper to taste. Stir well and serve with the lamb.

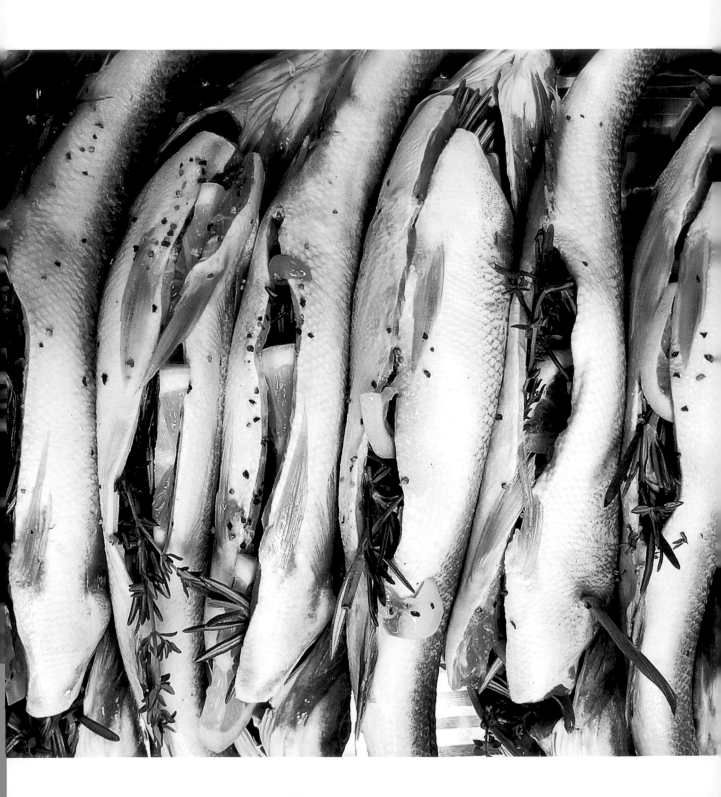

Fish

Americans are eating far more fish than we once did, and the availability of good fresh fish has improved mightily in the last ten years, thanks to increased demand based on appreciation of its taste and an understanding of its healthfulness. Salmon and small fish such as sardines and anchovies are among the most healthful foods, thanks to their oils, which are effective in reducing body cholesterol.

It pleases me to see whole fish, fillets, mollusks, and crustaceans arrayed on ice in a supermarket—it has become commonplace, not the exception. Fishmongers still prevail, especially in cities, and if you have one in your neighborhood I suggest you patronize it. The everyday selection may be impressive and special orders possible.

Children are naturally interested in animals and will find a visit to a fish store pretty fascinating, especially if live lobsters are swimming in a tank. They also enjoy knowing the basic types of fish, and, even more, how they move through the water. They may find it amusing to know that flatfish swim along horizontally, in a disklike fashion, have fins on both sides to propel them, and that they have both eyes either on one side or the other, depending on the species. Round fish swim vertically, weaving through the water, the way we usually imagine fish swimming, and have one eye on each side of their faces (see page 196).

Today many of us have increased our fish consumption for health reasons and because we have come to appreciate its taste, but I think preparing fish is still a challenging category for many home cooks. For whatever reason, even some confident cooks can be apprehensive when facing down a fillet of this or that fish.

For this and other reasons, I have arranged this chapter a little differently from the others. First, you will find a guide to buying fish. Following that, I have provided simple, basic preparations for fish. There are a few reasons for this: for one, once you've mastered these few methods, you will be able to apply them to a multitude of dishes; for another, you will learn to mix and match preparations and simple seasonings. Good fresh fish doesn't need and shouldn't be subjected to much handling, just some enhancing to bring out its own characteristics.

In the end, you will find fish convenient and easy for everyday meals. It doesn't need much preparation—even marinating time is short—and it cooks quickly. Grilled or pan-broiled fish steaks can satisfy carnivores, while a whole fish can be as festive as a roast. For kids, fish tacos and burgers are no-brainers.

I am fairly well convinced that overcooking fish is the main reason for failure and disappointment. So take great care not to leave the fish too long on the fire; when grilling, for instance, a few minutes on each side will do it. Fish will continue to cook for several minutes once off the fire.

Fish Basics

Buying Fish

There is nothing more important than freshness in fish. And nothing simpler than knowing what to look for: if you are buying a whole fish, check first that the eyes are clear, not at all filmy or cloudy; next, see that the color around the gills is red. Do this even if you mean to have the fish filleted, and don't buy any fish that falls short of these reliable clues. With minimal effort, something delicious can come from an excellent piece of fish, but sadly, no good end will come from mediocre or worse beginnings.

When you buy fish that has already been cut into a chunk (a section of the whole), filleted, or cut into steaks, look for bright color on the skin and, above all, that the flesh is compact and moist—avoid any fish with a hint of dryness and separation of the flesh. Fresh steaks and fillets will have a kind of sheen, or translucency to the flesh, and will not be dull.

And then there is the smell test. This is easy enough at a fish market, where you can take a whiff. What you want is a clean, oceany scent, not "fishiness."

What is true of finfish is true of crustaceans and bivalves: if it doesn't look good, it won't be good. Lobsters and whole crabs in tanks should be active, though sometimes they need a knock on the side of the tank to snap them out of their stupor. When picked up, a lobster should wave its claws about and curl its tail under. Soft and hard shell crabs lying on shaved ice or in crates of seaweed will respond to a tap on the shell.

Bivalves—clams, oysters, mussels—should be closed, but if they are slightly open and clamp back up if tapped, they still are alive and fresh. Avoid very light shells, which may be empty, or very heavy ones, which may be full of mud or sand.

Shrimp, the national favorite among shellfish, are nearly always frozen before they reach our markets and then are defrosted for sale; in any case, they should be shiny and moist-looking, with translucent flesh, firm to the touch, and not dry.

Preparing Fish

Once home, place the fish in a clean kitchen sink and gently rinse off any blood and slime. Slime, by the way, along with blood, is another good sign of freshness. Dry the fish with paper towels. If you can't cook your fish the day you buy it, put it in a glass or porcelain dish and cover it with plastic wrap; it will be fine for another day, but the best policy is always to cook fish as soon after buying as possible.

Unless you catch your own, whatever fish you cook should be scaled and gutted—cleaned—before you take it home.

How to Roast a Whole Fish

This may be my favorite method for cooking fish. The fish has direct, gently flavored taste and is juicy. Large whole fish suitable for roasting will vary depending on where you live, but great examples are striped or black bass, cod, snapper, and salmon. A chunk cut from the thickest part of a big fish can be treated in the same way as a whole fish; for example, you can get a two-pound piece from a five- to ten-pound fish. Plan on about a pound of whole fish per person from a fish that has its head and tail on. If you use a chunk from a large fish, six to eight ounces will do for each person. If you have leftovers, it is easy to toss them with some vinaigrette and serve over an herb salad for a light lunch.

Most fish need only basic seasonings; you don't want to compromise the delicate flavor of the fish itself. Here are some suggestions:

Sliced or roughly chopped lemons
Flat-leaf parsley sprigs
A few sprigs of thyme or lemon thyme
Thinly sliced garlic, shallots, onion, or leeks
Thinly sliced fennel and some fronds

I've also used other citrus fruits, such as tangerines and grapefruit, delicious with striped bass and salmon.

Here is a basic preparation for a whole fish and a set of flavoring components for roasting:

1 whole fish
1 tablespoon sea salt
1 tablespoon freshly ground pepper
1 lemon, quartered
1 tangerine, quartered
3 shallots, roughly chopped
1 medium leek, cut horizontally and washed clean
4 garlic cloves, crushed
½ bunch fresh flat-leaf parsley
½ bunch fresh lemon thyme
Olive oil, for brushing

Preheat the oven to 400 degrees.

After washing the fish, place it on a lightly oiled baking sheet. Season the fish inside with salt—sea salt if you have it—and a few grindings of pepper. Place whatever ingredients you have chosen into the cavity and scatter any extras around in the pan. You can sew the cavity closed with a larding needle and kitchen thread or close it up with a few thin skewers. A chunk needs only a skewer or some kitchen thread tied around it. Brush the fish with olive oil and season with salt and pepper.

Put the fish in the oven for 20 to 30 minutes, depending on its size. A fish is done when its flesh is no longer translucent, and flakes—you can test with a fork. Take care not to overcook. Remove the fish from the oven and let it rest for a few minutes. (You may like salmon to be slightly under-cooked, or medium-rare.)

Cut the string or pull the skewers out carefully. To serve the fish, pull the skin back to uncover the flesh. The next part can be intimidating to beginners, but it's easy once you get the hang of it and you may end up enjoying it as I do.

The idea is to lift the meat off the bones. Understanding basic fish construction helps: Fish are either round or flat. Round fish (bass, salmon) have a central backbone with a single row of bones that reach up to the dorsal fins and two rows that curve downward. Flatfish (flounder, sole, hali-but) are simpler, with two rows of bones that fan out to the dorsal and to the bottom. In either case, once you have removed the flesh from the top row of bones, it is easy enough to lift the skeleton itself. It doesn't matter if you don't do this perfectly at first. You will be amazed at how easy it is after just a few tries.

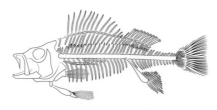

Round fish

Flatfish

Grilling Fish

Grilling fish is very similar to grilling meats (page 173). Large fish such as mahimahi, tuna, swordfish, and amberjack are usually sold already cut into boneless steaks. Round fish such as salmon and cod are cut along the grain and bone. In either case, steaks should be about one inch thick; plan on six to ten ounces per portion. I usually marinate fish before grilling, but not for as long as for meat because the porous flesh of fish will soak up the marinade very quickly and overwhelm the fish's own taste. Olive oil and lemon juice, a simple vinaigrette, or a combination of Asian flavors like light soy sauce and rice wine vinegar are enough. Besides giving flavor, the marinade will attract flames and nicely char the surface.

Hearty-flavored fish like tuna, mackerel, and cod are terrific when marinated briefly in the brine from pickled vegetables like green tomatoes or my Pickled Strawberries (page 322), which are particularly good on salmon.

Wipe the steaks and pour the marinade over—about 2 tablespoons for each steak. Prepare a charcoal fire or a stovetop grill. When the fire is ready, oil the grill with cooking spray or brush it with oil and grill the steaks for about 3 minutes per side.

Sautéing Fish

This is the method that takes the most patience; it also is the one you can do at the drop of a hat. Small whole fish and fillets take well to sautéing, and need only to be lightly floured before going into a hot pan with a little oil or butter. Set the heat at medium-high and adjust it as necessary so that the fillet browns nicely on one side. Flip it when you can begin to see the color at the edges and cook it for just one minute more on the second side. (A great chef once told me not to let the heat control me but for me to control the heat: that's why there is a knob.)

Sole (lemon, grey), flounder, snapper, bass, grouper, perch, barramundi, and monkfish fillets are just a few of the excellent choices for sautéing. Small whole fish such as smelts can be sautéed just like fillets.

Scallops can be cooked the same way as fillets. Season them and let them stand until the chill is off, then place them in a pan and moderate the heat. Once the scallops begin to brown at the edges, flip them, and cook them for only a minute or two on the other side.

Dressing the Fish

Fish takes well to light and bright flavors that emphasize freshness without overwhelming it. Sauces like my Parsley Mint Pesto (page 296), Katchkie Farm Fresh Salsa (page 312), and Salsa Verde (page 299) are excellent choices; Saffron Aioli (page 314) is the classic sauce for salt or fresh cod. Ginger Sauce (page 304) also can be used as a marinade.

Sauce your fish according to the rest of the menu—choose a salsa, for instance, if your sides have Mexican or Southwestern flavors.

FISH EVERY DAY:
A SHORT GUIDE TO FLAVORINGS AND PREPARATIONS

Salmon: dill and lemon

Tuna: soy, ginger, garlic

Halibut: thyme, fennel, citrus (grapefruit, orange)

Cod, snapper, and bass: Mediterranean flavors and ingredients such as olives, capers, tomatoes, rosemary

Flounder: fish and chips

Scallops: salt and pepper, then sear; serve with salad and herbs, grilled corn

Shrimp: barbecue, grill

1. Moroccan Tuna Skewers with Cucumber-Lemon Raita

I find harissa a good thing to always have on hand for quick everyday cooking. It is spicy, yes, but also complex enough to flavor a simple marinade like this one. The flesh of fish is more porous than most meat, so don't marinate the tuna for longer than two hours, and take care not to overcook it for the same reason—the heat will continue to penetrate after you take the skewers off the heat.

This meal reflects the everyday cooking of both India and North Africa, and the classic pairing of palate-cooling dishes like this typical raita with hot ones. Raitas are yogurt-based sauces that can be concocted from various spices and herbs; cilantro, for instance, could be substituted for the mint here, and lime juice for lemon. Yogurt probably originated in Turkey around 2000 B.C., and became an important food in Russia, the Balkans, the Middle East, and southern Asia, but less so in North Africa; it still makes a good companion to this Moroccan-inspired tuna. SERVES 4

2 hothouse or Persian
   cucumbers, peeled, seeded,
   and thinly sliced
2 cups plain Greek yogurt
3 tablespoons fresh lemon
   juice
2 tablespoons chopped fresh
   mint
½ teaspoon sugar
¼ teaspoon kosher salt
2 to 3 tablespoons harissa
   (see next page)
3 tablespoons canola or
   vegetable oil
2 pounds fresh tuna, cut into
   1-inch cubes
2 tablespoons chopped fresh
   flat-leaf parsley
Lemon wedges

Soak 4 bamboo skewers in water. Toss the cucumber, yogurt, lemon juice, mint, sugar, and salt together in a bowl, cover, and refrigerate for 3 hours.

About 2 hours before you plan to cook, mix the harissa and 1 tablespoon of the canola oil together in a bowl. Add the tuna cubes and stir to coat with the mixture, then thread them on the skewers. Cover the skewers and place them in the refrigerator.

Preheat a charcoal or indoor grill or place a heavy skillet over high heat. Brush the grill with some of the remaining oil, or pour just enough into the skillet to coat the surface.

Sear the tuna skewers for 30 seconds on each side, being careful not to overcook. Transfer to a serving platter, garnish with the chopped parsley, and serve with more lemon wedges and the raita.

HARISSA

Harissa is practically the ketchup of Tunisia and Algeria, the condiment of choice for everything from meat dishes and fish stews to couscous. The components of harissa vary from place to place and even from household to household, but hot chiles are the constant—this is basically a hot sauce—and most blends are flavored with cumin, coriander, or caraway. Sweet peppers, sometimes roasted, may go into a harissa blend, along with garlic or lemon juice. Harissa has become popular far beyond its North African roots and is easily found in supermarkets and online. I love the beautiful labels on some of the cans and tubes.

2. Mediterranean Fish Stew

The secret to this lovely, colorful, and flavorful stew is its rich orange-laced broth. The garlicky slices of toasted French bread are typical and may be served on the side, floated on top, or placed in the bottoms of the soup plates before the stew is ladled over. Follow the stew with a big green salad for a well-rounded meal.   SERVES 6

3 tablespoons olive oil

1 large onion, thinly sliced

2 medium celery stalks, cut thinly on the diagonal

8 garlic cloves, smashed

⅓ cup white wine

2 tablespoons tomato paste

3 pinches saffron threads

8 cups fish or shrimp stock, or a combination

¼ teaspoon red chile flakes

Two 3-inch strips orange zest

Juice of 1 orange

2 fennel bulbs, trimmed, cut crosswise into ⅓-inch slices (about 3 cups)

¾ cup peeled, seeded, and chopped tomatoes

1½ teaspoons kosher salt, plus more for seasoning fish

Freshly ground pepper

1½ pounds firm white-fleshed fish fillets, such as halibut, snapper, grouper, or cod

Place a large—6-quart or so—Dutch oven or soup pot over medium-high heat; pour in the oil, then lower the heat. Add the onion, celery, and garlic and cook until tender, stirring from time to time, 6 to 8 minutes. Add the white wine, tomato paste, saffron, stock, red chile flakes, orange zest, and orange juice and bring just to a simmer; continue to simmer, uncovered, for about 45 minutes, or until the liquid is reduced by about one-third.

Add the fennel and tomatoes and cook until the fennel is tender, about 20 minutes; add the salt and season with pepper to taste.

Season the fish fillets with salt and pepper. Cut the fillets into 1½-inch chunks. Add the fish, shrimp, mussels, and parsley to the broth and cook, gently stirring only once or twice to avoid breaking up the fish chunks, just until the fish and shrimp are cooked through and the mussels have opened, about 5 minutes. Serve in shallow bowls with Garlic-Rubbed Croutons and pass the Rouille at the table.

1 pound shrimp, peeled and
   deveined
1 pound mussels, washed and
   debearded
1 tablespoon chopped fresh
   flat-leaf parsley
Garlic-Rubbed Croutons, for
   serving (recipe follows)
Rouille, for serving
   (recipe follows)

Garlic-Rubbed Croutons

Day-old bread is fine to use for this.

Twelve ½-inch slices crusty French bread
¼ cup extra-virgin olive oil
Kosher salt and freshly ground pepper
1 large garlic clove, cut in half

Preheat the oven to 350 degrees.

Place the French bread slices on a small baking sheet and brush with the olive oil. Bake, turning once, until golden brown and crisp, about 10 minutes. While still warm, rub each crouton with one of the cut sides of garlic.

Rouille

This is a spicy mayonnaise-based sauce that blends nicely into the stew, and the spiciness can be adjusted to your taste. A bit more of the hot pepper puree that comes in a tube, such as ones from Italy, as well as Harissa (page 201) or a dash of hot sauce can be substituted for or used in addition to the cayenne. Taste as you add the seasoning as some can be very hot! Rouille is also traditionally dolloped onto vegetable and bean soups. If you happen to have a roasted pepper or want to get one from a deli, puree it and add some along with the hot pepper for a sweeter sauce.

½ cup mayonnaise
1–2 tablespoons hot pepper puree or harissa
1 small garlic clove, minced
¼ teaspoon cayenne pepper, optional

Mix everything together well. The sauce should be a little spicy and will add great zest to the stew.

FISH AND SUSTAINABLITY

Sustainability is a big issue throughout the food world, no more so than when we consider fish. I follow the Monterey Bay Aquarium Seafood Watch, which provides regional guidelines that help consumers make good choices from environmental and sustainable perspectives. Blue Ocean Institute is another excellent resource, with a wonderful website that children can easily navigate and learn from. Just as we delight in meeting farmers and learning about the journey a carrot takes from seed to field to plate, becoming knowledgeable about the origins of our fish or meat and poultry is essential.

3. Herb-Roasted Salmon

The rosemary sweet potatoes are a bit of a surprise, but they make a complementary accompaniment to the salmon. If sweet potatoes are not available, plain rice, Risotto (page 250), or couscous (page 245), can be substituted. SERVES 6

¼ cup chopped thyme leaves

¼ cup chopped rosemary leaves

1 cup chopped flat-leaf parsley leaves

2 cups olive oil

Six 5-ounce skinless salmon fillets

Salt and freshly ground pepper

Sweet Potatoes with Rosemary and Shallots (page 102), for serving

Herb Salad (page 25), for serving

Combine the herbs with the olive oil. Completely coat the salmon pieces with half the oil and herb mixture and set aside to marinate for 20 minutes.

Preheat the oven to 425 degrees.

Meanwhile, line a baking sheet with heavy-duty foil. Season the salmon with salt and pepper, place it on the sheet, and put the sheet in the upper third of the oven. Roast the fish for 8 minutes for medium-rare or up to 12 minutes to cook through.

Place the salmon fillets on six dinner plates and divide the potato wedges evenly among the plates. Top the fillets with the remaining herb salad and serve immediately.

4. Traditional Mexican Ceviche

love bright-tasting ceviches, especially as summer appetizers or for lunch. Ceviche goes way back in South America, and may even have been brought there by the Spanish, but it didn't really catch on for North Americans until the 1970s.

Treat this recipe as a departure point and customize your own versions, including using other citrus juices. Scallops, striped bass, and halibut, to name just a few, also take nicely to this treatment.

Ceviche creates a very good teaching moment to show kids that "cooking" does not happen only with heat. In ceviche, or cebiche or seviche (the spellings vary from country to country), the texture of the fish is transformed to a cooked state by the acid of limes or lemons in the marinade. The fish becomes firm and opaque and, generally speaking, no longer raw. Citric acid can take the fish just so far, however, and it is extremely important to use superfresh fish to avoid food poisoning and the parasites that only heat can eliminate.   SERVES 4 TO 6

1 pound kingfish (also known as king mackerel, cobia, and yellow amberjack; red snapper also can be used)

Juice of 10 limes

Pinch of salt

½ medium red onion, finely chopped

2 jalapeños, seeded and minced (see page 115)

¼ cup chopped fresh cilantro

¼ cup chopped green olives

¼ cup chopped celery, plus some leaves (optional)

1 avocado, peeled, pitted, and chopped or sliced

1 tablespoon olive oil

Salted crackers, for serving

Cut the fish into small pieces (1½ inches square, more or less). Place the fish in a bowl, cover well with the lime juice, add the salt, and stir. Place the bowl in the refrigerator for 2 hours and stir from time to time.

Remove the bowl from the refrigerator 5 minutes before serving and combine the fish with the onion, jalapeños, cilantro, olives, celery and leaves, avocado, and olive oil. Serve with the crackers.

The avocado and olives can be used to garnish the finished dish instead of mixing them in.

5. Pickled Salmon

If the idea of pickled fish startles you, think of it as a sweet-and-sour variation on the cold poached salmon theme, an excellent lunch or brunch dish, and in the category that also includes gravlax. Salmon takes well to being cured; I sometimes add a couple of green tomatoes or a thinly sliced red pepper to the fish while it is marinating. This makes for a very refreshing dish and is perfect as part of a buffet.   SERVES 4 TO 6

Four 6-ounce skinless salmon
    fillets
1 cup Katchkie Farm Ketchup
    (page 311) or good-quality
    store bought
1 cup cold water
¾ cup white vinegar
¼ cup sugar
1 medium Vidalia or yellow
    onion, thinly sliced
1 tablespoon packaged
    pickling spices
Pinch of salt

Fill a shallow pan or large skillet with water deep enough to cover the fish and bring to a boil. Add the salmon, lower the heat, and gently simmer for 5 minutes. Using a slotted ladle, carefully transfer the salmon to a shallow bowl or glass baking pan and set it aside to cool. Combine the remaining ingredients and pour the mixture over the fish; cover and refrigerate for 3 hours or overnight.

Carefully remove the fish from the brine and arrange it on a platter to serve.

The salmon will keep for 5 days.

6. Mom's Own Fish Sticks

My friend Jenifer Lang and her late husband, George Lang, were the proprietors of New York's beloved Café des Artistes. Jenifer is a well-known food authority—she is the editor of the American edition of *Larousse Gastronomique* and the author of *Jenifer Lang Cooks for Kids,* but she struggled to develop homemade and healthful fish sticks for her own children as good as the frozen kind so many of us grew up with and loved. Finally, after at least a dozen attempts, Jenifer had a winner, with this wheat germ and sesame seed coating. They don't taste exactly like the frozen fish sticks Jenifer's mother served on Friday nights, but they're very crisp and just as delicious—without all the additives.   MAKES 8 FISH STICKS

Cooking spray or olive oil

¼ cup dried bread crumbs

¼ cup wheat germ

¼ cup white sesame seeds

1 teaspoon paprika

½ teaspoon salt

1 egg

1 tablespoon water

¾ pound flounder, sole, or other white-fleshed fish fillets, cut into eight 1½-inch strips

Preheat the oven to 350 degrees.

Coat a baking sheet evenly with cooking spray or olive oil.

In a shallow dish, combine the bread crumbs, wheat germ, sesame seeds, paprika, and salt. Put the egg in another shallow dish with the water and beat with a fork to blend thoroughly.

Dip the fish pieces into the bread crumb mixture, then into the egg, and again into the bread crumbs.

Place the coated fish strips on the baking sheet and bake for 20 minutes, or until the fish is just cooked through; it should be flaky but not dry.

You can shorten the preparation time by keeping a batch of the dry coating mixture in a covered container in the refrigerator for up to three weeks. It's good for chicken fingers as well.

Math Moment

Cooking is a fun and practical way for kids to master their understanding of fractions. This recipe calls for ¼ cup each of wheat germ, bread crumbs, and sesame seeds. Ask your child to measure them out. What fraction of a cup do you have in all? How much more do you need to make a whole cup? If you wanted to double the recipe, how much would you need then? Here the visual makes the virtual instantly understood.

7. Red Snapper Fish Tacos with Pineapple Salsa

Even with all the delicious fish tacos popular today, these are really a super specimen, especially with the pineapple salsa. Children love them, and not just because they are eaten out of hand and great for a party. Most of the prep here involves sharp knives and high heat, chores better left to grown-ups, but children can do the assembly. Or you can let everyone construct his or her own taco at the table.

The dish is particularly good made with snapper, but other fillets, such as scrod or sea bass, can be substituted.

If you don't want to get an entire pineapple for the one cup needed here, lots of markets sell it already cut up; canned pineapple is not a good substitute.   SERVES 6

FOR THE SALSA
2 limes
2 tablespoons finely diced red
    onion
2 tablespoons finely diced red
    bell pepper
1 jalapeño, seeded and finely
    diced
1 cup finely diced fresh
    pineapple
1 avocado, diced
1 heaping tablespoon chopped
    cilantro

FOR THE TACOS
About ¼ pound large red
    radishes, enough to yield
    1 cup shredded
2 tablespoons olive oil
1 pound skinless red snapper
    fillets
Salt and freshly ground pepper
Twelve 6-inch white corn
    tortillas
½ cup sour cream

Zest and juice the limes together in a medium bowl. Stir in the onion, bell pepper, jalapeño, pineapple, and avocado; cover and refrigerate the salsa until ready to use.

Prepare a charcoal fire or a gas grill. Shred the radishes using a food processor fitted with the shredding disk, or use the coarse side of a box grater or a mandoline.

When the charcoal is white hot or the grill is medium hot, brush the grids lightly with some oil. Season the snapper well with salt and pepper and brush it with the remaining oil.

Wrap the tortillas in a clean, lightly dampened cloth and then in aluminum foil. Remove the salsa from the refrigerator.

Place the fillets on the grill and cook for about 3 minutes on each side, just until done; if they seem to be charring too quickly, move them away from the direct heat. Place the wrapped tortillas on the grill to warm through while the fish is cooking, turning the package once.

Remove the fillets from the grill and let them rest for about 2 minutes, then cut them into strips.

Stir the cilantro into the salsa. Unwrap the tortillas. Spoon the sour cream onto the tortillas, then divide the red snapper among them. Top with pineapple salsa and shaved radishes and serve.

8. Lime-Seared Scallops in Lemongrass Broth

Lemongrass can be nearly addictive, with its delicate lemony scent and flavor. No wonder it is pretty much indispensable in Thai cooking. I am seeing it more and more in ordinary supermarkets, and it is certainly available in Asian and specialty markets.

Get the largest scallops you can find for this recipe and remove any tough ligament that is still attached at the side.   SERVES 4 TO 6

4 teaspoons extra-virgin olive oil

1 teaspoon finely chopped tarragon

Zest and juice of 1 lime

4 garlic cloves, finely chopped

2 shallots, finely chopped

2 teaspoons peeled and minced fresh ginger

2 pounds fresh sea scallops

2 stalks lemongrass

1 tablespoon vegetable oil

1 teaspoon fish sauce

1 cup vegetable stock, homemade (page 38) or good-quality store bought

1 cup unsweetened coconut milk

2 tablespoons thinly sliced scallions or chives

Cooked white or basmati rice, for serving

Whisk together 2 teaspoons of the olive oil, the tarragon, lime zest and juice, and half the garlic, shallots, and ginger in a wide, shallow dish. Add the scallops, toss to coat, cover, and refrigerate for no longer than 30 minutes.

While the scallops are marinating, prepare the broth. Cut away the small pale bottom part of the lemongrass and peel off the tough outer leaves. Place the pieces on their sides and press down, with your palm or the side of a large knife, to bruise them. Heat the vegetable oil in a medium saucepan over medium heat; add the remaining shallots and slowly sauté until they are caramelized—richly browned but not burned. Add the remaining garlic and ginger and stir for about 1 minute.

Add the lemongrass and fish sauce to the pan and stir until fragrant, about 1 minute, then pour in the vegetable stock. Bring the sauce to a boil, then reduce the heat and simmer for about 20 minutes. Pour in the coconut milk and simmer for about 5 minutes longer. Set the sauce aside and keep it warm.

Meanwhile, drain the scallops of excess marinade and set them on paper towels for a minute or so to dry.

Place a large skillet over medium heat for about 2 minutes, then coat the surface with the remaining 2 teaspoons olive oil. When the oil is hot, gently add the scallops to the skillet without crowding them; sear the scallops in two batches if necessary.

Cook the scallops on one side for about 2 minutes, or until they are browned. Do not move them about or the searing process will be affected. Turn the scallops over and cook for 2 more minutes.

To serve, pour some of the warm sauce onto individual plates and set the scallops on the sauce; garnish with the scallions and place the rice to the side.

LEMONGRASS

Lemongrass is a hearty perennial plant grown in warm or tropical climates. Thanks to Thai and Philippine immigrants, crops now can be found in such seemingly unlikely places as Houston, Texas, often in backyards. The flavor of lemongrass is delicious in soups, poultry, fish, and meat; it also makes a delicious soothing tea.

Lemongrass stalks look a little like scallions, but are much tougher and fibrous and need to be well trimmed before they can be used. When shopping, look for firm stalks with good color—very pale yellow, nearly white at the bottom, green at the top.

9. Cilantro-Chile-Spiked Cod Burgers

These burgers make a good family dinner, but they are also terrific for casual weekend lunches with friends. Or make them into bite-size morsels for a cocktail or buffet party.

SERVES 6

1½ pounds cod, coarsely chopped

¾ cup panko (see page 218)

½ cup chopped fresh cilantro

¼ cup finely chopped red onion

2 jalapeños, seeded and minced

2 teaspoons Cajun seasoning

2 tablespoons mayonnaise

Juice and zest of 1 lime

2 garlic cloves, minced

1 teaspoon kosher salt

½ teaspoon freshly ground pepper

¼ cup yellow stone-ground cornmeal

2 tablespoons vegetable oil

2 tablespoons butter

6 hamburger rolls

1 avocado, peeled, pitted, and sliced, for serving

¼ cup sour cream, for serving

Place the cod, panko, cilantro, onion, jalapeño, Cajun seasoning, mayonnaise, lime juice and zest, garlic, salt, and pepper in a large bowl and, using your hands, mix gently until the ingredients are evenly incorporated.

Place the cornmeal in a shallow dish. Divide the cod mixture evenly into 6 balls, then form each into a patty about ¾ to 1 inch thick. Dredge the patties in the cornmeal.

Set a cast-iron skillet over medium-high heat and add the oil and butter; when they are hot but not smoking, place the patties in the pan. Cook until well seared on both sides and cooked through, 4 to 5 minutes per side.

Toast the rolls and serve the burgers with the avocado and sour cream.

Other fish, such as tuna or haddock, can be substituted for the cod.

Katchkie Farm Fresh Salsa (page 312) also makes a terrific garnish.

10. Salmon Burgers with Asian Flavors and Cucumber Slaw

I love these unusual burgers and make them often. They are particularly great when you have guests for lunch, so satisfying, and a nice change from meat burgers or the predictable chicken or tuna salads. Cod or halibut can be substituted for the salmon.   SERVES 4

FOR THE SLAW

1 medium cucumber, peeled
    and seeded
½ teaspoon salt
¼ cup peeled, julienned
    daikon
¼ cup peeled, julienned carrot
1 tablespoon fresh lime juice
2 teaspoons fish sauce
2 teaspoons minced cilantro

FOR THE BURGERS

1 teaspoon mirin
1 teaspoon minced Thai or
    other red chile
1 large egg white
1 tablespoon soy sauce
1 teaspoon sesame oil
Zest and juice of 1 lime
1 pound skinless salmon fillet,
    cut into ¼-inch dice (see
    Note)
Salt and freshly ground pepper
¾ cup panko (see page 218)
¼ cup minced scallions
1 garlic clove, chopped

To make the slaw, julienne or shred the cucumber and put it in a strainer. Toss with the salt; place the strainer over the sink or a bowl to drain for about 15 minutes. Squeeze out any excess moisture, rinse, drain, and pat dry. Toss the cucumber with the daikon, carrot, lime juice, fish sauce, and cilantro. Cover and refrigerate until ready to serve.

To make the burgers, preheat the oven to 400 degrees.

Whisk the mirin, chile, egg white, soy sauce, sesame oil, and lime juice and zest together in a medium bowl. Add the salmon, a pinch of salt, a few grindings of pepper, ¼ cup of the panko, the scallions, garlic, and shiso leaves, if using, and mix. Form the mixture into four patties.

Place the remaining ½ cup panko in a shallow dish. Dredge the patties in the panko to coat evenly on both sides. Heat the vegetable and olive oil in a large, nonstick ovenproof skillet over medium heat. Add the salmon patties and cook for 1 minute. Flip the burgers, then place the skillet in the oven; cook the patties until medium-rare, about 3 minutes. Remove the skillet from the oven.

Toast the buns. Place the burgers on the buns and top with the slaw.

4 shiso leaves, finely chopped
  (optional)
2 tablespoons vegetable oil
2 teaspoons olive oil
4 hamburger rolls

A fishmonger can cut up the fish for you, or you can do it with a good sharp knife. You can also do it in a food processor. The fish must be very cold. Cut it into chunks, then pulse in the processor just a few times to chop. Take care or you will end up with fish mush.

Shiso is an herb related to mint and basil; it is beautiful, dark green (though there is a rarer red version) with jagged edges. It has become popular and available; look for it at farmers' or Asian markets. But if you don't find it, you can substitute mint or Thai basil, or a combination, in this recipe.

PANKO

Panko is a very dry and flaky Japanese bread crumb that is made in a special oven, not from bread but from raw bread dough that is blown into the oven and instantly bakes into flakes. Panko has become very popular in the United States, to the point that you can find domestic brands on supermarket shelves, and for good reason—it stays crisper, crunchier, and drier when cooked longer than many traditional bread crumbs.

The story behind panko is that the Japanese wanted to replicate Wiener schnitzel in honor of the visit of an Austrian emissary. Japan is not a bread culture so making the crumbs and coating the veal cutlets was something of a revelation. In time tonkatsu, a breaded and fried pork fillet, became a fixture in Japanese cuisine, sometimes served over rice, sometimes on a bowl of noodle soup, and sometimes in a sandwich. The technology for producing the crumbs followed tonkatsu's popularity.

11. Black Cod with Coconut Basmati Rice Pilaf

The fish marinates overnight and the rice soaks for at least 30 minutes, so most of this delicious dish can be managed in advance. SERVES 2 TO 3

¼ cup sake

¼ cup mirin (see page 171)

4 tablespoons white miso paste

3 tablespoons sugar

2 or 3 black cod fillets (about 1 pound)

1 cup basmati rice

1½ cups cold water

3 green cardamom pods

3 thin slices peeled fresh ginger

3 sprigs cilantro

1 teaspoon kosher salt

1½ cups unsweetened coconut milk

1 tablespoon canola or other neutral-flavored oil

3 tablespoons chopped cashews

3 tablespoons thinly sliced scallions, white with about 1 inch of green parts

3 tablespoons toasted unsweetened coconut flakes

To make the marinade, mix together the sake, mirin, miso paste, and sugar thoroughly. Pat the fillets dry and place them in a shallow container with a cover. Pour all but ¼ cup of the marinade over the fillets, turn them, and cover the container. Refrigerate the fish overnight or up to 24 hours, turning a few times.

Place the rice in a strainer and rinse it under cold water until the water runs clear. Drain the rice well and transfer it to a large saucepan. Add the water, cardamom, ginger, cilantro, salt, and coconut milk. Let the rice soak for at least 30 minutes or up to 2 hours.

Remove the cod from the refrigerator about 30 minutes before cooking. Preheat the oven to 400 degrees.

Heat a heavy skillet—cast iron is ideal—or a stovetop grill. Gently wipe away any excess marinade clinging to the fillets. Lightly coat the pan or grill with the oil. Place the fish in the pan or on the grill and brown on the skin side, then transfer the fish to a baking sheet turning so the skin side is up and place in the oven; cook just until the flesh is firm to the touch and no longer translucent, about 10 minutes.

Meanwhile, bring the rice in its soaking liquid to a boil over medium-high heat. Stir a few times to keep the grains from clumping. Cook, uncovered, rapidly boiling, until most of the liquid is absorbed and the surface is covered with steamy holes, about 6 minutes. Reduce the heat as low as possible and cook, covered, for 5 minutes longer. Remove the pan from the heat and discard the cilantro, cardamom, and ginger. Fold in the chopped cashews, scallions, and coconut flakes.

Drizzle the cod with the reserved miso marinade and serve with the rice.

The marinade can keep the fish skin from getting crispy, so take care to shake the liquid from the skin before cooking—or remove the skin altogether.

12. Cynthia's Stuffed Bluefish—
A Taste of Summer

Cynthia Hayes and her family are like family to us. We have known one another for more than fifteen years, ever since we became country neighbors across a dirt road. Our children formed a little gang, climbing into tree houses, raking autumn leaves for colossal jumping piles, shucking corn for weekly barbecues, and sharing crazy sledding adventures down steep hills into snowbanks. Whether the day came to a close in front of a crackling fireplace or with long branches crowned with toasted marshmallows on summer nights, we shared endless meals punctuated by laughter, piles of dirty dishes, and good stories.

Cynthia's Sicilian family's name is DiMare—"of the sea"—and some of her relatives in America drifted back to islands and fishing, the ancient family trade. When she was young, she often visited her favorite aunt and uncle on Martha's Vineyard where fishing, often for blues, was a favorite activity. Cynthia's recipe is a typical straightforward way to treat good fresh fish.

Life happens around food.   SERVES 4

2 celery stalks, chopped

1 small onion, chopped

1 tablespoon olive oil, plus
   more if needed

1 garlic clove, finely minced

¼ cup chopped fresh flat-leaf
   parsley

1 cup bread crumbs

1½ pounds bluefish fillets,
   rinsed and patted dry

Preheat the oven to 375 degrees.

Sauté the celery and onion in about 1 tablespoon of the oil. Add the garlic and parsley. When the celery and onion are soft, add the bread crumbs and mix until moist; add more oil if necessary. Remove from the heat.

Pour a few drops of oil into an ovenproof glass baking dish. Place the fish in the dish, skin side down, and spread the stuffing over the flesh. Bake for 15 to 20 minutes, until the fish is firm.

Use a long metal spatula to remove the fish from the dish and take off their skin—it will naturally separate from the flesh—taking care not to break the fillets.

BLUEFISH

Bluefish can be found just about all around the world, though it may go by different names—in parts of Australia it's called shad, which is a different fish altogether in the United States. Like some people in the Northeast, bluefish go to Florida in the winter and start heading north again by April. In October, they head south again.

Pasta, Rice, and Grains

For close to ten years, a stubborn strand of linguine stuck to my kitchen ceiling. How did it get there? It was from a test our wonderful babysitter, Fiona, conducted with our children to see if the pasta was ready; if it stuck to the ceiling, it was ready to eat. That strand remained suspended above the kitchen table where we had family meals, a testimony to the children's love of pasta, but also to the spirit of playfulness and exploration that should be part of kitchen activities. I renovated the kitchen recently; letting go of that strand of linguine was nearly as poignant as leaving a kid at college for the first time.

Pasta, rice, and grains are endlessly adaptable to seasons and cultures, appealing to adults who enjoy a wide range of flavors and to children who simply find pasta and rice very satisfying. They are fun foods and simple to prepare. There may not be a parent on the planet who wouldn't agree that this is the no-worry category for kids' meals. Easy to make, endlessly adaptable, pasta, noodles, and rice also provide an efficient way to bring the edible plant world to the table.

On a list of all-time favorites, mac and cheese, any pasta with pesto, and any sort of dumplings will surely be at the top. The flexibility of creating a dish with new ingredients—or finding a way to weave in your leftovers—is the beauty of these foods.

The world of grains is worth knowing, especially as they are a good source of protein. Pasta and grain dishes are the ones teenagers will make for themselves as they start to tinker in the kitchen or when they first leave home and have to fend for themselves.

Pasta Rules

Pasta is easy to cook, but also easy to cook badly. The rules matter.

WATER   Start with a lot—four to five quarts per pound of pasta—in a large pot, and be sure it is cold. Harold McGee, a food scientist, has recently challenged this time-honored rule and reported that far less water is required to successfully cook pasta, but the jury, including—and especially—many Italian culinary experts, is still out.

SALT   Do not add salt until the water is boiling or about to boil—salt lowers the cooking temperature of water, not by much, but why wait longer than you need to? Wait until the water is rolling again before you toss in your pasta. Use sea salt, if possible, or kosher salt.

TIMING   The guidance on pasta boxes, especially imported brands, is quite reliable, but you are your own best judge. The usual expression for the doneness of pasta is "al dente," which translates to "to the tooth." The pasta should be tender, but not soft, still firm to the bite, but not hard. The only practical way to know is to bite a piece and pay attention—almost done and done may be just seconds apart. If you plan to cook the pasta in its sauce for a minute or so, or bake it, drain it even sooner than for al dente.

RINSING   Never rinse pasta unless you have cooked it as the first step in preparing a dish, for stuffing, for instance, or baking. In those cases, you want to cool the pasta and stop the cooking or it will become too soft as it bakes. There are those who rinse pasta to remove starch, but I say if you want to avoid starch, pasta isn't for you.

OIL   Except for a very few exceptions, like precooking for some dishes, never add oil to the cooking water. Some American cooks got the notion that the oil would keep the pasta from sticking together, which I guess is true, but it also keeps sauce from adhering. If you stir frequently, especially for about 30 seconds at the beginning, your pasta will not stick together.

PASTA WAITS FOR NO ONE   The greatest chefs and any Italian grandma agree on this. Have your ingredients ready and your family and guests at the table before the pasta finishes, then toss and serve. In some households, the cook's announcement, "I'm throwing the pasta in," translates to "Wash your hands, comb your hair, and get to the table, *subito.*"

TO DRAIN   The usual way is to pour the pasta into a colander set in the sink. This is fine, but carrying a pot of five gallons of boiling water can be daunting. A Chinese mesh strainer, the kind also used for pulling fried food out of hot oil, is good for this, as are tongs. I also like large pasta pots with perforated inserts; you still have to carry them to the sink, but instead of dumping the pasta into the colander, you simply pull the insert out.

TOSSING AND SERVING   The experts' secret is to remove about a cup of the cooking water just before draining the pasta. This water contains starch that can help bind the sauce and pasta, and it will lighten the sauce if it is thicker than you like. Start with just a tablespoon or two. You will be amazed at how effective this is.

In many preparations, the pasta can and should be tossed with the sauce or other ingredients over low heat; either return the pasta to the cooking pot, or turn it into the pan holding the sauce. Add a bit of oil or butter to taste. In any case, toss the pasta immediately after it is cooked, and then serve it. You might like to warm your serving bowl and dishes with hot water or at least keep the dishes near the stove as you cook.

I don't have to tell you that pasta is really endlessly variable, especially for family meals. One thing I've been doing in recent years is using whole-wheat pasta, especially with vegetables like green beans, broccoli, and spinach. There also is pasta made with farro wheat (page 255), which is delicious and super nutritious. For the first step of a vegetable and pasta dish, see my basic method for cooking greens (page 68); toss the pasta with the cooked vegetables and some of the pasta cooking water and you've got dinner. Add some roasted garlic or a bit of sautéed sausage, minced smoked turkey, a scoop of ricotta, or some pancetta for extra taste.

1. Spaghetti with Burst Cherry Tomatoes

Small tomatoes can now be found in any supermarket throughout the year. Nothing equals fresh local tomatoes, but these small varieties—cherry, grape, and so on—are a welcome alternative in the dark months. Most are grown in greenhouses and some are imported from places such as Israel and Mexico and have great flavor.

I leave all tomatoes out at room temperature, but these especially benefit from a few days of ripening to deepen their flavor and bring out their sweetness. I make it a point to always have some small tomatoes on hand for salads, salsas, and quick pasta dishes like this one. When cooking this with children, make sure you have plenty of extra tomatoes for snacking.

SERVES 4 TO 6

4 cups cherry or grape tomatoes (about 40 tomatoes)

2 tablespoons olive oil, plus more to finish

Salt

½ teaspoon sugar

2 garlic cloves, chopped

1 teaspoon red chile flakes

1 tablespoon chopped fresh oregano, or a pinch dried

1 pound spaghetti

Freshly ground pepper

Grated Parmigiano-Reggiano (optional)

Heat the oven to 400 degrees.

Put the cherry tomatoes, 1 tablespoon of the olive oil, a big pinch of salt, and the sugar in a large bowl and toss to coat the tomatoes well.

Line a rimmed baking sheet with a piece of parchment paper or aluminum foil. Pour the tomatoes onto the baking sheet, place them in the oven, and roast for 25 to 35 minutes, or until they collapse and their skins begin to char. Remove the tomatoes from the oven and let them cool slightly. Carefully lift the paper and pour the tomatoes and all their roasting juices back into the bowl.

Bring a large pot of water to a boil over high heat.

Heat the remaining 1 tablespoon oil in a large skillet over medium heat. Add the garlic and red chile flakes and sauté for about 1 minute. Add the roasted tomatoes with their juices and the oregano. Use a spoon to break up the tomatoes and cook until they are heated through.

When the water is rolling, add a big pinch of salt, drop in the spaghetti, and stir. Cook the pasta according to the package instructions for al dente. Remove and reserve some of the pasta cooking water, then drain the pasta.

Add the pasta and about 1 tablespoon of the reserved cooking water to the tomato sauce. Stir and toss to thoroughly coat the spaghetti. Add a tablespoon or so of the remaining pasta water if the sauce is too dry or thick; drizzle with olive oil and season with salt and pepper to taste. Turn the pasta into a serving bowl or individual bowls and pass the cheese, if using, at the table.

The tomatoes can be roasted and kept at room temperature for several hours or for a day or two in advance and refrigerated until needed.

For a different twist, add 2 cups diced eggplant to the tomatoes before roasting, and sprinkle the final dish with grated ricotta salata.

Or throw about ½ pound of rock shrimp or other small peeled shrimp into the skillet with the tomatoes, cook and stir for about 2 minutes, then add two generous handfuls of baby arugula and stir just to wilt.

Basta la Pasta

Perhaps because pasta appeals to people of all ages, many charming and whimsical names have been assigned to pasta shapes. Share some with your children. Start with the English elbow, the shape of choice for the all-important mac and cheese, and then move on to Italian. You might stage a demonstration and let them choose what they'd like. I suggest you keep the strangolapreti, or strozzapreti, "priest-strangler," for adult amusement.

Here are some good ones for kids to learn:

1 Orecchiette . . . little ears
2 Cappelletti . . . little hats
3 Capelli di angelo . . . angel's hair
4 Chicche . . . this word allegedly came from baby talk and means "sweets" or "candy"
5 Farfalle . . . butterfly
6 Lumache . . . snail's shells
7 Penne . . . pens or quills
8 Paglia e fieno . . . straw and hay; a combination of white and spinach noodles
9 Vermicelli . . . another word for spaghetti. It means "little worms" Yuk!
10 Stelle and stelline . . . stars and little stars
11 Conchiglie . . . shells
12 Fusilli . . . spirals
13 Gigli . . . lilies; a pretty small shape
14 Occhi . . . eyes
15 Ruote . . . spoked wheels
16 Tubetti . . . little tubes
17 Fazoletti, fazzolettini . . . handkerchiefs, small handkerchiefs; a good shape to fold over a simple filling

New shapes continue to appear; a few years ago some top Italian graphic designers were invited to come up with designs for pasta. One of the most popular to come out of the challenge was radiatori, or "radiators," a short, ridged shape that is excellent for holding sauce.

1

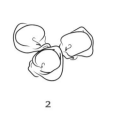

2

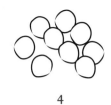

3

4

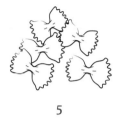

5

6

7

8

9

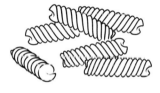

10

11

12

13

14

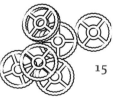

6

7

15

16

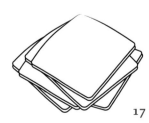

17

2. Penne with Roasted Cauliflower

Here is another example of stale bread becoming an appealing ingredient in a dish. Particularly in the poor southern regions, Italian home cooks often grated it (*pangrattato*) onto pasta in place of more expensive cheese. Now such dishes are part of the pasta canon, revered for themselves.   SERVES 4

4 tablespoons olive oil, plus more for the baking sheet

1 small cauliflower (about 1 pound)

Salt and freshly ground pepper

1 cup fresh flat-leaf parsley leaves

1 tablespoon grated lemon zest

1 tablespoon capers, rinsed and drained

1 pound penne

½ teaspoon red chile flakes

1 cup garlic croutons, coarsely crushed (recipe follows)

Place the oven rack at the highest position and preheat the oven to 475 degrees. Thinly coat a baking sheet with a bit of olive oil.

Trim the cauliflower and cut it from top to bottom into thin slices, about ¼ inch thick. Toss the cauliflower with 2 tablespoons of the olive oil, spread it in a single layer on the prepared sheet, and season with salt and pepper. Place the sheet on the rack and roast the cauliflower for 18 minutes, or until lightly browned.

Place a large pot of water over medium-high heat.

Pulse the parsley, lemon zest, and remaining 2 tablespoons oil in a small food processor or chop them together on a cutting board until a chunky mixture forms. Add the capers and pulse until they are coarsely chopped.

When the water is at a rolling boil, add a big pinch of salt, drop in the penne, and stir; cook the pasta, stirring from time to time, until al dente, according to the package directions, about 9 minutes. Remove and reserve ½ cup of the cooking water and drain the pasta.

Toss the pasta with the cauliflower, parsley sauce, and red chile flakes in a large serving bowl; add the reserved cooking water as necessary if the dish seems too thick.

Sprinkle the garlic croutons over and serve from a serving bowl or divide among four individual bowls.

> Coarse bread crumbs, lightly sautéed or baked with 1 or 2 minced cloves of garlic and a bit of olive oil, can be substituted for the croutons.

Make Croutons with the Kids

Croutons are fun and easy to make with kids, and also reinforce the idea of reusing ingredients. Take 4 or 5 slices of stale bread and have the kids cut them into ½-inch squares by slicing the bread into strips (crusts can stay on), then cutting in the other direction. You can let them sit for half an hour to dry out further. In a bowl, mix together ½ cup olive oil, ¼ teaspoon garlic powder, ¼ teaspoon salt, and ¼ teaspoon pepper and toss with the bread cubes till evenly coated.

Lay the bread cubes out in a single layer on a baking sheet and put into a preheated oven at 325 degrees for about 15 to 20 minutes. Keep an eye on them; you don't want them to burn. You will find that your helpers will snack on the croutons, so consider making twice as many as you will want for your recipe! By the way, unwanted grilled cheese sandwiches, even on the stale side, make excellent croutons (but keep these refrigerated).

3. Sweet Potato Gnocchi

These melt-in-your-mouth little dumplings combine rich and sweet tastes. There are definitely fun chores for children here, especially the rolling of the little pieces of dough and making the typical indentations you see on gnocchi, which will also speed up the process of forming them. This is cooking *casalinga,* homemade, so don't worry if the gnocchi are less than perfect—the word can even mean homely, in the best sense.

My favorite sauce for this is brown butter and crisp-fried sage (as used in Creamy White Polenta with Sage and Brown Butter, page 254), or you could simply heat the sage with the brown butter. A light tomato sauce would also be lovely.   SERVES 10 TO 12

2 red-skinned sweet potatoes (2 pounds), rinsed, patted dry, and pierced all over with a fork

One 15-ounce container fresh ricotta cheese, drained in a sieve to remove excess moisture, overnight or for about 2 hours (factor in time to drain the ricotta before you begin)

1 cup finely grated Parmigiano-Reggiano

2 tablespoons (packed) light brown sugar

2 tablespoons plus 2 teaspoons salt

½ teaspoon freshly grated nutmeg

About 2¾ cups all-purpose flour

Sage and brown butter sauce (see page 254)

Preheat the oven to 375 degrees.

Line a large baking sheet with parchment paper, place the sweet potatoes on it, and bake until soft, about 40 minutes. Alternatively, the potatoes can be cooked in a microwave oven, on a plate, and then baked for 5 minutes on each side. Let the potatoes cool to room temperature.

Cut the sweet potatoes in half lengthwise and scrape the flesh into a medium bowl; mash with a fork and transfer 3 cups to a large bowl. Add the ricotta cheese and blend well. Add the Parmigiano-Reggiano, brown sugar, 2 teaspoons of the salt, and the nutmeg. Mash again to blend well. Mix in the flour, about ½ cup at a time, until a soft dough forms.

Turn the dough onto a floured surface and divide it into 6 equal pieces. With your palms flat, roll each piece into a 20-inch-long rope about 1 inch in diameter. Sprinkle the dough and your work surface lightly with flour as needed if the dough is sticky. Cut each rope into 20 pieces, then roll each piece over the tines of a fork to indent lightly. Transfer the pieces to a baking sheet.

Bring a large pot of water to a boil over high heat; add 2 tablespoons of salt. When the water returns to a rolling boil, begin to add the gnocchi, working in batches of 10 or so. Cook the gnocchi until tender, 5 to 6 minutes. As they finish cooking, remove the gnocchi with a skimmer or slotted spoon to a colander. Divide the gnocchi among shallow bowls, spoon the sauce over, and serve at once.

This makes a generous amount. If you don't need it all for one meal, the prepared gnocchi can be frozen. Place the uncooked gnocchi on a baking sheet and put it in the freezer. Once they are frozen, dust the gnocchi lightly with flour and store them in a freezer bag. To cook, drop the still-frozen gnocchi into boiling water as above—do not defrost before cooking.

4. Fettuccine with Shredded Zucchini, Fresh Ricotta, and Lemon Zest

I realize that this seems almost too simple to mention, but it is such a perfect dish, and a good solution to a high-summer extravagance of zucchini and mint. And unlike some pasta dishes, it is light enough for a first course. I grate an additional bit of lemon zest over the finished dish.   SERVES 4 TO 6

Salt

1 pound fettuccine

4 tablespoons extra-virgin olive oil

3 or 4 garlic cloves, finely chopped or grated

Zest of 1 to 2 lemons

2 medium-large or 4 small zucchini, cleaned but not peeled, and shredded

Freshly ground pepper

¼ cup chopped fresh flat-leaf parsley

¼ cup chopped fresh mint

1 cup fresh whole-milk ricotta cheese, at room temperature

Place a large pot of water over high heat. When the water is at a rolling boil, add a big pinch of salt, drop in the fettucine, and stir.

Cook the pasta, stirring from time to time, according to package directions for al dente, usually about 12 minutes. Meanwhile, heat the olive oil in a large skillet over medium heat. When the oil is warm, add the garlic and sauté until golden, about 1 minute. Add the lemon zest and cook for 30 seconds longer. Increase the heat to medium-high, add the zucchini, and cook, stirring, until tender, 2 to 3 minutes. Season with salt and pepper.

Remove and reserve about ½ cup of the cooking water, then drain the pasta and quickly toss with the zucchini, parsley, and mint. Spoon on the ricotta and toss lightly again, add small amounts of the cooking water to lighten the cheese to the consistency you like, and serve.

Zucchini is easy to shred on the large holes of a box grater, with the shredding attachment of a food processor, or with a mandoline (page 80).

The Language of Cooking

Like "al dente" (page 226), "dandelion" is another word connected to the Italian for "teeth": *dente di leone*—lion's teeth. Kids love knowing this sort of thing, especially if they can connect something they eat with a wild animal. They've seen pictures of those teeth, now show them the plant, which just might be growing on your lawn. The French is similar: *dent di lion.* And while our word, "teeth," is quite different, "dental," "dentist," and "denture" are all related to those foreign words.

Another good word from the Italian here is "ricotta," which means "recooked," referring to the process of making the cheese. *Rifatti* means "remade," and is used for what we call leftovers, because Italian—and French—cooks like to give them a second life in dishes like frittatas, salads, or sauces for pasta.

5. Pasta with Artichokes and Eggs

This will remind you of spaghetti carbonara, a pasta dish made with eggs that cook as they are tossed with hot pasta. In this meatless version, we keep carbonara's cheese, but artichokes replace the pork. The recipe comes from our friend the well-known cookbook author and Italian food authority Giuliano Bugialli.   SERVES 4 TO 6

1 lemon

3 large artichokes

¼ cup olive oil

2 tablespoons unsalted butter

1 medium onion, preferably
    red, chopped

2 garlic cloves, minced

About ¼ cup chopped fresh
    flat-leaf parsley

Salt

Freshly ground pepper

1 pound rigatoni

2 extra-large eggs, at room
    temperature

2 tablespoons grated Pecorino
    Romano, Siciliano, or
    Parmigiano-Reggiano
    cheese, plus more for the
    table if desired

Squeeze the lemon through a strainer into a large bowl of water.

To prepare the artichokes, trim the stems flush at the bottom. Break off all the dark outer leaves until only very light greenish-yellow ones are left, with just a bit of dark green at the tips. Turn the artichokes on their sides and slice them horizontally; you will be left with about the bottom third of each. Cut the artichokes into quarters and remove the chokes with the tip of a knife (a grapefruit spoon is also good for this). Slice each quarter into 3 or 4 pieces and drop them into the bowl of water and lemon juice.

Place a large skillet or sauté pan over medium heat. Pour in the olive oil, then add the butter. When the butter has ceased bubbling, add the onion and garlic; stir for about 3 minutes, then add the parsley. Drain the artichokes and add them to the pan. Cover the pan, reduce the heat to low, and cook the mixture for 10 minutes, stirring from time to time.

Bring a large pot of water to a boil over high heat.

Add 1 cup of water to the artichokes and continue cooking until the artichokes have absorbed most of the moisture and are very soft, reduced almost to a sauce.

When the water comes to a boil, add a big pinch of salt, drop in the rigatoni, and stir. Cook, stirring from time to time, according to the package directions for al dente, usually about 10 minutes.

Meanwhile, break the eggs into a large serving bowl and whisk them lightly; whisk in the cheese and salt and pepper to taste. Drain the pasta well, then turn it into the bowl. Mix gently but thoroughly—the eggs will cook in the heat of the pasta; stir in the artichokes and pan juices and serve in individual bowls.

Pass additional cheese at the table, if desired.

ARTICHOKES

Virtually 100 percent of this country's artichokes are grown around the little town of Castroville, California, in the heart of the Central Coast farm region.

Castroville is close enough to San Francisco to make a terrific family day trip, even when the town is not holding its annual Artichoke Festival. Several restaurants on the main street do everything imaginable to offer more and better ways to prepare artichokes: dips, soups, tarts, omelets, pizza, pasta, and, of course, fried . . . and it does seem that some of the largest artichokes you will ever see are cooked and served right where they were grown. For children, the main attraction is the giant artichoke sculpture in front of the restaurant named, yes, the Giant Artichoke—the sculpture is taller than the building.

I have seen local artichokes at New York's Union Square Greenmarket. Those came from a farmer in New Jersey; apparently, small family farmers, mostly Italians, still produce them in the southern part of the state. We had a small crop at Katchkie a couple of years ago and now are planting more and are very excited at the prospect. We think our valley, with its warm days and relatively cool nights, is somewhat similar to the California coastal region.

Baby artichokes, by the way, are simply the ones that grow lowest on the stalk; the big guys are at the top, and the artichokes are arranged downward in a size-based hierarchy.

6. Mac 'n' Very Cheesy

Yes, this does seem like an awful lot of cheese, but there is no mistake in the amounts here. We serve this at Dizzy's Club Coca-Cola, the renowned club at Jazz at Lincoln Center in New York—it's a little hot, and goes nicely with cool jazz.

At Dizzy's, the mac 'n' cheese is an appetizer size served with a salad. You can do the same, or have it as a side to a main dish. Otherwise, this will be enough for at least eight as a main course with a vegetable side.   SERVES 8 TO 12

1 pound elbow macaroni
Salt
Freshly ground pepper
20 ounces shredded Cheddar, plus more for topping if desired
8 ounces shredded Swiss cheese
8 ounces shredded Monterey Jack cheese with jalapeños
4 ounces grated Parmigiano-Reggiano
1 cup sour cream
1 teaspoon dry mustard
1 teaspoon cayenne pepper, or to taste
1 egg
6 ounces half-and-half

Bring a large pot of water to a rolling boil, add a big pinch of salt, drop in the macaroni, and stir. Cook until barely al dente, about 5 minutes; the macaroni will cook more as it bakes. Drain and rinse under cold water.

Preheat the oven to 375 degrees.

Mix the remaining ingredients together in a large bowl, then stir in the macaroni to blend well. Season to taste with salt and pepper.

Spoon the mac and cheese into individual 6- or 8-ounce ramekins or one large baking dish, $9\frac{1}{2} \times 12 \times 3$ inches deep. Sprinkle on the extra Cheddar, if using, place the ramekins or dish in the oven, and bake until bubbly and browned on top, 15 to 20 minutes.

THE STORY OF NOODLES

There is hardly a place on the earth where flour and water are not turned into noodles of one shape or another. Marco Polo did not bring noodles back from China as legend has it. The earliest Italian cookbook, which was written in Florence long before Marco went off on his travels, includes pasta recipes, and there is evidence that some versions of pasta were eaten in ancient Roman times (the word "lasagna" comes from a Latin word).

However, it is easy to believe that noodles in one form or another were already a part of the Chinese diet when Polo arrived. The Chinese culture was already old and quite advanced, and the reverence for excellent cooking had long been established.

7. Vegetable Lasagna

This is a big project but always worth it! When I decide to make my vegetable lasagna, I will usually make a few pans—one for the meal ahead, one for the freezer, and one for Farmer Bob. Lasagna freezes beautifully (I first cut each batch into manageable thirds) and it is always helpful to be able to pull out a wedge for a late-night comfort meal or a surprise visitor. You can enlist lots of help in putting together the cheese mixture, making your own tomato sauce, selecting and slicing the veggies, and, of course, assembling the many layers— the process of mapping out the ingredients is good work for a young scribe.

When you see my ingredients, you will understand why I say that we grow vegetable lasagna at Katchkie Farm. By late July and into September, I get all my vegetables from the field—peppers, onions, garlic, eggplant, zucchini, chard, and, of course, the tomatoes and herbs. I welcome any variations and additions. I will gather herbs and add them, including our parsley, basil, oregano, and thyme. Many times I end up with more prepared vegetables than needed for the lasagna. I then use those extras in a frittata or quiche; I add the cheese mixture and bake them in individual dishes for forty-five minutes.

This lasagna is quite open to interpretation; you may want to add or subtract an ingredient, or tweak the amounts and kinds of cheeses. For instance, I recently substituted 1 pound of quark, a soft cheese similar to cottage cheese, for 1 pound of ricotta—delicious.

Here are the basics, with details to follow. I've also included my schematic drawing; it always guides me as I construct the lasagna. You will need a deeper pan than the usual lasagna or other baking pan to accommodate this. A 13-x-9-inch roasting pan is better because it will be deeper, around 3 inches; I also like a deep gratin pan that I can bring to the table.   12 SERVINGS

THE COMPONENTS

2 to 3 quarts tomato sauce, organic if possible

Cheese filling

Prepared vegetables

1 bunch Swiss chard, tough leaves and ribs trimmed away, washed and thinly shredded

Olive oil, for the chard and pans

Make the cheese filling: Mix all the ingredients together and reserve.

Prepare the vegetables: Toss the zucchini, yellow squash, eggplant, onion, garlic, and bell peppers with a bit of olive oil and season with salt and pepper. Lightly cook the vegetables as you wish: grill, sauté, or roast in the oven (page 80). If you are using roasted tomatoes, roughly chop them and add them to the cooked vegetables, then set the vegetables aside.

Sauté the chard in a skillet with a little olive oil, just to wilt it, about 3 minutes. The chard can be added to the other cooked vegetables or kept separate.

Preheat the oven to 350 degrees.

Lightly oil a deep 9-x-13-inch baking pan.

1 pound precooked lasagna
  noodles (see box for
  guidance) or fresh lasagna
  noodles
1 cup shredded mozzarella
2 sliced tomatoes
¼ cup grated Parmigiano-
  Reggiano

FOR THE CHEESE FILLING

3 pounds fresh ricotta
¾ cup grated Pecorino
  Romano
3 large eggs
1 bunch flat-leaf parsley,
  chopped
1 bunch basil, cut into
  chiffonade (page 163)
Leaves from 5 sprigs thyme

FOR THE VEGETABLES

½ medium zucchini, sliced
  into thin disks
½ medium yellow squash,
  sliced into thin disks
1 medium eggplant, peeled,
  sliced, and lightly salted; let
  the eggplant sit on paper
  towels for about ½ hour,
  then rinse and pat dry
1 medium yellow onion, sliced
5 cloves garlic, chopped
2 red bell peppers, or 1 red and
  1 yellow or orange, seeded
  and sliced
Olive oil for dressing the
  vegetables
Salt and freshly ground pepper
A few roasted tomatoes,
  optional (page 82)

Thoroughly combine the ingredients for the cheese filling.

Assemble the lasagna: Lightly cover the bottom of the pan with one-third of the tomato sauce. Lay three pieces of pasta side by side over the sauce. Spread about one-third of the cheese filling over the pasta (you might find it helpful to use your fingers). Add another layer of pasta, then another third of the tomato sauce, then about half the prepared vegetables. Layer on another third of the cheese filling, another layer of pasta, and the remaining vegetables; if you have kept the chard separate, lay the strips over the vegetables. Add the remaining cheese filling, cover it with the remaining tomato sauce, and sprinkle the mozzarella evenly on top. Lay the sliced tomatoes evenly across the top and sprinkle with the Parmigiano-Reggiano.

Cover the dish loosely with foil and bake in the oven for 45 minutes. Remove the foil, turn the temperature up to 375 degrees, and bake for an additional 20 minutes. Remove the dish from the oven and let it rest before cutting and serving.

Sometimes the lasagna will bubble over when cooking. You might want to place a sheet of aluminum foil under the pan or on the bottom of your oven.

Mapping My Lasagna

I keep this sketch handy to remind myself how to construct lasagna.

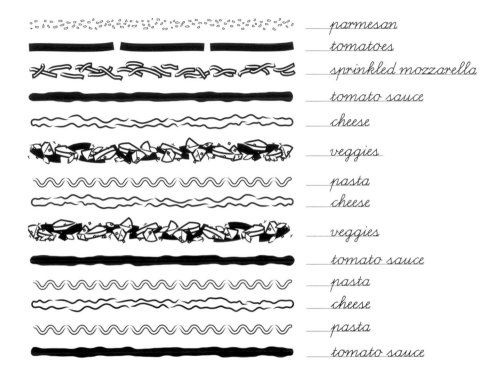

parmesan

tomatoes

sprinkled mozzarella

tomato sauce

cheese

veggies

pasta

cheese

veggies

tomato sauce

pasta

cheese

pasta

tomato sauce

Katchkie Favorites

8. Why We Like Couscous

Couscous seems so much like a grain that it sometimes surprises people to learn it really is a kind of tiny pasta found throughout North Africa and parts of the Middle East. "Couscous" also refers to the dish of endless variations that may involve meat and vegetables or, my favorite versions, just vegetables, a kind of stew of carrots, squashes, and chickpeas.

In the old days, couscous was made by rolling bits of moistened semolina wheat and pushing them through a series of ever-smaller sieves. Today's couscous is quite the opposite: machine-made and presteamed, it can be found in just about any supermarket and is nearly an instant dish, faster to cook than rice.

At Katchkie Farm, we sauté about a cup of diced yellow squash and some red onion, combine it with a couple cups of cooked whole-wheat couscous, and lots of basil and parsley, and dress it with a drizzle of good olive oil and a dusting of lemon zest. Try other combinations: zucchini, tomatoes, cucumbers, cooked fresh or dried beans, and other herbs—just about anything featured in the produce section or at a farm stand. Couscous is a great side dish, good for buffets or as a substitute for rice. Very young eaters like it with some butter and a light grating of Parmesan.

9. Crescent Moon Vegetable Dumplings

Corinne Trang, author of several books on Asian cooking, has demonstrated dumpling making at the Sylvia Center. The idea of making Chinese dumplings may be intimidating to grown-ups, but if you think about it, it is very close to the sorts of craft projects children do all the time. And this is one of those times when little fingers are an advantage. The kids can help with the assembly of the filling, even prepping some ingredients, but an adult should handle the stove chores. This could be a great weekend project for the family, or the main activity at a small kids' party.   MAKES ABOUT 60 DUMPLINGS

1 cup plus 2 tablespoons soy sauce

2 tablespoons light sesame oil

1 large garlic clove, thinly sliced

1 scallion, thinly sliced

½ cup roughly chopped fresh cilantro

1 red hot chile, seeded and minced (optional)

1 pound firm tofu, drained

One 1-inch piece fresh ginger, peeled and minced

½ bunch spinach (or ½ bag baby spinach leaves), minced

6 shiitake mushrooms, stems removed, caps minced

1 teaspoon dark sesame oil

Freshly ground pepper

½ cup flour

60 fresh round wonton or dumpling wrappers (see Note)

Put 1 cup of the soy sauce in a small bowl.

Heat the oil in a skillet over high heat, then add the garlic, scallion, cilantro, and red chile and stir-fry until fragrant and the scallion is lightly golden, about 2 minutes. Transfer to the bowl with the soy sauce and stir; this will be the dipping sauce.

Combine the tofu, ginger, spinach, mushrooms, dark sesame oil, and pepper to taste in a large bowl and mix thoroughly. Set the filling mixture aside.

To assemble the dumplings, pour some water into a small bowl. Dust a baking sheet with the flour. Put a wrapper on the palm of one hand. Dip your opposite pointer finger in the water and run it across the outer ½-inch edge of the wrapper. Put a heaping teaspoon of filling in the center of the wrapper and fold the wrapper into a half-moon, pressing the wet edges together to seal. Place the dumpling on the floured baking sheet (see illustrations, page 248). Repeat with the remaining wrappers and filling.

Bring a large pot of water to a boil over high heat. Working in small batches (about 10 pieces at a time), lower the dumplings into the water, stirring a couple of times so they do not stick together. Once the dumplings rise to the surface, cook them for another 1 to 2 minutes. Using a slotted spoon, transfer the dumplings to a soup plate or large bowl. Drizzle lightly with the remaining 2 tablespoons soy sauce and serve with the dipping sauce on the side.

Nowadays, dumpling wrappers can be found in most super-markets, often frozen. If you can, get fresh ones at an Asian market, where they are made daily. Or check for freshness if you buy packaged wrappers—if they separate when you ruffle the edges they are good; if they seem damp or stick together, avoid them.

Have a Dumpling Party!

For a children's party, arrange individual plates, lightly dusted with flour, for the assembly step so that everyone can work on his or her own dumplings, then let the children deliver the finished dumplings to an adult stationed at the stove for cooking. If you have a couple of pots of water going, and another adult to help, the dumplings can be ready in no time. This also could be a great opportunity to develop chopstick skills—and add to the hilarity. One-piece trainer chopsticks just for kids are available, some with animal characters on top. How's that for a party favor, along with copies of these shaping illustrations?

How to Shape Dumplings

1. Take a wrapper.

2. Dip your fingertip in the water, dab the inside edge of the wrapper with your wet finger, and put the filling in the center.

3. Fold the dumpling in half to form a half-moon (or semicircle), pressing the wet edge until it sticks.

10. Vegetable Soba Noodles

Japanese soba noodles are usually made with a combination of wheat and buckwheat flours ("soba" means "buckwheat" in Japanese). The proportions of each vary from region to region and there is even a special and expensive version that is 100 percent buckwheat. Soba are generally thicker than other Asian noodles, but some are thinner, so their cooking times can vary. Seven to 8 minutes is typical, but thin soba may cook in 5 to 6.

Soba noodles deliver more nutrition than regular pasta, with protein and vitamins B_1 and B_2.

SERVES 4

1 pound soba noodles

$\frac{1}{3}$ cup plus 1 tablespoon vegetable oil

2 tablespoons peeled and minced ginger

2 tablespoons minced garlic

2 tablespoons chopped scallion

$\frac{1}{3}$ pound edamame (page 57), steamed and shelled

1 small or $\frac{1}{2}$ medium bok choy, julienned

$\frac{1}{2}$ red bell pepper, seeded and julienned

$\frac{1}{2}$ pound bean sprouts

2 tablespoons vegetarian oyster sauce

$\frac{1}{4}$ cup light soy sauce

$\frac{1}{4}$ cup dark soy sauce

1 tablespoon sugar

2 teaspoons sesame oil

Bring a large pot of water to a boil, drop in the noodles, and stir. Cook the noodles according to the package directions until just tender, about 10 minutes. Drain, rinse well under cold water, and drain again. Toss the noodles with 1 tablespoon of the oil and set aside.

Heat the remaining $\frac{1}{3}$ cup oil in a wok or large sauté pan and add the ginger, garlic, and scallion and cook, stirring, for about 1 minute. Add the edamame, bok choy, bell pepper, and bean sprouts and stir-fry until the vegetables begin to wilt. Add the noodles and toss to combine.

Add the oyster sauce and cook, stirring, until the noodles are heated through and the vegetables are tender. Finish with the light and dark soy sauce, sugar, and sesame oil and cook for 2 minutes more.

11. Basic Risotto

This is my basic formula for a risotto to accompany main courses, especially braised saucy dishes; add a pinch of saffron threads to serve with the classic osso buco Milanese. For a first or main course, see the list of variations below. SERVES 4 TO 6

1 quart chicken or vegetable stock, homemade (page 38) or good-quality store bought

1 tablespoon vegetable oil

3 tablespoons unsalted butter

1 small shallot, chopped

¼ cup minced onion

1½ cups Arborio rice

½ cup white wine

Kosher salt

¼ cup grated Parmigiano-Reggiano

Heat the stock to a simmer in a medium saucepan, then lower the heat to keep it hot.

Heat the oil and 1 tablespoon of the butter in a large, heavy-bottomed saucepan over medium heat. When the butter is melted, add the shallot and onion and sauté for 2 to 3 minutes, or until slightly translucent.

Add the rice to the pot and stir it briskly with a wooden spoon to coat the grains well with oil and butter. Sauté for another minute or so until you detect a slightly nutty aroma, but do not let the rice brown.

Add the wine and continue to cook, while stirring, until the wine is fully absorbed. Stir in 1 teaspoon of salt.

Add a ladle of hot stock and 1 teaspoon of salt to the rice and stir until the liquid is fully absorbed; lower the heat if the rice seems to be sticking. When the rice appears almost dry, add another ladle of stock and repeat the process; continue, adding ladles of hot stock and stirring the rice until the liquid is absorbed. While it cooks, you'll see that the rice will take on a creamy consistency as it begins to release its starch.

The risotto is ready when the grains are tender but still firm to the bite, but not crunchy, which will take 20 to 30 minutes. If you run out of stock before you reach this point, add water, small ladles at a time.

Stir in the remaining 2 tablespoons butter and the cheese; taste and add more salt if needed.

TRY THESE VARIATIONS ON BASIC RISOTTO

Toward the end of cooking, stir in:

- Sautéed or roasted wild or cultivated mushrooms (page 81), dried mushrooms (page 119), or a combination; finish with grated Pecorino Romano cheese.
- Fresh tomatoes, seeded and chopped
- Herbs, such as basil, thyme, and parsley
- Lemon juice and zest
- Fresh peas, cut asparagus, cooked artichokes, chopped greens; this is a good use for leftover vegetables
- Seafood—chopped fresh shrimp, scallops, boned fish fillet. Add cooked seafood at the very end, or raw seafood when you think the risotto is about 5 minutes from finished. With this version, omit the cheese.

12. "Fried" Black and Gold Rice

My friend the chef Bill Telepan shared this rice recipe with me. Bill is nothing short of remarkable. With a child in a New York City public school, he became involved with school lunch years before the national movement began. And if anyone knows the recipe for leadership and change, it is Bill; he helped create Wellness in the Schools, an organization through which parent volunteers, school personnel, and local chefs are inspiring healthful eating. His passion for local food has been his signature and the flavors he coaxes to the table

connect us to seasonal bounty. I love bumping into Bill on the street, in the market, or in his restaurant, usually in his chef coat and jeans; I am constantly learning from him.

Varieties of black rice are grown throughout Asia, in Japan, Indonesia, Thailand, and China, where it was once known as "forbidden rice," which meant that no one but the emperor could have any. There also is an Italian black rice, riso Venere, hybridized with Asian strains and grown in the northern rice-growing region. Black rice is aromatic, with a nutty taste, and is more nutritious and less glutinous than white rice. **SERVES 6 TO 8**

1 bunch asparagus
3 tablespoons vegetable oil
2 eggs, beaten
1 bunch scallions, white and about 1 inch green parts, thinly sliced
1 cup cold cooked black rice (see headnote)
1 cup cold cooked Carolina Gold or brown rice
½ cup cooked peas
4 tablespoons vegetable stock, homemade (page 38) or good-quality store bought
Salt

If the asparagus are thin to medium, snap the ends; if they are fairly thick, trim the ends and, with a vegetable peeler, lightly peel the lower third of the stalks. Pour water into the bottom of a steamer and bring it to a boil. Put the asparagus in the top of the steamer, place it over the bottom, cover, and cook until the asparagus are just tender, 5 to 7 minutes, depending on the thickness of the stalks. Remove the asparagus from the steamer and set aside.

Heat 1 tablespoon of the oil in a small sauté pan over high heat. When the oil is hot, add the eggs and scramble until cooked through, 4 to 5 minutes. Chop the eggs up with a spatula and set the pan aside.

Heat the remaining 2 tablespoons oil in a large pan over medium-high heat; when the oil is hot, add the scallions and cook for 1 minute. Add the rice and peas and sauté for another minute; add the stock and cook the rice until the liquid is evaporated, about 5 minutes. Season with salt to taste and stir in the cooked eggs.

Divide the rice among four warm bowls or plates and top with the asparagus.

13. Brown Basmati Rice Salad

The apples, red pepper, and raisins give this dish a nice touch of sweetness, while the onion and lime juice give a sparkle of acid. See the list below for more suggested ingredients, or come up with your own. While I suggest using brown rice, this recipe works well with just about any rice you want to cook up. I love this more healthful version.   SERVES 6

1½ cups cooked brown basmati rice at room temperature

1 crisp green apple, peeled, cored, and chopped

1 red bell pepper, seeded and chopped

¼ cup yellow raisins

2 scallions or 1 medium red onion, chopped

2 tablespoons fresh lime juice

1 tablespoon canola or olive oil

2 teaspoons chopped fresh cilantro

½ teaspoon turmeric

½ teaspoon curry powder

Salt

In a large bowl, mix together the rice, apple, bell pepper, raisins, scallion, lime juice, oil, and cilantro. Season with the turmeric, curry powder, and salt to taste. Let the salad sit for a few hours before serving at room temperature.

TRY THESE VARIATIONS FOR A DIFFERENT TWIST

Wild rice, white basmati, or long-grain brown rice

Quinoa substituted for rice

Chopped apricots

Pine nuts

Chopped walnuts

Pomegranate seeds

The proportions for cooking brown basmati rice are the same as for regular white rice: 2 cups water or other liquid to 1 cup rice. However, brown basmati will take longer to cook, 35 to 45 minutes.

14. Creamy White Polenta with Sage and Brown Butter

Leftover polenta can be cut into squares and then reheated in a small pan and served with maple syrup and eggs for breakfast. Or dust it with Parmigiano-Reggiano and crisp it under a broiler. Delicious. SERVES 4

4½ cups water

1 cup coarse stone-ground white polenta, cornmeal, or grits, preferably organic

¼ cup heavy cream

¼ cup finely grated Parmigiano-Reggiano

1 teaspoon salt

¼ teaspoon freshly ground black pepper

1 cup cooking oil, such as canola or corn oil

18 sage leaves, washed and dried

4 tablespoons butter

Bring the water to a simmer in a 3- to 4-quart heavy saucepan. Add the polenta in a slow stream, constantly whisking until incorporated. Simmer, stirring occasionally with a long-handled wooden spoon, until the liquid is absorbed and the polenta is thick but still soft, about 30 minutes. The consistency will be like a loose risotto. Stir in the cream, 2 tablespoons of the Parmigiano, and the salt and pepper.

While the polenta is cooking, heat the oil in a small saucepan. When the oil is quite hot but not smoking, drop in the sage leaves for 5 to 10 seconds, or until they are crisp—this will happen very quickly. Remove the leaves with a slotted spoon, drain them on paper towels, and set them aside.

Melt the butter in another small saucepan or skillet and cook over medium heat until it is golden brown and develops a nutty aroma and flavor; take care not to let it burn.

To serve, place a portion of polenta on each plate, drizzle 1 tablespoon of brown butter over each serving, sprinkle with the remaining Parmigiano-Reggiano, and top with a few fried sage leaves. Serve immediately.

You could also try this version: Omit the oil and sage leaves; dollop 2 tablespoons of mascarpone on each serving and sprinkle with chopped flat-leaf parsley.

The Greatest Grains

It pleases me that grains are becoming as popular for their good taste as much as for their goodness. Chefs and food writers have made grains newly fashionable and interesting; grains have lost their dreary hippie health food associations, though they remain appealing for being low in carbohydrates and, in some cases, as an alternative to wheat. Nearly every supermarket now stocks even the once "exotic" grains such as quinoa.

FARRO is a great example, a nutty-tasting strain of hard wheat from Italy, and found only in specialty markets until just a few years ago. Farro is as versatile as it is nourishing—it supposedly fortified Roman troops, and long before that was snack food for dinasaurs. It is delicious in soups, salads, and even desserts; a traditional Tuscan torta is made with orange-scented ricotta and farro. Substitute farro for rice in a traditional risotto recipe (page 250) to make a farrotto. **Spelt** is sometimes passed off as farro, but it is different when cooked; farro keeps some of its bite, while spelt becomes soft. Both farro and spelt also are ground into flour; farro turns up in pasta, spelt in bread, and both are delicious.

WHEAT BERRIES also are often confused with farro. Though not the same, they can be used similarly. Both need a longer cooking time than other grains, as long as 40 minutes, but you can cut the time by soaking them in water for half an hour or longer, or even overnight.

BUCKWHEAT—actually a fruit seed—is the stuff of Japanese soba noodles and Russian porridge, gluten free and high in fiber. Americans are more familiar with **bulgur,** if only as the main ingredient in tabbouleh. Both buckwheat and bulgur, which has already been boiled and cracked, cook in about 15 minutes, making them two more candidates for side dishes in everyday meals.

CRACKEDWHEAT, another variety, also has been cracked and cooks quickly.

QUINOA is a supernutritious ancient grain, grown for thousands of years in South America. Quinoa didn't catch on outside its region for centuries, probably because its hard bitter shell was off-putting to early European explorers. This taste can be washed away by soaking the tiny seeds in successive water baths until the water is clear, but most of the quinoa in markets today has been pretreated, so you can skip this step. Quinoa's mild flavor makes it highly versatile. Like rice and couscous, it is good at the side of tastier, even spicy dishes. Cook quinoa in twice its volume of liquid just to a boil, lower the heat, add a big pinch of salt, and simmer for about 15 minutes. Or cover the pot when the liquid is at the boil, remove it from the heat, and let it sit for about 30 minutes. Either way, the results should be fluffy and tender. A bit of oil or butter can be added, along with herbs. Quinoa can be dressed as a warm or room temperature salad with the addition of toasted nuts and dried cranberries or added to the liquid in a stewed dish for the final 15 or 20 minutes of cooking. Quinoa is highly digestible and makes a good early food for children. Unknown to most of us just a few years ago, quinoa now is as ubiquitous as rice. I recently found, in an ordinary small-town supermarket, black quinoa, which I'd only ever seen in a specialty market, and a quinoa relative, kañiwa, a tiny, mahogany-colored seed that cooked up nutty and crunchy.

MILLET is actually the small seed of various grain plants, much of which goes into birdseed, animal fodder, and beer, but it is becoming more popular for the table. Millet has a mild sweetness and crunchy texture. It cooks quickly, in about 15 minutes, in twice its volume of water or broth. It makes a good warm cereal or a side dish similar to rice, and it can be added to soups and stews.

BARLEY Don't underestimate this grain, which has as much histori-cal importance as wheat; barley has sustained people and animals since ancient days, and has been used as much in potables—alcoholic and non-alcoholic—as in food. Like other grains, barley is versatile. Of course, we adore our all-time favorites like mushroom-barley soup, but barley deserves an equal place as a side dish and can be prepared by the same method as risotto (page 250). I've come across various strains lately, including black and purple types; the purple retains some chewiness and is particularly good combined with other grains or in soup. Combine cooked barley with greens in a gratin or use it in a salad, as I do with farro (page 258).

Whole grains are the least processed, with only their outer hulls removed, leaving the nutrient-rich bran and germ intact. High nutrition comes with some inconvenience as these grains need longer cooking time than pearled, or polished, grains that have had the bran layers—and much of the fiber—removed.

15. Farro Salad with Peas, Cucumber, and Chervil

Here we have a perfect mix of fresh and elegant spring flavors. This can begin a meal or be all you need at the side of fish, roasted chicken, or grilled lamb. SERVES 6 TO 8

4 cups water

1½ cups farro

Salt

½ pound sugar snap peas, strings removed

1 English cucumber, washed but not peeled, seeded, and thinly sliced

About 1 cup cherry tomatoes, halved

1 teaspoon Dijon mustard

2 tablespoons white balsamic vinegar

Freshly ground pepper

¼ cup extra-virgin olive oil

¼ cup snipped chives, plus 1 teaspoon for garnish

¼ cup chopped flat-leaf parsley, plus 1 teaspoon for garnish

¼ cup chervil leaves, plus 1 teaspoon for garnish

Combine the water and farro in a medium saucepan. Add 2 teaspoons salt and bring to a boil over high heat. Reduce the heat to medium-low, cover, and simmer until the farro is tender, about 30 minutes (see page 255). Drain well and rinse under cold water, then transfer to a large bowl to cool.

Meanwhile, bring a medium pot of water to a boil and add a pinch of salt. Blanch the sugar snap peas for 3 minutes, then plunge them into a bowl of ice water to refresh.

Add the snap peas, cucumber, and tomatoes to the farro and toss to mix well.

Whisk the mustard, vinegar, and a few grindings of pepper together in a medium bowl; slowly drizzle in the olive oil, whisking to emulsify; add salt to taste. Pour this vinaigrette over the salad, add ¼ cup each of the chives, parsley, and chervil, and toss well.

Sprinkle the remaining herbs over the salad before serving.

The Language of Cooking: *Emulsify*

When we say "emulsify" in cooking, we mean to meld ingredients together. This term is frequently applied to making salad dressings and other types of sauces that often involve fats such as butter or oil that bind themselves to other ingredients. For instance, when oil and vinegar or lemon juice are vigorously whisked together they become creamy, opaque, and stable. Mayonnaise is a classic example of an emulsified sauce; the oil is literally absorbed by the egg yolks and the result is a thick, stable sauce.

16. Dinah's Farro with Roasted Eggplant, Red Pepper, and Olives

Dinah Herlands Foer is my eldest niece and has been a vegetarian for several years, though from time to time she reminisces about carnivorous meals at home as a child. In a nod to sustainably raised meats (free range, drug free, humanely raised and slaughtered), she and her husband will enjoy beef, lamb, or chicken—from a source they are familiar with—on a special occasion. Otherwise, this represents a typical meal for them.

The Italian farro is nice, nutty, and a bit crunchy with the other classic Mediterranean ingredients here.   SERVES 4 TO 6

Salt

1½ cups farro

1 medium eggplant

Olive oil or cooking spray for coating

2 red bell peppers

½ cup good kalamata olives, pitted and roughly chopped

¼ cup olive oil

2 tablespoons fresh lemon juice

Grated Parmigiano-Reggiano, to finish (optional)

Shredded basil leaves, for garnish (optional)

Preheat the oven to 400 degrees.

Bring a large pot of water to a boil. Add a big pinch of salt and the farro; reduce the heat to medium and cook the farro just until tender, about 30 minutes (see page 255).

Slice the eggplant into medium-thick slices, toss with olive oil or spray both sides lightly and evenly with a vegetable cooking spray, and sprinkle with salt. Place the slices on a baking sheet and roast in oven, turning once, until nicely browned on both sides, 10 to 15 minutes.

Slice the peppers and toss with olive oil and salt. Place the slices on a baking sheet. Roast until shriveled and browned, about 10 minutes.

When the eggplant and peppers are cool enough to handle, roughly chop them, taking care not to lose their juices. Toss the vegetables with the farro and stir in the chopped olives.

Whisk the lemon juice with 4 tablespoons olive oil. Toss the farro and vegetables with ¼ cup of the dressing and let it sit for about 30 minutes before serving. Toss again with the remaining dressing, grate cheese over the salad, and sprinkle with the basil, if using.

To turn this into an entrée, add about 1½ cups cooked chickpeas, or a regular-size can, drained and rinsed, to the farro.

Crumbled feta can be used instead of the Parmigiano-Reggiano. The dish can be made ahead up to the final steps and refrigerated, then brought back to room temperature before serving.

17. Barley Risotto

The highly talented Michael Anthony is the executive chef at Gramercy Tavern, now nearly twenty years old and one of New York's best and most popular restaurants. His barley risotto, shared here, is less a traditional expression of risotto and more a celebration of carrots and their sweetness. The carrots are cooked separately and layered with the barley, bound by the toasted quality of the grain and the spiced nuts. Treat yourself by using any variety of carrots you may find at the farmers' market in fall; we find ours at the Union Square Greenmarket.

As busy as he is as a chef and father, Michael manages to devote enormous amounts of time to working with children.   SERVES 10

4 tablespoons olive oil

1 cup minced onions

1 tablespoon plus 1 teaspoon minced garlic

2 cups pearl barley

Salt

8 to 10 cups vegetable stock, homemade (page 38) or good-quality store bought, or water

1 teaspoon peeled and minced fresh ginger

1 teaspoon toasted coriander seed

2 cups peeled and sliced carrots plus 4 tablespoons minced carrots

2 cups minced leeks, white part plus about 1 inch of green

2 shiitake mushrooms, trimmed and thinly sliced

Place a medium pot over low heat and pour in 2 tablespoons of the olive oil. When the oil is warm, add the onions and let them sweat until they are translucent but not colored. Add 1 tablespoon of the garlic and cook until fragrant, about 1 minute, then stir in the barley to coat it thoroughly with oil. Add a pinch of salt and pour in 5 cups of the vegetable stock, enough to cover the barley. Bring to a boil over medium heat, then lower the heat and simmer gently until tender, about 20 minutes.

Meanwhile, place another medium pot over low heat, pour in the remaining 2 tablespoons oil, the remaining 1 teaspoon garlic, the ginger, and coriander and sauté for 5 minutes; do not let the garlic burn. Add the sliced carrots and cook, stirring occasionally, for 2 minutes; do not let the carrots brown. Pour in 2 cups of stock, add a pinch of salt, and simmer until the carrots are tender, 5 to 10 minutes.

Transfer the carrots and the cooking liquid to a blender or food processor and puree until smooth.

Stir the 4 tablespoons minced carrots, leeks, and mushrooms into the cooked barley and simmer until tender, adding vegetable stock ½ cup at a time as needed to reach desired consistency, creamy like a good risotto, about 10 minutes. The amount of stock you use will depend on the heat under your pan, the amount absorbed by the carrots and barley as they cook, and your desired consistency. Stir the butter, carrot puree, cheese, and herbs into the barley. Season with salt and pepper to taste.

Garnish each serving with 1 teaspoon of the spiced nuts, if using.

1 tablespoon butter

3 tablespoons Parmigiano-Reggiano

2 tablespoons chopped fresh herbs (one part each flat-leaf parsley, chives, and tarragon)

Freshly ground pepper

Ground Spiced Nuts (recipe follows; optional)

Ground Spiced Nuts

This spiced nut mixture can be made ahead and kept in a tightly closed jar for several days. The nuts are delicious on their own—before grinding as for this dish—as a little snack as well. Makes about 2 cups.

½ cup almonds

½ cup pistachios

⅓ cup pine nuts

¼ cup coriander seeds

3 tablespoons sesame seeds

2 tablespoons cumin seeds

1½ teaspoons black peppercorns

1 teaspoon fennel seeds

1 teaspoon salt

Toast the nuts in a pan over low heat, stirring frequently and taking care not to let them burn, about 5 minutes, and set aside. Toast the remaining ingredients in a similar manner; the spices are ready when they release their fragrance.

When both the spices and nuts are cool, roughly grind them together in a food processor, using the pulsing button, or with a mortar and pestle, until the mixture resembles very coarse sand.

18. Late Summer Barley Salad with Roasted Portobello Mushrooms

With corn, tomatoes, and basil joining mushrooms and walnuts, this dish bridges the end of summer to early fall. If you have the time, marinate the mushrooms for a few hours before grilling and finishing the dish. This is another specialty of my niece Dinah Herlands Foer. SERVES 4

4 large portobello
  mushrooms

3 garlic cloves, minced, plus 1
  whole clove

4 tablespoons olive oil, more
  if needed

1 to 2 tablespoons balsamic
  vinegar, or to taste
  (optional)

2 tablespoons red wine or red
  wine vinegar

2 tablespoons low-sodium
  soy sauce

3 or 4 sprigs fresh oregano

2 or 3 sprigs fresh rosemary

Salt and freshly ground
  pepper

Kernels from 2 ears corn (see
  page 109)

Leaves from about 6 sprigs
  basil, plus extra for garnish

1 cup (packed) arugula

½ cup chopped walnuts

¼ cup grated Parmigiano-
  Reggiano (optional)

¾ cup grape or cherry
  tomatoes, cut in half

1½ cups cooked barley

Wipe the mushrooms clean and remove the stems. Place the mushrooms in a baking dish large enough that they are not overlapping. Combine the minced garlic, 1 tablespoon oil, vinegar, wine, and soy sauce and pour the mixture over the mushrooms. Place the oregano and rosemary sprigs under and over the mushrooms; sprinkle the mushrooms with salt and pepper and set them aside.

If the corn kernels are young and tender, they need no cooking. Otherwise, blanch them by dumping them into boiling water for 1 to 2 minutes, then refresh them quickly under cold water and drain them well.

Combine the basil, arugula, walnuts, garlic clove, cheese, and the remaining olive oil in a food processor and puree, adding small amounts of oil as needed to make a thick pesto. Season to taste with salt and pepper. Toss about half the pesto with the barley while it is still warm, then stir in the corn kernels and tomatoes.

Remove the mushrooms from the marinade and pat them dry. Grill the mushrooms over a charcoal fire or on a kitchen grill or broil them until nicely browned. Let the mushrooms sit for 10 minutes, then remove them from their cooking juices (reserve juices for another use, like stock or soup, or discard).

Arrange the barley salad on a serving platter. Slice the mushrooms and place them on the barley or serve the barley on individual plates and top each serving with a whole mushroom. Top with dollops of the remaining pesto and garnish with basil leaves.

This can be made in advance, but keep the barley and the mushrooms, along with their cooking juices, separate until you are ready to serve. If you refrigerate the components, bring them to room temperature before serving.

Eggs and Other Morning Food

Cooking eggs and making pancakes are activities for the entire family—from toddlers to grandparents. The results are always delicious and the dishes are simple to prepare, requiring little time. Cracking eggs usually wins the prize for favorite kitchen task (closely followed by licking the bowl). One of my most cherished kitchen items is a stoneware cup from Vermont that has a protruding nose with large nostrils and actual holes. It separates egg yolks and whites in the most unconventional way. Can you picture it as the whites emerge from the nostrils—to the laughter and groans of my little helpers!

Egg dishes—from huevos rancheros to quiche and frittatas—capture global culinary diversity with very approachable methods and flavors. Challenge your young eaters to find how different food cultures prepare eggs or make a crepe and bring the recipe to the kitchen for a new adventure. And think of your pancakes as canvases waiting to be personalized. I pull frozen summer fruits from the freezer to produce a stack of strawberry or blueberry pancakes in the dead of winter. Chocolate chips and bananas get attention from my assistants year-round as well.

If you have the opportunity, buy some superfresh eggs—laid that day—and do a little show-and-tell with your children. Crack one of the farm eggs into a bowl and crack a supermarket egg into another. The first thing they will notice is the vivid color of the yolk—sometimes nearly orange—of the newly laid egg. Point out also that the fresher egg is more "set up," rounder and firmer-looking, with a thick white circling the yolk. Finally they will notice the deeper, richer, "eggier" taste once it is cooked.

1. Vegetarian Breakfast Burrito

12 eggs

6 tablespoons milk

2 teaspoons olive oil

½ cup red or yellow diced
onion

2 or 3 medium tomatoes,
diced (3 cups)

1½ cups fresh corn kernels
(from about 4 ears)

¼ cup diced green bell
peppers

¼ cup diced red bell peppers

Salt and freshly ground
pepper

Six 6-inch flour tortillas

3 tablespoons minced scallions

1 cup shredded Cheddar

1 cup Katchkie Farm Fresh
Salsa (page 312)

Preheat the oven to 350 degrees. Crack the eggs into a deep bowl and whisk in the milk.

Heat 1 teaspoon of the olive oil in a large skillet over medium heat. Add the onion and cook, stirring, until translucent; add the tomatoes, corn, and bell peppers. Cook just until the vegetables are beginning to be soft and fragrant. Remove the pan from the heat and blot the surface of the ingredients with paper towels to remove excess liquid; transfer the vegetables to a bowl.

Return the pan to the heat, add the remaining oil, and pour in the eggs. Reduce the heat to medium-low. Season the eggs with salt and a few grindings of pepper. Don't stir; let the eggs begin to set before scrambling, about 2 minutes.

Wrap the tortillas in foil and place them in the oven to warm, about 10 minutes. Spoon the vegetable mixture onto the eggs. With a wooden spoon, start to scrape the eggs from the edge of the pan to the center, forming large soft curds.

Continue scraping along the bottom of the pan to redistribute the eggs as they cook. When the eggs still look wet but are no longer liquid, gently mound them into the center of the pan.

Turn off the heat but leave the skillet on the burner. Fold in the scallions and cheese. Leave the eggs in the warm pan to finish cooking, stirring once or twice, about 2 more minutes.

Remove the tortillas from the oven. Spoon an equal amount of the egg mixture near the center of each tortilla, top with salsa, and gently roll them to create a snug wrap.

The Chickens—and Eggs—of Katchkie Farm

Katchkie Farm is almost exclusively dedicated to produce, but we always have chickens; our free-range brood—usually around fifty—is fed grain and allowed to scavenge for little bugs in the garden. We have a number of heirloom and unusual breeds that we call our rainbow egg layers, because we have Cuckoo Marans that lay dark brown ("chocolate") eggs, Araucanas that lay green and blue eggs, and others that lay pink, brown, and white eggs. We collect eggs daily; children who visit the Sylvia Center cook them and there are even enough for us to use in our cafés, fried, on Katchkie Farm salads.

A day at the Sylvia Center invariably ends at the chicken coop. Spring visitors are likely to see fluffy baby chicks, always a delight. The children—first or second graders—seem to know to be very quiet around drowsy babies; big smiles, "shhhh," and suppressed giggles are standard coop behavior. They pet and hold the chickens and feed them greens. And they are amazed by the different-colored eggs that come from different-colored chickens.

2. Sylvia Center Frittata

This is one of the dishes the children make when they visit Katchkie Farm. They first harvest the ingredients, which change through the growing season. This is a good balanced dish for a hearty weekend brunch, lunch, or light supper, and a good example of how versatile eggs are.   SERVES 6 TO 8

3 tablespoons olive oil

1 medium onion, chopped

4 to 6 cups assorted seasonal
   vegetables (see "The Year
   in Omelets," next page)

10 eggs

Salt and freshly ground
   pepper

3 to 4 tablespoons chopped
   herbs (see "The Year in
   Omelets," next page)

½ pound feta cheese

Heat the oil in a large skillet or frying pan over medium heat. Add the onion and sauté, stirring, until softened but not browned, about 3 minutes. Add the seasonal vegetables, beginning with the harder ones (such as winter root vegetables) and continuing to the softer ones.

Beat the eggs in a bowl; season with salt and pepper to taste.

When the vegetables are soft, add the herbs, spread the vegetables into an even layer, and pour the eggs into the pan, then crumble the cheese over. Lower the heat to medium-low and cover the pan. Cook until the eggs are set but not dry, 5 to 7 minutes. Cut into wedges and serve.

3. The Year in Omelets

The children who visit the Sylvia Center cook exclusively from Katchkie Farm crops, so their omelets are based on whatever is ready to pick. I suggest you follow that notion and let your omelets reflect what's available, season to season. Make your choices with your children at a farmers' market or even the supermarket.

Among the herbs, parsley is a given and chives are always wonderful with eggs; basil goes well with green beans and tomatoes, thyme with potatoes. And so on. Omelets are an excellent way to introduce foods and flavors, and let the kids participate.

Of course, my scheme follows our particular location; yours may be different, earlier if you are south or way west of the Hudson Valley, later to the north and Midwest, but you get the idea: let the season and the market be your guide.

Winter Roasted potatoes, onions, roasted sweet potatoes, garlic, dried herbs, dried tomatoes, fresh or dried mushrooms. Roasted winter squash, onions, and leeks. Or try a sweet omelet with fruit preserves or chutney and with a fresh cheese, such as goat, ricotta, or mozzarella.

Spring By April, green is beginning to pop out. All sorts of wild greens are available, from dandelions to upland cress. Look for fiddleheads and ramps and mushrooms. I have an ironclad rule—*no* asparagus out of season! By May you can finally have some, along with early greens such as spinach, green garlic, assorted herbs, mushrooms, early onions, and scallions.

Summer June is good for chard, peas, herbs, spinach, garlic scapes, broccoli rabe, broccoli, scallions, and green beans. July gives you zucchini; green beans; tomatoes; herbs; broccoli; tender young green tops from radishes, beets, and turnips; and zucchini blossoms.

August into September Onions, peppers, tomatoes, eggplant, herbs, corn, green tops, leeks, and garlic.

Anytime and always Cheeses, onions, potatoes, and herbs.

In any season, leftovers, vegetables in particular, can almost always be worked into omelets. My Vegetable Lasagna (page 242) leads inevitably to Sunday omelets.

4. Scrambled Eggs

We often hear that the simplest preparations are the ones culinary students are judged by—an omelet, a roasted chicken—so I asked our chef at Great Performances for a definitive method for this most everyday of dishes: scrambled eggs.

I will add only that ingredients matter as much as method. So get the best eggs you can find. We bring our Katchkie Farm eggs to the New York Greenmarket; I love their deep-yellow yolks and the way they retain their domelike shape when you crack them into a bowl or pan—two signs of freshness. I know that more and more good, fresh, and organic eggs are available from small chicken farmers all over; they deserve our support, and you will see and taste the difference.

This is a good early cooking lesson for children. They will thank you when they are in college.

SERVES 6

12 eggs

6 tablespoons milk

1 tablespoon butter

Salt and freshly ground
  pepper

Crack the eggs into a bowl that's deep enough to support vigorous whisking. Thin the egg mixture with the milk. Whisk the mixture until the eggs and milk are well combined.

Heat the butter in a large skillet over medium heat. When the butter starts to bubble, pour in the eggs. Reduce the heat to medium-low. Sprinkle a big pinch of salt and a few grindings of pepper over the eggs. Let them begin to set before you stir them.

Add any additional ingredients you like (see Note for suggestions). With a wooden spoon, start to scrape the eggs from the edge of the pan to the center, forming large, soft curds.

Continue scraping your spoon along the bottom of the pan to redistribute the eggs as they cook. Do not rush this process, and lower the heat or pull the pan off for a few seconds if you feel the eggs are drying or hardening.

When the eggs look wet but are no longer liquid, gently mound them into the center of the pan. Turn off the heat but leave the skillet on the burner for about 1 minute. The scrambled eggs will continue to cook from the heat of the pan and from their own heat. Stir once more before serving.

What can go into scrambled eggs is limited only by your taste and imagination. Soft scrambled eggs with cottage cheese are a very good early dish for young children. Here are some suggestions:

- ½ cup shredded, crumbled, or grated cheese such as mozzarella, Cheddar, Parmesan, or goat or cottage cheese
- Herbs: about 2 tablespoons of each or about ½ cup mixed, such as parsley, thyme, tarragon, chervil, and chives
- 2 or 3 scallions, chopped
- Sliced sautéed mushrooms
- 1 medium tomato, chopped
- Salsa and sour cream
- Cooked broccoli with Cheddar

Don't be tempted to add salt to the eggs before they are in the pan as this may toughen them.

5. Shakshuka

I discovered shakshuka for the first time in the Galilee region of Israel, in the small town of Rosh Pina. It was love at first bite not only because of the great taste, but also because the presentation was perfect. Every ingredient must have come from within ten miles of the café, including the olive oil used to sauté the vegetables. The shakshuka was served in a small cast-iron pan—just the right amount for one hungry individual, plus a few bites to share with friends. I incorporated this dish into my repertoire and brought it to the Sylvia Center, where it became a signature locavore item.

Shakshuka is open to personal taste and variation, so do not hesitate to incorporate whatever is in your fridge or at the farm stand. These ingredients are for two portions, but you can increase the amounts and divide them among individual ovenproof dishes or make one larger shakshuka.

SERVES 2

2 tablespoons olive oil

1 onion, chopped

1 red or yellow bell pepper, seeded and chopped

½ teaspoon chopped jalapeño (optional)

¼ teaspoon sweet paprika

¼ teaspoon cumin

1 teaspoon sugar

4 plum tomatoes, chopped

2 garlic cloves, chopped (optional)

Cayenne (optional)

Salt and freshly ground pepper

¼ cup tomato sauce

4 chard leaves, sliced crosswise into thin ribbons (optional)

½ cup cubed, sautéed eggplant (optional)

2 eggs

1 tablespoon chopped flat-leaf parsley

Pita bread, warmed

Preheat the oven to 400 degrees.

Heat the olive oil in a 10-inch cast-iron pan and add the onion. Sauté the onion until it begins to soften, then add the pepper. If you like a spicy bite, this is the moment to also add the chopped jalapeño. Cook for 10 minutes, until the mixture begins to brown and continues to soften. Stir in the paprika, cumin, and sugar, then the tomatoes, garlic, if using, and cayenne to taste, if using; season with salt and pepper to taste. Add the tomato sauce and cook slowly for another 15 minutes; take care that the mixture does not get dry and add a little water if necessary.

Stir in the chard and eggplant, if using.

Crack the eggs on top of the mixture and place the pan in the oven for about 10 minutes. Take care as the eggs bake; you want the yolks to remain loose. Sprinkle the dish with the parsley just after removing it from the oven.

Serve with the pita.

OATS

When the health benefits of oat bran were identified about twenty years ago—its soluble fiber can help to lower body cholesterol—a kind of fad erupted. Muffins in particular became a favorite highly palatable, bran-delivery system. When one food journalist decided to analyze a typical coffee-shop bran muffin she discovered that its benefits were offset stunningly by high daily percentages of fat and calories: the average American muffin, like so much of our food, had been supersized and oversweetened.

The fact remains, though, that oat bran and oatmeal are beneficial in a sensible diet. They can help lower cholesterol and are high in complex carbohydrates and some vitamins. Your grandmother may have cited oatmeal as good "to stick to your ribs," by which she meant, whether she knew it or not, that because it is digested slowly, it can provide more energy longer—excellent for schoolchildren and athletes of any age.

Food should neither be a fad, nor should we eat, or feed our families, prescriptively. Food that is good for you is most likely good to eat—it will taste good. People I know who are sensible and moderate omnivores usually developed their eating habits when they were growing up—something to keep in mind as you feed your own children.

6. Katchkie Seasonal Fruit Salad with Minted Yogurt

I love the delicate flavor and dainty round shape of Spain's Marcona almonds, but you can substitute any other variety here. Marconas are popular to nibble with drinks, and you may find them already prepared for that purpose—sautéed in good olive oil and sprinkled with sea salt and thyme leaves. They are nearly addictive, but for this dish you want plain ones.

Needless to say, any other fruits you fancy besides those listed can go into the mix.

SERVES 6 TO 8

1 cup Marcona or other almonds (not skinned, salted, or seasoned), roughly chopped

3 tablespoons honey

½ cup plain yogurt

3 tablespoons chopped fresh mint, plus additional sprigs for garnish (optional)

8 cups ripe, local, seasonal fresh fruit: strawberries, blueberries, blackberries, raspberries, sliced peaches, apples, halved apricots, melon balls—alone or in any combination that pleases you

Preheat the oven to 300 degrees.

Place the almonds on a baking sheet and put them in the oven; toast the almonds until they are light golden brown, tossing a few times, 5 to 10 minutes. Remove the almonds and set them aside.

In a small bowl, whisk together the honey, yogurt, and chopped mint until well mixed. In another bowl toss the fruit together carefully; divide it among individual serving bowls. Scatter the almonds over the fruit and top with a dollop of the minted yogurt. Garnish with a fresh mint sprig, if desired.

7. Katchkie Farm Granola

Making your own granola is easy, and only a bit time-consuming. It also is cheaper and better than most store-bought granola. And you know what's in your own granola—less sugar, for one thing. Needless to say, this recipe can be varied—dried pears can replace the apple rings; dried cranberries or cherries can be added or substituted for some of the apricots.

I often make a delicious parfait by layering our granola, yogurt, and chopped fresh pears, beginning and ending with granola. Fresh berries are also good. This is a really nice brunch dish. If you have an ice cream machine, use it to make frozen yogurt, and top it with granola for a healthful dessert. MAKES ABOUT 3½ QUARTS (24 SERVINGS)

⅓ cup dried unsulfured apricots

⅓ cup dates

⅓ cup dried apple rings

3 cups rolled oats

1 cup unsweetened shredded coconut

1 cup sunflower seeds

¼ cup flaxseeds

⅓ to ½ cup maple syrup

¼ to ⅓ cup canola oil

⅓ cup dried unsweetened cranberries

Preheat the oven to 325 degrees for 30 minutes.

Chop the apricots, dates, and apple rings.

Mix the oats, coconut, sunflower seeds, and flaxseeds together in a large bowl. Spread the mixture on a baking sheet, in two batches if necessary to make even layers. Toast in the oven for 15 minutes, stirring once or twice.

Return the granola to the bowl and toss it quickly and thoroughly with the maple syrup and canola oil. Return it to the baking sheet, spreading it out evenly again. Bake for another 15 minutes. Let cool.

Transfer the granola back to the mixing bowl and combine it with the apricots, dates, apple rings, and cranberries.

If you don't think you'll get through this big batch within two or three weeks, pack some into jars or storage bags and keep it in the freezer. Children can help here: give them the bags and scoopers or measuring cups of the approximate amount you want to put in each.

8. Homemade Muesli

I like the nutty taste rye brings to this muesli mix. Rye flakes are made from groats that have been rolled, like oats; they can be found in health food stores and also in some supermarkets that carry the bigger brands of specialty cereals and grains. Rye is high in fiber and lower in gluten than other grains.   SERVES 4 TO 5

2 cups rolled oats
¼ cup rye flakes
¾ cup raisins
½ cup dried berries, such as
   blueberries or cranberries
½ cup dried date pieces
½ cup slivered almonds
⅓ cup raw unsalted
   sunflower seeds
½ cup yogurt, for serving
¼ cup milk, for serving

Mix together the oats, rye flakes, raisins, berries, dates, almonds, and sunflower seeds. Store the muesli in airtight containers.

For each serving, combine about a cup of the muesli with the milk and yogurt and let it stand at room temperature for 30 minutes.

9. Buttermilk Pancakes

Pancakes seem so American to me that I tend to keep them in a discrete category, unrelated to all those foreign versions—French crepes, Indian dosas, Chinese scallion pancakes, Mexican tortillas—as much as I love them all. Perhaps it is the uniquely American maple syrup that seems to make pancakes ours and ours alone, or that pancakes are so ubiquitous, one of the foods that binds us together, coast to coast, day or night.

Making pancakes—cooking batter on a hot surface—is a clear demonstration for children of the baking process; they can see it right before their eyes. So, along with letting them drop the batter onto the griddle and, with guidance, flip the cakes, you can deliver some basic food science: the baking powder and soda that they mixed into the batter contains carbon dioxide that begins to produce bubbles that expand as they get hot. They can see this as the pancakes begin to puff and rise and bubble on the surface, and they can see it in the texture of the steamy cakes on their plates. When they move on to biscuits, cakes, and, most interesting of all, bread, they will know what is happening even if they can't see it all. As our editor put it, "Pancakes are Baking 101." SERVES 4 TO 6

4 tablespoons unsalted butter,
   plus 1 more for the griddle
1 cup all-purpose flour
1 cup whole-wheat flour
2 teaspoons baking powder
1 teaspoon baking soda
½ teaspoon salt
3 tablespoons sugar
2 large eggs, lightly beaten
3 cups buttermilk

If you are using a griddle, preheat it to 375 degrees; preheat the oven to 175 degrees and place a heatproof serving platter or baking sheet in the oven.

Melt the butter in a small saucepan and let it cool a bit.

Place the flours, baking powder, baking soda, salt, and sugar in a medium bowl and stir to combine. Add the eggs, buttermilk, and the melted butter; whisk to combine, but do not overbeat—the batter should have small to medium lumps.

If you are not using a griddle, place a large, heavy frying pan over medium-high heat. Test the pan or the griddle by sprinkling it with a few drops of water; if the water bounces off the surface, it is ready.

Brush the griddle or pan with butter. Pour about ½ cup of the batter onto the griddle for each pancake, placing them 2 to 3 inches apart; a medium-size ladle is good for this.

When the pancakes have bubbles on top and are slightly dry around the edges, flip them over. Cook until the pancakes are golden on the bottom, about 1 minute more. Repeat the process with the remaining batter; place the finished pancakes in the oven. Serve warm with your favorite accompaniments.

The Primitive Pancake

The pancake's ancestors were the earliest form of bread, or baking itself for that matter. Long before the earliest ovens, people made thin batter from grains and milk or water and perhaps eggs, and cooked them on fire-heated stones or in earthenware pots over open fires.

The Pueblo Indians of the American Southwest still make this sort of bread, which is called piki. The batter is brushed onto the hot stone and then quickly peeled off—piki is as thin and crackly as tissue paper. Three sheets are rolled together to eat. For special celebrations, the Pueblos may add color to the batter and produce pink, blue, or yellow piki. The Sardinian *carta da musica* has a similar parchmentlike characteristic.

It baffles me that so many people persist in thinking that buttermilk is high in fat because of its name, when in fact there isn't any butter in it at all. In the olden days, when butter was churned from whole milk, the cream-free milk was left behind. A few flecks of golden butter might have strayed into the milk, but buttermilk was, and is, a low-fat product.

Unless you get it from a small dairy, the buttermilk you buy today will be a commercial product almost invariably made from skim or nonfat milk, though whole-milk buttermilk can still be found. This buttermilk has been "cultured" by the addition of lactic acid bacteria; it has a clean, refreshing taste and is thicker than regular milk. It brings a nice tang and tenderness to baked goods.

When I'm out of buttermilk, I sometimes duplicate the effect in simple baked goods like biscuits or pancakes by adding some plain yogurt to milk.

10. Brioche French Toast

ere is a celebration of dairy and eggs. Use the freshest eggs and richest milk and cream you can find. And this is a good weekend project for children—make the challah on Friday or Saturday and let them follow up with this yummy dish for Sunday morning or even for dessert. Of course, store-bought challah or brioche or any kind of bread, including baguettes or whole-wheat breads, can be made into French toast.   SERVES 6

1 loaf day-old brioche or
    challah bread
6 large eggs
½ cup superfine sugar
2 cups milk
2 cups heavy cream
1 teaspoon ground cinnamon
Pinch of freshly grated
    nutmeg
4 tablespoons butter, melted
    and cooled to room
    temperature

Cut the bread into 1-inch slices. Whisk the eggs, sugar, milk, and heavy cream together in a large bowl. Add the cinnamon and nutmeg and whisk to combine. Lay the bread slices in a shallow baking dish and pour the egg mixture over them; let the bread sit until it begins to absorb the liquid, 2 to 3 minutes, then flip and let sit for 2 or 3 minutes more. The custard mixture should be almost completely absorbed.

Preheat the oven to 200 degrees. Place a baking sheet or ovenproof serving platter in the oven.

Place a large skillet over medium-high heat and coat the bottom of it with butter. Add 3 or 4 slices of soaked bread and cook until they are golden brown and crisp on the bottom; flip and cook on the second side, adding more butter to the pan as necessary. Transfer the finished slices to the baking sheet in the oven to keep warm while you continue the process with the remaining bread and butter.

Serve the French toast immediately, with powdered sugar, maple syrup, fresh berries, or any other of your favorite toppings.

What makes toast "French"? A good question. In this country, the name is given to bread soaked and cooked in some sort of combination of milk and eggs, because it came to us through the French settlers of New Orleans and Canada, among other places. The French name is *pain perdu,* or "lost bread"—meaning stale bread, which is usually wasted. But you could call it lost and found bread, because when it is made into tasty French toast it really has found a new life.

It is hard for us to believe today but wheat, and anything made from it, was a bit of a luxury until fairly modern times, and therefore bread was not to be wasted, even when it got old and hard. Our "French" toast probably goes back to medieval days, and can be found in most countries, especially European ones, but even in Asia and Africa. In England, this is known as "eggy" bread, and in some places, including France, it also is served for dessert.

THE MAGICAL, MYSTERIOUS EGG

As the snow melts and the ground begins to thaw, we see small signs of renewed life at Katchkie Farm. And our hens respond to the lengthening days; they begin to lay eggs in profusion. Even in the age of factory-raised eggs and year-round supplies, the natural cycle kicks in.

Eggs have been a symbol of life, renewal, and even sacredness since pagan times—including the belief that the very world was a kind of egg, with the sky and the land as its two halves.

So it is not surprising that eggs have prevailed in both Easter and Passover holidays as potent symbols of rebirth and redemption. For kids celebrating Easter, what is more delightful than hunting brightly colored eggs hidden among the daffodils? At a Passover seder, permission to eat the egg—dipped in salt water and followed by matzo, horseradish, and charoset—signals the imminent arrival of dinner.

Condiments

1. Bob-A-Que Sauce

2. Basil Pesto

3. Parsley Mint Pesto

4. Sage and Arugula Pesto

5. Salsa Verde

6. Chimichurri Sauce

7. Spicy Cranberry Sauce

8. Spicy Coriander-Coconut Chutney

9. Ginger Sauce

10. Caramelized Onion Relish

11. Hummus

12. *Katchkie Favorites:* Katchkie Farm Hummus

13. Katchkie Farm Ketchup

14. Katchkie Farm Fresh Salsa

15. Katchkie Farm Tomato Preserves

16. Saffron Aioli

17. Blueberry Jam

18. *Katchkie Favorites:* When You Have Too Many Apples

19. Hasty Pickles

20. Pickled Green Tomatoes

21. Pickled Strawberries

22. Kimchi

Everyday dishes and simple preparations can be endlessly varied with tasty—but simple—relishes and sauces. I am fascinated by this category of food and can spend hours wandering up and down the condiment aisles of gourmet stores and upscale supermarkets. Condiments are the barometer of food trends, and one often sees the peaks and valleys of popularity on these shelves. Historically, many condiments were devised as ways to preserve food. Pickling is a prime example.

Though the definition of "condiment" is "food seasoning used at the table," condiments can be so much more. Frequently, we love our condiments to the point that we gravitate to dishes that are merely vehicles for enjoying the dip, spread, or relish. Salsa—a great accent to anything from eggs to chicken to meats—is a classic, especially with tortilla chips. I find I am looking for excuses to enjoy our Katchkie Ketchup and will dip veggie sticks in it. Gabrielle Langholtz, the editor of *Edible Manhattan* magazine, confided that after she got her first jar from me as a gift, she drank it all straight from the bottle, before she was even three blocks away! And then there's pesto, with which I am so nearly obsessed that it drives endless meals, especially when my herb garden is at its height.

Condiments, used strategically, can cajole a reluctant eater to enjoy a new taste.

1. Bob-A-Que Sauce

Farmer Bob Walker, the master of all he surveys at the farm, and resident chef, developed this excellent sauce. It can be mopped on ribs or chicken as they cook on the grill or set on the table as a sauce—or both. A California native, Bob loves the spicy flavors of Mexican cooking. His sauce has a kick. Bob cooks for himself almost nightly, and sometimes for his friends, usually dishes with a southwestern spin and always with a good helping of organic vegetables.

This recipe may yield more than you need, but it keeps well in the refrigerator and is an obviously good thing to have on hand. Whatever seasonal apple you have will do.

MAKES ABOUT 1 QUART

1 pound ripe tomatoes, cored and roughly chopped

1 cup cider vinegar

1 cup peeled, cored, and diced apple (about 1 large apple)

¼ cup dark or light brown sugar

¼ cup tomato paste

2 tablespoons minced green bell pepper

2 tablespoons minced white onion

½ teaspoon peeled and minced fresh ginger

½ teaspoon tamarind paste (see page 168)

1 garlic clove, minced

¼ teaspoon dry mustard

⅛ teaspoon chipotle chili powder

⅛ teaspoon allspice

Salt and freshly ground pepper

Combine all the ingredients, except the salt and pepper, in a medium pot over medium heat. Simmer for 30 minutes or until the mixture thickens; stir from time to time to prevent scorching.

Remove the pot from the heat and set aside to cool a bit. Put the sauce into a blender or the work bowl of a food processor and process to a thick puree.

Season to taste with salt and pepper and adjust the other seasonings as well. Or add more cider vinegar, if needed, to thin the sauce.

2. Basil Pesto

This is a fairly typical basil pesto, but I like to add some of Sprout Creek Farm's Toussaint cheese to mine. For one thing, it is a fine, award-winning cow's milk cheese, with a subtle milky flavor and a smooth texture; as it ages, it becomes more complex and can be used as a grating cheese. It adds some richness to the texture as well as to the taste of the pesto.

Another reason I use Toussaint cheese is that Sprout Creek, which was founded by the Society of the Sacred Heart, is a Hudson Valley neighbor with a mission similar to ours at the Sylvia Center. Sprout Creek is a working farm with educational programs for children and adults. The belief at Sprout Creek Farm is clear and principled: "Children will protect each other and our Earth if they are helped to appreciate it." MAKES 1½ CUPS

3 cups basil leaves

3 garlic cloves

¾ cup freshly grated
   Parmigiano-Reggiano

3 tablespoons freshly grated
   Sprout Creek Farms
   Toussaint cheese (see
   above) or increase the
   Parmigiano accordingly

Scant ¼ cup pine nuts,
   lightly toasted

½ cup extra-virgin olive oil,
   plus more if necessary

Kosher or sea salt and freshly
   ground pepper

Combine the basil, garlic, cheeses, and pine nuts in a food processor or blender and process, pulsing, to achieve a rough chopped mixture.

With the machine running, slowly pour in the olive oil until it is combined with the herbs. Add salt and pepper to taste and process to the desired consistency—less for a more textured, rustic pesto or more for a smoother one; add more oil if desired. If you are making pesto for pasta, use some of the pasta cooking water to thin the sauce to the point you like.

See page 298 for keeping and storing pesto.

PESTO

I've always loved pesto, but once I had a farm and was able to grow things on a grander scale than in the back garden, it also became a means to an end, helping to justify my herb obsession, along with my avid seed collecting. I have become such a well-known seeker of seeds that people bring me all sorts. As a result, just among the basil, I have opal, lemon, chocolate, mint, and Thai, as well as some Iranian basil cultivated from seeds I was given by my friend Nazli (I don't ask, they don't tell). Consequently, my pesto repertoire is notable.

Making first-rate pesto is not difficult. Once you master the simple technique involved, you too can follow your own instincts, moving beyond basil and pine nuts to pestos composed of whatever herbs are in the garden or the market. Let Italy, where numerous regional and seasonal variations abound, guide you: in Sicily, almonds and tomatoes are used along with the local basil; in Liguria, besides the iconic basil pesto, there is a walnut, pine nut, and spinach version, and a garlic- and nut-free combination of parsley, basil, mint, butter, cream, and Parmigiano-Reggiano dresses spinach tagliatelle. Pesto is closely bound to our notions of summery stuff, but a big-flavored pesto such as one of dried porcini, tomatoes, rosemary, and Pecorino Romano cheese sounds lovely for cooler days.

Making pesto can also be instructive for children, a way to let them taste and test. Line up a few different herbs, including some familiar ones such as parsley and mint, then taste them along with some others that will expand their palates, like sage, chervil, tarragon, or one of the less common basils. You might arrange them from mildest to most intense. Let the children describe the characteristics of each. Then let them help design a pesto for dinner; once the herb has been decided, move on to the nut and cheese. And remember my almost never-fail rule: if they make it, they will eat it.

There are many opportunities for kids to participate here, from pulling the herbs from the plants to pouring the oil and other ingredients into the food processor, to cracking and shelling the walnuts, using nimble little fingers to pick out the pieces. Kids love the pulse feature on the food processor. And using an old-fashioned mortar and pestle is an excellent activity; if you can tolerate the inevitability of a little mess, pounding the ingredients can be an entertaining and enlightening cooking lesson for you and your child—at least once (see page 298).

The Language of Food: *Pesto*

"Pesto" comes from *pestare,* the Italian word for "to pound or grind."
And the Italian word for "pestle" is *pestello.* Clearly, this is a sauce
married to its technique.

3. Parsley Mint Pesto

Along with corn, the summers of my youth were defined by mint growing like crazy around the back of our country house. Some people consider mint a garden nuisance, but I don't mind it, especially in late summer when its little purple flowers appear. There are many varieties of mint, but spearmint and peppermint are by far the most common. You may find other kinds at farmers' markets or plant stores; some of them are more subtle or complex in flavor—less pepperminty.

But at least in summer, there is rarely a reason to buy mint—if you plant just a bit, you will have all you need for pestos like this one (good with cold meats or fish, potatoes, and green beans) and plenty for cool mint tea or lemonade, or to toss over fruit salads and cold tomato soup. I even use a few leaves in my green salad.   MAKES 1½ CUPS

½ cup blanched whole
   almonds, toasted
1 small garlic clove
½ cup (packed) flat-leaf
   parsley leaves
1 cup mint leaves
1 cup basil leaves
½ cup extra-virgin olive oil,
   plus more for drizzling
1 heaping tablespoon
   crumbled ricotta salata
Kosher or sea salt and freshly
   ground pepper

Place roughly half of each ingredient, not including the ricotta salata, salt, and pepper, in a food processor; don't worry about proportions, all will be combined later. Pulse until well chopped. Pour the mixture into a bowl.

Repeat with the remaining ingredients, then stir to combine well. Stir in the ricotta salata and salt and pepper to taste. Drizzle a bit of olive oil over the pesto to keep it from darkening and let it rest for 5 to 10 minutes before serving.

4. Sage and Arugula Pesto

The flavors here are pretty assertive, so choose this pesto for boiled small whole potatoes or toss it with whole-wheat pasta. Use it as a sauce with pork, grilled steaks, or seafood.

MAKES 2 CUPS

1 cup extra-virgin olive oil

4 garlic cloves, 3 whole and 1 minced

½ cup shelled walnuts

4 cups (loosely packed) arugula leaves

½ cup sage leaves

½ cup grated Parmigiano-Reggiano

Salt and freshly ground pepper

Heat about 1 tablespoon of the oil in a small skillet over medium heat. Add the whole garlic cloves and sauté until they are golden brown, about 5 minutes; do not let the garlic burn or it will become bitter. Pour the garlic and oil from the pan and set them aside.

Toast the walnuts in the skillet over medium heat until golden, 1 to 2 minutes. Remove the walnuts from the heat.

Put the arugula, sage, walnuts, and both the sauteed and minced garlic in a blender or a food processor; pulse to mince the ingredients.

With the machine running, or while pulsing the food processor, slowly pour in the remaining oil and blend just until the ingredients are well incorporated.

Scrape the mixture into a bowl and stir in the cheese. Season with salt and pepper to taste.

Try This at Home

Pesto is one of the dishes that came into everyday American cooking with the arrival of the food processor, a machine that simplified a technique that previously had required time, persistence, and muscle. As with some other classic sauces that have existed since the culinary pre–machine age, a mortar and pestle was used to achieve creamy results. In the case of pesto, various herbs, oil, cheeses, and nuts were pounded and ground together, and then the oil was painstakingly added to incorporate it. Making pesto was laborious.

I'm all for reducing the labor intensity of home cooking, especially when it expands the cook's repertoire, but I recommend making certain dishes (bread and pastry also come to mind) the traditional way, at least once or twice, just to get a feel for the authentic results. After that, you can make your machines do your bidding, learning to work and control them to produce the right results.

For the basic proportions, use the Basil Pesto recipe (page 293) here. Wash and dry the basil leaves, then put them in the mortar with the garlic and salt to taste and grind the mixture to a creamy consistency with the pestle. Incorporate the nuts using the same method, and then the cheese. Dribble the oil in very slowly so that it will emulsify with the other ingredients. Let everyone take turns adding the oil.

An authentic pesto is uniform and balanced, not oozing oil and not, by the way, intensely garlicky. So, once you know what your goal is, you can move on to a machine. Whether you are using a blender or a food processor, add the oil quite deliberately, pulsing carefully to incorporate it. Keep a light hand with all the ingredients and you will achieve a credible machine-made pesto.

How to Keep Pesto

Pesto will keep in the refrigerator for at least a few days under a thin layer of olive oil—this keeps the herbs from becoming dark and bitter. (I find it keeps even longer than just a few days.) Pesto can be kept frozen for at least a month. Combine all the ingredients with the exception of the cheese in a container with a good seal and top with oil. Defrost at room temperature, not in the microwave, and stir in the cheese before using. Small portions can be frozen in ice cube trays and popped out when needed to top off a piece of fish or chicken or to stir into green beans or broccoli or a hearty soup like minestrone.

5. Salsa Verde

It wasn't so long ago that tomatillos were a true specialty item, rarely seen outside a can. But the tomatillo is easily cultivated and now widely available fresh in supermarkets. We grow tomatillos at Katchkie Farm to the great joy of some of the workers there who come from Mexico. This salsa verde is typical of the ones made at Katchkie, simple and straightforward. I like the clean but emphatic, slightly tart taste. Serve this with chips or as an accompaniment to Mexican dishes.

Peeling tomatillos can be a sticky job, so if you're working with children, keep a little bowl of water on hand to rinse fingers between tomatillos. Once in a while, a "shell" comes off almost intact and can be hung like a tiny lantern. MAKES 1 (GENEROUS) PINT

¾ pound tomatillos (8 to 12, depending on size)
¼ cup chopped white onion
¼ cup fresh cilantro leaves
2 teaspoons fresh lime juice
Pinch of sugar
1 jalapeño or serrano chile, seeded and chopped (see page 115)
Kosher salt and freshly ground pepper

Preheat the broiler. Remove the papery husks from the tomatillos and rinse them well.

Cut the tomatillos in half and place them, cut side down, on a foil-lined baking sheet. Place the sheet under the broiler until the tomatillos are lightly blackened, 5 to 7 minutes.

Place the tomatillos, onion, cilantro, lime juice, sugar, jalapeño, and salt and pepper to taste in a food processor or blender and pulse until they are combined and finely chopped, but take care not to overblend or puree the mixture.

Adjust the seasonings to taste, and chill the salsa in the refrigerator before serving. The salsa will keep, refrigerated, for several days.

TOMATILLOS

You may be forgiven if you still believe the tomatillo to be some sort of tomato. The name is Spanish for "little tomato" and salsa verde is nearly as ubiquitous as tomato salsa, but this little fruit is, in fact, related to the gooseberry. You can see some resemblance in the papery outer covering or "shell." Tomatillos are dainty nutritional powerhouses, loaded with potassium and high in vitamins C and A, but low in calories.

6. Chimichurri Sauce

This is my version of the classic South American green sauce. I serve it with grilled skirt steak, but it goes just as well with other cuts, including burgers. If you want just one sauce for grilled beef, this is it. Make it an hour or so before serving to let the flavors blend.

MAKES 1 CUP

½ cup extra-virgin olive oil

2 teaspoons fresh lime juice

½ teaspoon red chile flakes

Leaves from 1 bunch flat-leaf parsley, chopped

Leaves from ½ bunch cilantro, chopped

2 teaspoons Worcestershire sauce

2 tablespoons red wine vinegar

1 teaspoon minced garlic

1 teaspoon minced shallot

Salt and freshly ground pepper

Combine all the ingredients, adding the salt and pepper to taste.

7. Spicy Cranberry Sauce

Another gift to my personal repertoire, and now this book, from my friend Dan Barber. This cranberry sauce begs to be on the Thanksgiving table and is equally good with duck or pork. I have a friend who spoons cranberry sauce onto her morning yogurt, along with some granola.   MAKES ABOUT 2 CUPS

Zest of 1 orange, julienned

Zest of ½ lemon, julienned

Juice of 1 orange

Juice of 1 lemon

One 12-ounce package
   cranberries

½ large red onion, finely
   diced

2 cups port

2-inch piece fresh ginger,
   peeled and julienned

3 tablespoons dark brown
   sugar

1½ teaspoons kosher salt

¼ teaspoon freshly ground
   white pepper

½ teaspoon cinnamon

2 tablespoons Grand Marnier
   (optional)

Heat the orange and lemon juices in a small saucepan over medium heat, add the zests, and cook until soft, about 10 minutes; do not let the mixture boil. Set aside.

Meanwhile, place the cranberries, onion, port, ginger, brown sugar, salt, pepper, and cinnamon in a saucepan over medium heat and cook, stirring occasionally, until the cranberries have cooked down and the mixture is thick, about 15 minutes. Stir in the Grand Marnier, if using, citrus zest and the juice. Set aside to cool, and serve at room temperature.

The cranberry sauce can be made in advance and kept, refrigerated, for several weeks.

8. Spicy Coriander-Coconut Chutney

It is by now well established that there are those of us who really like cilantro, and the rest of the world. I recently read that there may be a physical reason that some people are so averse to cilantro, sometimes to the point of hostility; thankfully, I do not have that affliction.

I like all sorts of chutneys; this one is great as part of a condiment selection with curried dishes, as well as with grilled chicken, lamb, or shrimp.   MAKES 1½ CUPS

1 cup cilantro leaves and
    tender stems
3 green serrano chiles, seeded
    and chopped (see page 115)
½ cup grated fresh coconut
    or shredded unsweetened
    dried coconut
1 cup canned unsweetened
    coconut milk
1 teaspoon peeled and grated
    fresh ginger
1 to 3 tablespoons fresh
    lemon juice
1 teaspoon kosher salt, plus
    more if needed
1 teaspoon sugar
2 tablespoons vegetable oil
1 teaspoon black mustard
    seeds
4 fresh curry leaves, coarsely
    chopped (optional)
Freshly ground pepper

Combine the cilantro with the serrano chiles, coconut, coconut milk, ginger, 1 tablespoon of the lemon juice, the salt, and sugar.

Heat the vegetable oil in a small skillet over medium heat. Add the mustard seeds and curry leaves, if using, and stir until they are fragrant and toasted, taking care not to let them burn, 4 or 5 minutes.

Pour the mustard seeds and curry leaves, along with the sautéing oil, into the cilantro mixture and stir to blend thoroughly. Adjust the seasonings with additional lemon juice, salt, and pepper to taste.

9. Ginger Sauce

I am partial to this sauce for fish; it has lots of flavor on its own but manages also to enhance rather than overpower it. This recipe yields more than you need for four or six servings; it can be cut by half, or you can freeze it. I like to have it on hand for pretty much any fish preparation. It is good as a marinade as well as a sauce, but be sure it is chilled or at room temperature for a marinade.   MAKES 5 TO 6 CUPS

1 tablespoon vegetable oil

½ onion, finely chopped

2 garlic cloves, minced

¼ cup peeled and minced fresh ginger

¼ cup vegetable stock, homemade (page 38) or good-quality store bought, or water

2 cups sugar

1 piece star anise

1 cup white vinegar

1 cup white wine

1 cup light soy sauce

1 cup ketchup, homemade (page 311) or good-quality store bought

Salt and freshly ground pepper

Place the oil in a small skillet and set it over medium heat. Add the onion, garlic, and ginger, and cook until the onion is soft.

Put ¼ cup of the stock in a medium saucepan and stir in the sugar and the star anise. Cook over medium heat, without stirring, until the liquid clears and becomes medium caramel in color. Off the heat, add the vinegar and wine and stir to combine, then add the onion mixture, soy sauce, and ketchup. Simmer the sauce, stirring, until it thickens enough to coat the back of a spoon, about 10 minutes. Season the sauce with salt and pepper to taste.

To make a thicker sauce or a glaze, dissolve 4 teaspoons cornstarch in 4 teaspoons water; when the mixture is smooth, stir it into the sauce and cook for 5 minutes, while stirring.

10. Caramelized Onion Relish

Having a farm has deepened my admiration for the centuries of inventive cooks who devised ways to "put food by," meaning to put it away for the winter months. Necessity and a horror of wasting even the most bountiful crop led to preserving and a vast, marvelous culinary category. On the savory side, that includes ubiquitous pantry items like pickles and relishes. I can't say I ever thought much about where they came from, besides a store, but now I watch my crops in anticipation of making condiments like this delicious relish.

This recipe makes a generous amount, and keeps well, but can be halved.

MAKES 3 CUPS

½ cup extra-virgin olive oil, plus more to finish

8 cups diced red onions (about 6)

5 tablespoons light brown sugar

1 cup red wine vinegar

½ cup fresh orange juice

1 tablespoon minced fresh rosemary

1 tablespoon orange zest

Salt and freshly ground pepper

Heat the olive oil in a large saucepan over low heat.

Toss the red onions with the sugar to coat them, then add them to the pan and cook for 10 minutes, until they are soft but not browned, stirring occasionally to prevent scorching.

Add the vinegar and orange juice to the pan. Cook until the mixture is thick and jamlike and the liquid has evaporated. Stir in the rosemary and orange zest; season with salt and pepper.

Top the onions off with a thin coating of olive oil when you are ready to store them. The relish can be packed into jars and kept, refrigerated, for a month or longer; the thin coating of olive oil keeps it fresh and moist. The relish will keep, refrigerated, for 2 weeks or longer.

PRESERVED LEMONS

Preserved lemons are a kind of pickle used in North African cooking, particularly in Morocco, where they are indispensable for tagines; it is impossible to imagine what Moroccan cuisine would be without them. Preserved lemons are also typical in Indian cooking, often as an accompaniment to rice dishes. Lemons are preserved for the usual reasons: to avoid wasting the great crops that are gathered during their growing season, and later to have them on hand when fresh ones are scarce.

You needn't be making a Moroccan dish, however, to find preserved lemons useful. They are good in seafood, veal, lamb, and rice dishes as well as with chicken; in southeast Asia, bits of preserved lemon are sometimes added to soups. Preserved lemons can be found in specialty food shops, in some supermarkets, and online. It usually takes just one to brighten a dish; the flavor is deeply lemony, but not spicy unless hot spices have been added to the pickling mix. And remember it's just the skin you want, so always discard the flesh.

HOW TO MAKE PRESERVED LEMONS

Making preserved lemons is easy, and it's a good way to engage and teach children a simple but ancient culinary process: using salt and acid to preserve foods. There are shades of differences among methods, but the objective is the same: you want to pack the lemons in jars with salt and enough lemon juice to cover them. After that, you just wait.

Have on hand at least ½ cup kosher salt, 1 or 2 lemons more than you plan to preserve, and a clean 1-gallon canning jar.

Start with 8 or 10 lemons (enough to fill the jar), scrub them well, and trim the stem ends. Cutting through just the skin, but not into the flesh, score each lemon into four even sections, starting from the top, nearly, but not all the way to the bottom. Leave the skin attached. Do this over a bowl to catch the juice.

Sprinkle some of the salt into the bottom of the canning jar. On a board or work surface, roll the lemons around in more of the salt or use your fingers to push it into the cut skin, and then pack them into the jar tightly, letting some of the juice squish out. Alternatively, you can simply sprinkle salt over each layer of lemons as you pack them. Use about a tablespoon of salt for each lemon. The jar should be well filled with lemons, and the oozing juice should nearly cover them. Sprinkle a final 2 tablespoons of salt over the top and close the jar tightly.

Leave the jar out at room temperature for a few days, turning it upside down from time to time. At this point the lemons should have begun to soften and exude even more juice, but if they are not fully covered, top them off with some freshly squeezed juice from additional lemons.

Place the jar in the refrigerator; your lemons should be ready in about three weeks—you will know when the skins are soft—and will keep for at least six months. If you have a cool cellar you might keep the jar there, but you are the best judge of that.

Before the jar is closed, various spices can be added, including peppercorns, a cinnamon stick, a fresh bay leaf, coriander seeds, or a hot dried chile or two.

Opinion varies on the type of lemons to use, whether thick- or thin-skinned, but in any case, it is the skin you will use in recipes, after the flesh is scraped away. Though more expensive, sweet, juicy Meyer lemons make great preserved lemons, but any type will do if they are ripe and on the small side.

For homemade gifts, pack the lemons into smaller jars, three or four each. Your child may like to give one to her teacher at holiday time; it will be something she made and unique—not another scented candle! And let her make her own labels.

11. Hummus

This is my Israeli nephew Eytan's recipe. I've included a hummus recipe here because I think this bean-based dish functions primarily as a dip. Hummus is very nutritious thanks to the chickpeas, which are high in protein, calcium, and mostly polyunsaturated fat, along with high fiber. It's a good thing to remember for kids' lunches or snacks. You could include a small container in a lunchbox, along with cut-up raw vegetables and wheat chips, pita wedges, or chapatis (page 340).

Hummus varies almost from cook to cook, but it is always a garlicky dish. If you would like less garlic emphasis, roast all eight in this recipe and omit raw ones.

MAKES ABOUT $2\frac{1}{2}$ CUPS

2 cups dried chickpeas
$\frac{1}{8}$ teaspoon baking soda
   (optional)
Juice of 3 lemons
2 garlic cloves and 6 roasted
   garlic cloves (page 98)
1 teaspoon salt
1 teaspoon cumin
1 teaspoon freshly ground
   pepper
A scant $\frac{1}{2}$ cup tahini

Place the chickpeas in a large bowl and cover them well with water; soak overnight or for about 8 hours. Drain the chickpeas and place them in a large pot with the baking soda, if using (see Note), cover with plenty of water, bring to a low boil, and cook until soft, about 1 hour. Drain, retaining about 1 cup of the cooking water, and refresh the chickpeas under cold water. Place the chickpeas in a food processor with the lemon juice, garlic cloves, salt, cumin, and pepper and process to a rough mixture. Add the tahini and continue to process, adding small amounts of the reserved cooking water, until the mixture is thick and smooth. Adjust to taste with additional amounts of salt, cumin, and pepper.

Some hummus experts recommend adding baking soda to the water when you cook beans in order to cut down on their gassy smell and effect. Don't overdo it though, as too much can give off a soapy smell.

Katchkie Favorites

12. Katchkie Farm Hummus

At the Sylvia Center, we make a quick hummus using supermarket ingredients; we call this Hummus in a Hurry. Just drain and rinse one large can of chickpeas and put them in your food processor with ½ cup tahini, the zest and juice of a lemon, a small garlic clove (or omit it), and a big pinch of ground cumin and process until the mixture is quite smooth. Add a little water or olive oil if necessary to thin to a consistency you like. Season to taste with salt, pepper, and additional cumin.

SESAME SEEDS

The lightly roasted seeds of the sesame plant are ground into a paste and used extensively throughout the Middle East, India, and Asia; they may be hulled or unhulled. Sesame seeds are rich in minerals such as iron and magnesium; the mineral content is even higher if the seeds are not hulled.

13. Katchkie Farm Ketchup

This is one of the most successful products we've developed for sale to support the Sylvia Center. Feel free to interpret this recipe to your own taste—you may like it spicier or more acidic; I like the ketchup to have some texture, but you may like a smoother sauce. For me, the main thing is that we came up with ketchup that has an edge of sweetness without the cloying characteristic of many other brands.

We love hearing that Katchkie Ketchup beats out Heinz in casual taste tests. And though I encourage you to do side-by-side taste testing, many children, my son included, are so accustomed to the commercially flavored product that they prefer it. Don't give up! With time, the true flavors of the tomato and the integrity of the recipe will prevail! MAKES 1 PINT

1 tablespoon canola or other
   neutral flavored oil
2 tablespoons chopped white
   onion, organic if possible
4 cups (32 ounces) canned
   crushed organic tomatoes,
   drained
½ teaspoon cider vinegar
1 tablespoon tomato paste
   (see Note)
¼ teaspoon Ancho chili
   powder
½ teaspoon ground coriander
1 teaspoon Worcestershire
   sauce
1 teaspoon brown sugar
½ teaspoon molasses
Kosher salt

Heat the oil in a medium saucepan over medium heat. Add the onion and sauté until translucent and fragrant, but not browned, about 5 minutes. Add the tomatoes and vinegar and simmer for 10 minutes, stirring from time to time.

Let the tomato mixture cool to room temperature, then puree it in a blender or a food processor to your desired consistency.

Return the mixture to the pan, add the tomato paste, chili powder, and coriander, and simmer for 5 minutes. Add the Worcestershire sauce, brown sugar, molasses, and a pinch of salt and simmer for 5 more minutes. Taste and adjust seasoning with additional salt, chili powder, and coriander. Let the ketchup cool, then store it in jars, refrigerated. It will last a long time.

You can find very good quality tomato paste, both imported Italian and domestic, that comes in tubes; use what you need and then keep the tube in the refrigerator. This eliminates the curse of canned tomato paste: what to do with the rest after you use just a bit. If you do use canned paste, though, you can keep what's left by measuring out small amounts—tablespoons are ideal—and freezing them. Plop the measured amounts out onto a plate or into an ice cube tray, put it into the freezer for about 30 minutes, then transfer the frozen pieces to plastic bags.

14. Katchkie Farm Fresh Salsa

This is the most basic of salsas, ready to take its usual place alongside guacamole and chips or to act as a condiment with just about anything, particularly grilled or Mexican dishes. Add more jalapeños or a hotter variety of chile (see page 115), or more lime juice or even a splash of vinegar as you like. The most significant ingredient is the tomato; to me, a salsa made with indifferent or underripe tomatoes is merely ceremonial and ultimately disappointing. So look for the best tomatoes in season, or be patient if the ones you have are not quite ripe.

Most children past the age of three will enjoy this salsa, as it is pretty mild, and children like to dip. Serve it with good-quality organic tortilla chips, or crisp some up in the oven for a healthful snack.   MAKES 3 CUPS

6 medium ripe tomatoes,
   diced
¼ medium white onion,
   diced
1 jalapeño, minced (see page
   116)
Leaves from 8 fresh cilantro
   sprigs, roughly chopped
1 garlic clove, minced
Juice of 1 lime
¼ cup olive oil
½ teaspoon salt

Combine all the ingredients in a mixing bowl and toss thoroughly. Let the salsa stand for 15 minutes before serving; adjust seasonings to taste.

This will keep for a few days in the refrigerator.

Leftover salsa, especially when it is more juice than substance, is a good quick marinade for fish or chicken.

15. Katchkie Farm Tomato Preserves

Like any preserves, this can be used on bread or toast. It is good on sandwiches, with cheese, as a substitute for ketchup, or as a condiment for grilled meats or vegetables. This recipe yields a lot, but it can be halved. The preserves make a great gift when packed into pretty pint jars, and they keep as well as any jam or preserves.   MAKES 4 QUARTS

4 cups malt vinegar

5 cups white sugar

1 tablespoon salt

5 pounds ripe tomatoes, roughly chopped

2 pounds onions, chopped

1 garlic clove, minced

½ teaspoon cayenne pepper

1 teaspoon ground cloves

1 teaspoon ground allspice

1½ teaspoons ground ginger

Place the vinegar, sugar, and salt in a large pot over medium heat. When the sugar is dissolved, add the remaining ingredients and lower the heat to maintain a simmer. Cook, stirring from time to time, until the mixture is reduced and thickened, 1 to 3 hours (see Note).

Remove the pot from the heat and set aside to cool to room temperature. Pass the preserves through a food mill into a large bowl. Transfer the preserves to jars, and store, refrigerated, for up to 6 months.

The time needed to thicken the preserves can vary widely and depends on the amount of liquid in the tomatoes.

16. Saffron Aioli

Garlic was introduced to southern France by Crusaders returning from the Middle East. It caught on fast. This mayonnaise-like sauce looms large in Provençal and Catalan cuisines, among others. In Provence it is at the heart of the Grande Aioli, a feast that may include at least one type of seafood—salted codfish is more or less requisite—meat or chicken, and numerous raw and cooked vegetables, including potatoes, chickpeas, and hard-boiled eggs. Still today, a Grande Aioli (or *Aioli Monstre*) might be a village affair, with long tables set out in the square, usually to celebrate the local saint's day.

This version is a shortcut; I add the distinguishing saffron and garlic to already-made mayonnaise, homemade or store bought. If you are not up to mounting a complete Grande Aioli, try it with hot or cold seafood—mussels, codfish, and lobster are splendid—or roasted or grilled chicken at room temperature and simple boiled potatoes. Another traditional use of aioli is to spoon it onto a hearty fish soup or stew. It is great to have on hand.

MAKES A LITTLE MORE THAN 1/2 CUP

Big pinch saffron threads
   (about 8), crumbled
1/2 teaspoon hot water
1/2 cup mayonnaise
1 garlic clove, chopped
1 teaspoon Dijon mustard
1 tablespoon extra-virgin
   olive oil
1 teaspoon fresh lemon juice
1/8 teaspoon salt
1/8 teaspoon freshly ground
   pepper

Put the saffron threads into a small cup with the water and let it stand for 5 minutes. Puree the saffron threads and soaking liquid with the remaining ingredients in a food processor or a blender until smooth. Adjust the seasonings to taste and serve immediately or keep, refrigerated, for several days.

Herb Aioli

Omit the saffron and stir in 2 teaspoons finely chopped fresh flat-leaf parsley, 1 teaspoon finely chopped fresh tarragon, 1 teaspoon rice wine vinegar, and salt and pepper to taste. Other herbs, such as chives, thyme or lemon thyme, or basil may be substituted. Let your menu and your herb patch guide you.

SAFFRON

The price of saffron can come as a shock—$15 or more for a gram—at least until you consider its cultivation and harvesting. Around two football fields of a particular type of crocus are needed to yield enough stigmas for a single kilogram, and the harvesting remains a hands-on process. Fresh saffron threads will be bright reddish orange and not dry or broken; buy saffron in well-sealed glass vials from a store that has a good turnover and store it in the freezer.

High-quality saffron comes from Iran, India, Spain, and Italy, among other places, where it defines a great range of dishes from paella and bouillabaisse to biryani and Milan's traditional risotto. Thanks to early spice traders saffron shows up as well in baked goods like English breads and Sweden's saffron buns.

17. Blueberry Jam

Beth Linskey and her products have been fixtures at New York's Greenmarkets from the beginning, and Beth herself is often on the scene, a cheerful little woman under a heavily beribboned straw hat, who, if you catch her eye, may say, "Hi, I'm Beth, and I make jam." Beth's Farm Kitchen operates out of an old farmhouse in Stuyvesant Falls, New York, not far from Katchkie Farm. She started about thirty years ago with just one terrific recipe for strawberry jam and now has about ninety products, all small-batch production. Beth was a big help to us when we were developing our own products; for a time we even made our ketchup at her place, and Beth helped with the tomato jam and refined the salsa. Some days I would pick up the phone to hear her say, "This needs to be tweaked!" Beth really held our hands; she's been a good neighbor and supporter of the Sylvia Center.

Thinking about making fruit jams and jellies makes me want to go pick an enormous flat myself! There is nothing more rewarding than taking a trip to a "pick your own" field and loading up on more berries than you know what to do with . . . because you *do* know! Outings to pick fruits are some of the most memorable moments in my family. And homemade jam makes a perfect gift for the holidays or for a teacher. Children can be enlisted to design labels, which you can have printed up, and to help choose jars. They will be quite thrilled with their accomplishment.   MAKES FOUR TO FIVE 8-OUNCE JARS

3 to 4 pints blueberries
½ teaspoon lime juice
2 teaspoons prepared calcium powder*
Water
1⅓ cups granulated sugar
2 teaspoons Pomona's Universal Pectin

Mash enough blueberries to yield 4 cups. Combine the berries and the lime juice in a pot with the calcium water* and stir thoroughly. Bring the mixture to a boil over medium heat.

Meanwhile, whisk together the sugar and powdered pectin.

When the blueberries are at a rolling boil, stir in the sugar and pectin mixture, then bring the mixture back to a rolling boil. When the jam "sets up"—when it is quite thick and holds a loose shape and is no longer fluid—pour it into hot sterilized glass jars and cap them immediately.

* Powder and instructions for preparation of calcium water are included with packages of Pomona's Universal Pectin.

Red, White, and Blueberries

You probably know that Maine is famous for its blueberries; the little state produces 25 percent of our domestic crop, making it the largest grower in the world. If you visit Maine in the summer, try to find one of the towns that holds a seasonal blueberry festival. But wherever in the state you may be, a lobster dinner followed by blueberry pie ranks as one of the greatest possible meals, quintessentially American.

18. When You Have Too Many Apples

I almost always have homemade applesauce in my fridge. I make a batch whenever the apples in the fruit bowl are beginning to get past their eating-out-of-hand stage. Applesauce is great at breakfast, especially for a light morning meal; spoon some onto oatmeal or have it with yogurt and granola. For babies, a good early food is squash and apples cooked together and then pureed. At my house applesauce above all is required at the side of Potato Latkes (page 99).

If you are confident that no pesticides have been used, you needn't peel your apples. Otherwise, peel and core them, chop 4 or 5 of them very roughly, and toss them into a pot with a splash of orange juice, apple juice, or just water—you don't need much, as the apples will begin to ooze their own moisture soon enough. Season with a pinch of salt and brown or turbinado sugar to taste. If you want a chunky result, the apples will probably break down well enough on their own; for a smoother sauce, or if you kept the skins on and they are still too big or thick, put the sauce through a food mill or use an immersion blender; the ideal texture is up to you.

For variation, add grated fresh or dried ginger, cinnamon, nutmeg, allspice, or even warm Asian spices such as turmeric or five-spice powder; a pinch of garam masala can turn simple applesauce into a sophisticated side to lamb or pork. Or add a handful of raisins, currants, or dried cranberries.

APPLES

At Katchkie Farm, we use apples from nearby orchards. But wherever you are, you can optimize the seasonal bounty by choosing the best variety available and putting it to its optimal use. If, for instance, you love the Macoun, you will want to focus on its relatively early but short season and then move on to Honeycrisp and Golden Delicious, two eating apples that will be around for several months. The best cooking apples—Idared, to name one—will not be as satisfying out of hand as a sweet Jonamac or Spartan. For pies as well as eating, Cortland and Granny Smith are superb, and the Rome is good for baking. And if you are brewing your own cider, use the most tart varieties.

As with tomatoes, some wonderful old apple varieties are again being cultivated. There may be some very local ones where you live—look for them at farmers' markets. Other types are more generally available across the country. Apples fall into two main types—sweet and tart—but those descriptions do no justice to the subtleties in their tastes. I urge you to expand your apple palate when you come across an apple new to you. And if you want to have a taste test with children, it is hard to imagine a food better than apples—they've been eating them forever, so they will be open to the experiment. I've found that tasting anything on its own is not particularly revealing, but when you go, for instance, from a Honeycrisp to a Granny Smith, the difference can be significant.

So, generally, sweeter varieties like Crispins, Honeycrisps, Gala, Fuji, Macoun, and Golden Delicious are good for eating out of hand or in salads, while the tarter Empires, Baldwins, and Cortlands are good for baking, sauce, or pie. But many varieties are nearly all-purpose, like the sweet-tart Jonagold and Pink Lady. Some apples deliver it all—Granny Smith, for instance, is a nice, crisp, sweet-tart apple for eating and holds up nicely in a pie.

19. Hasty Pickles

You don't have to go to the store for pickles, and you don't have to wait for your own to mature, either. When the cucumber harvest comes in at Katchkie Farm, we use this method for quick pickles. If you are using Kirbys, the traditional pickle cucumber, use around eight; if they're large, use four or five.   MAKES 32 OUNCES OR 1 QUART JAR

8 Kirby cucumbers
Kosher or sea salt
1½ cups water
½ cup white vinegar
1 cup sugar
A few allspice berries
1 bay leaf

Scrub, but don't peel, your cucumbers. Slice the pickles about ¼ inch thick. Put the slices in a large colander and set it over a bowl or in the sink. Sprinkle the cucumbers with kosher or sea salt to draw out excess water.

Meanwhile, make a brine: pour the water and white vinegar into a medium pot; add the sugar. Toss in the allspice berries and the bay leaf.

Bring the mixture to a boil, then let it cool to room temperature.

Rinse the salt from the cukes, squeeze them gently, and let them soak in the brine for 3 to 6 hours, refrigerated, before serving; the pickles will keep for about 5 days.

Quick pickle making is great for kids—there is no cooking, so everyone can help.

The cucumbers can be sliced in a food processor fitted with the slicing disk, or on a mandoline.

20. Pickled Green Tomatoes

I begin pulling still-green tomatoes from their vines when the first hint of frost is in the air. I cook them up, of course, but I also put some by to enjoy pickled; these are especially good with smoked fish.

Small or medium tomatoes are best, but above all, be sure they are completely green, with no sign of ripeness.   MAKES 5 PINTS

About 2 pounds small to
   medium green tomatoes
4 medium white onions
¼ cup kosher salt
4 green or red bell peppers,
   seeded and roughly
   chopped
½ teaspoon celery seeds
½ teaspoon mustard seeds
1 tablespoon whole allspice
1 tablespoon whole cloves
1 cup granulated sugar
1 quart white vinegar

Wash the tomatoes and slice them horizontally, about ½ inch thick, or cut them into quarter wedges if they are on the small side. Peel and slice the onions, also horizontally, about ½ inch thick. Place the tomatoes and onions in a large colander set over a bowl or in the sink, sprinkle them with the salt, toss, and leave them for about 8 hours or overnight.

Tie the spices up in cheesecloth. Place the vinegar and sugar in a large nonreactive pot (a heavy enameled one is perfect) and add the spice pack. Simmer for ½ hour.

While the brine is simmering, rinse the tomatoes and onions well under cold water, shake off the excess water, and divide them, along with the bell peppers, among five hot 1-pint sterilized mason jars.

If necessary, bring the brine back to a boil and ladle it into each of the jars, just to cover the vegetables. Cool to room temperature and store the jars in the refrigerator.

21. Pickled Strawberries

The first time I tried them, I was a little surprised at how well strawberries take to pickling; the warm spices and hot jalapeños accent the fruit's sweetness. I particularly like these with grilled fish. If you have other leftover wine, like champagne, on hand, it can be substituted in. Sake is good, too. The liquid, or brine, left from these pickles is good in a marinade for chicken or fish; it adds acid and a distinctive flavor.   MAKES ABOUT 1 QUART

1 quart fresh ripe
　strawberries, hulled and
　washed
½ cup golden raisins
1 cup roughly chopped
　orange segments, seeds
　removed
⅔ cup jalapeños, seeded
　and finely chopped
　(see page 116)
1¼ cups white wine
1¼ cups sugar
½ teaspoon salt
½ teaspoon cayenne pepper
2 cinnamon sticks, each
　broken into 2 or 3 pieces
4 whole cloves

Layer the strawberries, raisins, oranges, and jalapeños in a gallon container with a lid.

Bring the wine, sugar, salt, cayenne, cinnamon, and cloves to a boil in a large nonreactive saucepan. Reduce the heat and simmer for 10 minutes. Pour the hot syrup over the fruit. Let cool to room temperature, cover, and refrigerate for 24 hours before serving. To serve, remove the fruit from the liquid with a slotted spoon.

22. Kimchi

When did we non–Korean Americans discover kimchi? When did we begin to regard it as just another condiment in the fridge door? When did we look for local and varied specimens at farmers' markets, and then when did we start making our own? This is the American food experience. In some ways we are hopelessly parochial, in others, as cosmopolitan as anyone; once the unknown becomes familiar, we embrace it. We can thank our diversity. Each generation brings new waves of immigrants, and immigrants bring their food; if we aren't exactly a melting pot, we do have a very wide table. Kimchi is a good example, an everyday necessity to Koreans that has worked its way into the American pantry. You know something has caught on when mass-market producers push it onto supermarket shelves.

This kimchi recipe is from Soonjo Lee, the friend of a friend of mine. Her recipe is a North Korean style—her father was from Pyongyang, which is now in North Korea. There, according to Soonjo, they prefer a lighter tasting kimchi; as you go farther south, the flavors become more intense, with more salted anchovy and spicy red pepper powder in the mix. Traditionally, Koreans store kimchi in clay pots and bury them in the earth in the fall, usually in November, before the ground freezes. Soonjo remembers that as a child "there would be three days of making kimchi in huge pots, four or five feet tall! In those days, we waited for the cabbage harvest and then made our year's supply of kimchi."

You will need a weight of some sort to press the cabbage. Soonjo uses a flat rock of about 2 pounds—and she cleans it in the dishwasher. If you don't have a rock, a can of food will do, but put it in a plastic bag before placing it on the cabbage.   MAKES 1 GALLON

2 medium Korean (Napa) cabbage, about 4 pounds

2 cups coarse sea salt, Korean if available, plus more for seasoning

12 cups water

1 Korean radish or Japanese long radish

2 to 3 tablespoons Korean red pepper powder or ground fresh pepper

Cut the cabbages in half, vertically, then in half again, to make 8 wedges.

In a large bowl, combine the salt and water, stir to dissolve, and add the cabbage. Soak the cabbage until the leaves are wilted, 5 to 8 hours, turning the bottom leaves of the wedges to the surface from time to time so they will be evenly salted.

When the cabbage is wilted, rinse it two or three times in cold water and drain in a colander.

Shred the radish. In a large bowl, mix the radish with the red pepper powder and the sugar so that the radish is coated. Add the shrimp, oyster, if using, garlic, and ginger and combine well; mix in the scal-

1 tablespoon sugar

2 tablespoons salted tiny
   baby shrimp or fish sauce

One 2-ounce fresh oyster

1 tablespoon chopped garlic

1 tablespoon chopped ginger

1 small bunch scallions,
   including green parts,
   trimmed and chopped

7 or more dried anchovies

lions. In the same bowl, separate the mixture into eight more or less equal portions.

Place one of the cabbage wedges on a work surface. Hold the wedge with one hand and layer one portion of the radish mixture between the leaves, mainly at the thick white bottom. Fold the top leaves over the bottom, press gently, and place the folded piece in the jar. Repeat with the remaining wedges. Place a two-pound weight on top. Be sure there is enough room above the weight to allow for the liquid that will exude and for the bubbling that will occur as the mixture ferments. Leave the jar at room temperature overnight.

Prepare an anchovy broth. Bring 2 or 3 cups of water to a boil. Add the dried anchovies and simmer for 15 to 20 minutes, to dissolve the anchovies. Strain the liquid, discard the anchovies, and let cool to room temperature.

Pour the clear broth into the jar. Set the jar into a shallow pan or other container to catch any liquid that bubbles over. Keep the jar at room temperature until it begins to ferment, 2 or 3 days, and then store it in the refrigerator. The kimchi can be transferred to smaller jars at this stage.

Disposable food handler's gloves are good to wear when mixing the spicy mixture and when stuffing it into the cabbage wedges.

It is impossible to predict exactly how long it will take for the kimchi to ferment. More salt will hasten the process, as will storing it in a warm room.

The cabbage can also be cut into 1 to $1\frac{1}{2}$-inch squares. This will hasten the fermenting process, which is good if you want to use the kimchi soon, but the kimchi will not last as long as it does when fermented slower.

Korean red pepper powder, fish sauce, and dried anchovies, as well as sea salt from Korea, can all be found in Asian markets, as well as in the many supermarkets that now have good Asian food sections.

Round-headed cabbage can be substituted for Napa and Japanese radishes for the Korean ones.

Breads, Pizza, and Muffins

Most of us who cooked when we were little began with baking, simple things like biscuits and cookies; this is an alluring activity for adults and children, a time to be cozy together in the kitchen. There is the fine mess that can be made with flour and the fun of rolling out dough, cracking eggs, or trying, perhaps giddily, to level off measuring spoons—in short, the delicious abandoning of control.

I have a friend whose earliest cooking memories are of baking with her mother, including making yeast-raised bread. It was exciting, and she loved going down to the warm basement to check the progress of the rising dough and to deliver it back up to the kitchen when it was ready. And then, of course, the punch-down! Along with giving her pleasant memories, baking bread as a child meant my friend never knew the curious intimidation that afflicts so many home cooks when they face a recipe involving yeast.

So I've included a first bread for children to make, knowing it may also be the first for their grown-ups. And there are recipes for foccacia and pizza, with lots of healthful variations on the basics, and the quick and easy chapatis that we make with children at the Sylvia Center. The other lesson here is more subtle but no less significant: good bread will ruin anyone's taste for the soft, highly processed, and nearly tasteless stuff that still sits on market shelves.

1. A Child's First Bread

This is a traditional white bread, perfect for children—it demonstrates the essential process and results in a loaf any kid will like for toast, sandwiches, or, after a few days, for French toast or bread pudding. MAKES TWO 9-INCH LOAVES

1 package (¼ ounce) or 1
    scant tablespoon active dry
    yeast
3 tablespoons sugar
2½ cups warm, not hot,
    water (110 degrees)
6½ cups unbleached bread
    flour, plus more for
    kneading
1 tablespoon kosher salt
3 tablespoons butter or lard,
    at room temperature
Canola or other neutral-
    flavored oil or cooking
    spray

Mix together the yeast, sugar, and water in a large bowl. Add 2 cups of the flour, then stir in the salt and butter. Set the bowl in a warm spot for about 10 minutes, until the mixture is foaming.

Add the remaining 4½ cups flour, ½ cup at a time, mixing well after each addition. When the dough begins to form a mass and pull away from the sides of the bowl, turn it out onto a lightly floured surface. Knead the dough until it is smooth and elastic, 8 to 10 minutes: push the dough away from you with the heel of your hand, then turn it back over itself and repeat. Dust the dough and your work surface very lightly with flour if it is sticky. You can test the dough's readiness by pulling off a small piece and stretching it lightly; it is ready when it seems nearly translucent.

Lightly coat a large bowl with oil. Place the dough in the bowl and turn to coat it lightly all over. Cover the bowl with a clean damp cloth and set it in a warm, draft-free place until the dough is doubled in volume, about 1 hour.

Lightly oil two 9-x-5-inch loaf pans. Deflate the dough by punching it down with your fist, then turn it out onto a lightly floured surface. Knead the dough lightly again, just a few turns, and divide it into two equal pieces; form each piece into a loaf the length and width of the loaf pans and pinch the underside together to form a seam.

Fit the loaves into the pans, seam side down, and cover them with the damp cloth. Let the loaves rise until doubled, about 40 minutes.

Preheat the oven to 425 degrees.

When the loaves are ready, place them in the oven, lower the heat to 375 degrees, and bake for about 30 minutes, or until the tops are golden brown. You can also test for doneness by carefully removing a loaf from a pan and tapping the bottom—it will sound hollow when it is ready.

Turn the loaves out onto baking racks and resist the temptation to slice into them before they are cool—about 1 hour.

You can substitute about ½ cup whole-wheat flour for ½ cup white.

Kids love to see yeast bubble up. Experiment with them—put some yeast in a bowl and feed it with a sprinkle of sugar. They love to imagine those little particles chomping on a sweet snack and getting bigger!

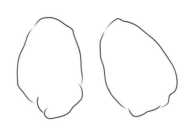

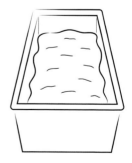

THE BONUS OF BREAD PAST ITS PRIME

Some of us grew up with bread that was suspiciously resistant to growing stale (thanks to the magic of artificial preservatives). But traditional bread—the sort of bread that loses its freshness in a day or two and grows stale quickly, made by dedicated bakers—has made a big comeback in the past several decades, now to the point that it can be found just about anywhere.

Stale bread gave our ancestors fits; they really couldn't afford to waste food, and anyway, it just seemed wrong. We are less frugal today, and often too quick to throw food into the trash, which is too bad—there is a rich legacy from the cooks of leaner times: bread pudding (page 126), French toast (page 285), croutons (page 233), bread soups and salads (panzanella, page 10), stuffings (page 125), even bread crumbs, all came from the need to be thrifty. In time these dishes and ingredients entered the home cook's canon; now I have to plan ahead to make something like a bread pudding, to be sure the bread will be stale enough.

Salvaging stale bread is just one way to use extra food. At least once a week, take stock of what is in the fridge, and if you have a child, do this together. "How can we use this?" is a great springboard to a creative discussion about what to cook and can be a lot of fun. Making a new dish is a positive way to use leftovers, much better than the dreary prospect of just reheating something that has lost its luster. The more experimentation and the fewer rules, the more ownership a child can feel toward cooking. Pasta, soup, and omelets are good opportunities for reusing leftovers and for teaching children frugality and respect for food.

2. Rosemary Focaccia

Focaccia is a simple, relatively flat Italian bread typical of Genoa and other parts of Liguria. It has become enormously popular in the United States as well, riding the wave of excellent bread made by skilled bakers to be found all over the country.

This recipe produces a simple, tasty focaccia, good with salad or soup, or to split and use for sandwiches; it is also excellent breakfast bread. I've given several variations below; these are particularly good as appetizers with a glass of wine.

Measuring, then sifting, then measuring again will teach children something about how air—and patience—play a part in cooking. MAKES ONE PAN OF FOCACCIA, SERVES 6 TO 8

1 package (¼ ounce) or
   1 scant tablespoon active
   dry yeast
1 teaspoon sugar
1 cup warm, not hot, water
   (about 110 degrees)
2⅔ cups all-purpose flour,
   plus more for kneading
½ teaspoon salt
5 tablespoons extra-virgin
   olive oil
1 tablespoon cornmeal or
   semolina
Leaves from 3 sprigs fresh
   rosemary
1 teaspoon sea salt

Mix together the yeast, sugar, and water in a small bowl and set it in a warm place for 10 minutes, or until foamy.

Put the flour and salt in a large mixing bowl. Make a well in the center and pour in the yeast mixture and 2 tablespoons of the olive oil. Using a wooden spoon, stir until well combined; the dough will be shaggy. Use your hands to bring the dough together in the bowl.

Turn the dough onto a lightly floured surface and knead it for 10 minutes, or until it is smooth and elastic; shape the dough into a ball. Lightly coat a large bowl with olive oil. Place the dough in the bowl and turn to coat in oil. Cover the bowl with plastic wrap or a damp, clean kitchen towel and set it in a warm, draft-free place until the dough is doubled in size, about 1 hour.

Lightly coat a 9-x-13-inch (or approximate) baking pan with olive oil and sprinkle the surface with the cornmeal. Punch the dough down with your fist, then turn it onto a lightly floured surface; knead until the dough is smooth and elastic, 2 to 3 minutes. With your fingers, press the dough into the prepared baking sheet and brush it with olive oil; set it aside to again double in size, about 30 minutes.

Preheat the oven to 400 degrees.

When the dough is ready, press dimples onto its surface with your fingertips. Poke little bunches of the rosemary leaves into the dough, spacing them evenly. Drizzle or brush the dough generously with the remaining olive oil and sprinkle it with the sea salt. Place the pan in a preheated oven for 20 minutes. Brush again with the olive oil and bake for an additional 5 minutes. Transfer the pan to a wire rack; serve the focaccia warm or at room temperature, sliced into squares or rectangles.

VARIATIONS

There are endless possibilities for delicious focaccia toppings. Here are a few of my favorites.

Tomato Focaccia   Omit the rosemary. Cut 6 ripe plum tomatoes into ¼-inch-thick slices and arrange them over the dough when it is ready to go into the oven; sprinkle with fresh oregano leaves from 6 sprigs. Drizzle with olive oil and sprinkle with sea salt and 1 teaspoon sugar. Bake as above, but for 10 to 15 minutes longer.

Cheese Focaccia   Omit the rosemary. When you shape the dough for rising, work ½ cup finely grated Parmigiano-Reggiano and ¼ cup finely chopped chives into the dough mixture. Continue as for rosemary focaccia.

Cheese and Bacon Focaccia   Add ¾ cup grated cheddar cheese and 2 or 3 strips finely chopped cooked bacon to the dough mixture. Finely slice 1 small onion and distribute the rings over the dough when it is ready for the oven. Continue as for rosemary focaccia.

Garlic Focaccia   Garlic can be combined with the rosemary, or the rosemary can be omitted. Thinly slice 6 large garlic cloves and distribute the slices over the surface of the dough. Continue as for rosemary focaccia.

Olive Focaccia   Omit the rosemary. Combine ½ cup pitted and sliced kalamata olives with the flour mixture. Continue as for rosemary focaccia.

Basil Focaccia   Omit the rosemary. Add ¼ cup loosely packed, finely shredded basil and ¼ teaspoon freshly ground pepper to the dough. Continue as for rosemary focaccia.

Focaccia Traditions

In his book on the cooking of Liguria, *Recipes from Paradise,* the Italian food authority Fred Plotkin writes about the annual Festa della Focaccia held in Recco, a town renowned for Liguria's traditional cooking, and for its foccacia in particular. In a given year, as many as fifteen thousand people may attend, and more than half a ton of flour may go into the various focacce produced. Among the events is a lesson in focaccia-making for the town's eighty or so nursery school children, led by its expert bakers. The idea behind all food festivals is to celebrate, and to connect a community to food as part of its identity. Another reason is to teach those specialties to the next generation in order to pass them along; the people of Recco are quite serious about preserving their focaccia.

3. Whole-Wheat Pizza

This dough is terrific, wholesome, useful, and endlessly variable. The recipe here is for the traditional Margherita pizza with tomato, basil, and mozzarella; if you must choose just one, this is it. Fortunately, life offers more choices, so a list of other toppings follows.

This recipe can also be made as a flatbread with simple toppings such as olive oil, garlic, and rosemary—nice to serve alongside a hearty soup for a satisfying family supper.

MAKES ONE 12-INCH PIZZA

2 tablespoons warm, not hot, water (about 110 degrees)

½ teaspoon active dry yeast

1⅓ cups all-purpose flour, plus more for rolling the dough

⅓ cup whole-wheat flour

½ cup cool water

1 teaspoon kosher salt

Olive oil

Cornmeal, for dusting

½ cup tomato sauce

4 ounces fresh mozzarella, shredded

Basil leaves, roughly chopped or julienned (optional)

Pour the warm water into a mixer; sprinkle in the yeast and let stand until the yeast dissolves, about 15 minutes (it will not be foamy at this stage).

Add the flours, cool water, and salt to the yeast mixture; mix on medium-low speed for 4 minutes. Let the dough rest for 5 minutes, then mix on medium speed until it is smooth, elastic, and just slightly sticky, about 3 minutes. If your mixer has a dough hook, you may use it at this stage.

Lightly coat a medium bowl with olive oil. Gather the dough into a ball, transfer it to the prepared bowl, and turn to coat it lightly all over. Cover the bowl with plastic wrap and let it sit in a warm, draft-free place until the dough is doubled in size, about 2 hours. (Alternatively, place the dough in the refrigerator overnight. Remove 2 hours before you're ready to make your pizza so the dough can rise.)

Preheat the oven to 450 degrees.

Sprinkle a baking sheet generously with cornmeal. Roll the dough out on a lightly floured surface to a 12-inch round; transfer the dough to the baking sheet.

Spread the sauce over the dough, sprinkle on the cheese and basil, if using, and drizzle with a bit of oil. Bake for 10 to 15 minutes, until the edges are puffed and brown, but not burned. Remove the pizza from the oven, cut into wedges, and serve at once.

The possibilities for topping pizza are limited only by your imagination. Greens, for instance, are good with sausage or ricotta; prosciutto with fresh ricotta; fontina with tomatoes. Here are a few suggestions.

A handful or two of chopped, cooked (blanched) greens,
    such as spinach, chard, or escarole
Cooked Italian sausage, chopped or thinly sliced
Pancetta, thinly sliced or minced
Prosciutto
Fresh ricotta or ricotta salata
Fontina
Anchovies
Chopped or sliced fresh tomatoes, or cherry tomatoes
Caramelized onions
Grilled or broiled eggplant slices, tomato sauce, ricotta salata

PANCETTA

Pancetta is an Italian bacon that, like the bacon you know, also comes from the belly of the pig, the *pancia,* but is mildly seasoned, salt-cured, and air-dried, not smoked, which results in a different flavor and texture. Pancetta has become quite widely available, even in supermarkets.

4. Chapatis

These are the Indian flatbreads also known as roti, and we make them with the children at the Sylvia Center. These tasty breads are quick—the dough is unleavened but does need to rest—and simple and fun to make. And short of the in-and-out-of-the-oven part, there is nothing even a quite small child can't do. We serve chapatis with Hummus (page 308), but they can be used like wraps, with just about any filling.

Like cookies, these chapatis can be done in batches; they cook so quickly that one batch can be baking while the next is being rolled out. Let the kids roll the balls as evenly as possible—they needn't be perfect—and press them into circles. The challenge will delight them and make them appreciate your cooking for them all the more.   MAKES 16 PIECES

3 cups all-purpose flour, plus more for kneading the dough

1 cup whole-wheat flour

1 teaspoon salt

2 tablespoons butter, melted and cooled, or ¼ cup olive oil

1½ cups warm water

Preheat the oven to 450 degrees.

Mix the flours and salt together in a bowl. Stir in the melted butter.

Add the water gradually, stirring, until a soft dough is formed. Knead the dough on a lightly floured work surface for about 5 minutes. Shape the dough into a ball, return it to the mixing bowl, and cover it with a clean cloth. Let the dough rest for at least 20 minutes but not longer than 2 hours.

Divide the dough evenly into 16 pieces and shape each into a ball. Lightly flour your work surface. Use a rolling pin to roll each ball of dough into a circle about 4 inches in diameter; they do not need to be perfect rounds. Prick the chapatis all over with a fork.

Arrange the chapatis on baking sheets—as many as they will hold—and bake until browned, about 7 minutes. Remove the chapatis from the sheet and let them cool on wire racks.

5. Carrot Bread

This quick bread is good for breakfast, in a lunch box, or after school. It is sweet enough for a child's palate but also packed with nutrition from the carrots and whole-wheat flour. It is a favorite with the Sylvia Center kids, who love to grate the carrots, zest the oranges, and beat the eggs.

For people who don't like nuts or are allergic to them, the pecans can be omitted and the results will still be excellent.   MAKES ONE 9-INCH LOAF

Canola, peanut, or corn oil,
   for the pan
1⅓ cups all-purpose flour,
   plus more for the pan
1½ cups shredded carrots
1 cup boiling water
1 cup firmly packed light
   brown sugar
¼ cup plus 1 tablespoon
   vegetable oil
1 teaspoon grated orange zest
1 cup whole-wheat flour
2½ teaspoons baking powder
1 teaspoon baking soda
½ teaspoon salt
½ teaspoon cinnamon
2 large eggs, lightly beaten
½ teaspoon pure vanilla
   extract
½ cup chopped, toasted
   pecans or walnuts
   (optional)

Preheat the oven to 350 degrees. Coat a 9-×-5-inch metal loaf pan with the canola oil and dust it with flour.

Place the carrots in a bowl and pour in the boiling water; add the brown sugar, vegetable oil, and orange zest. Let the mixture cool for about 10 minutes.

Stir the flours, baking powder, baking soda, salt, and cinnamon together in a large mixing bowl; make a well in the center. Stir the eggs and vanilla into the carrots, then pour the mixture into the well of the dry ingredients. Add the pecans, if using, then stir with a wooden spoon until well combined—do not use an electric mixer.

Pour the batter into the prepared pan and bake on the center rack of the oven for 1 hour, or until a cake tester comes out clean and the sides have begun to come away from the pan. Place the pan on a wire rack to cool, then turn the bread out and cut it into 2-inch squares.

6. Buttermilk Biscuits

You might agree that buttermilk makes the best biscuits, flaky and just a little tangy. I make these little ones to serve with soups or salads; at Great Performances, we use them for dainty ham or roast beef sandwiches, shortcakes, and breakfast biscuits, cut in three-inch rounds.

Biscuits are good for a first baking lesson. A three-year-old can easily stir the dry ingredients, and little fingers are ideal for pinching fat into flour and even for folding the dough. With a bit of help with pouring the buttermilk and cutting the biscuits—do this together—a child can just about manage the entire process. The sense of pride he will feel when he carries the biscuits to the table will more than make up for a messy floor and counter.

MAKES 10 TO 12 MINIATURE (2-INCH) BISCUITS OR EIGHT 3-INCH BISCUITS

2 cups all-purpose flour, plus more for folding the dough
1 tablespoon plus 1 teaspoon baking powder
¼ teaspoon baking soda
¾ teaspoon salt
2 tablespoons cold butter
2 tablespoons cold vegetable shortening
1 cup chilled buttermilk

Preheat the oven to 450 degrees.

Combine the flour, baking powder, baking soda, and salt in a large mixing bowl. Using your fingertips, rub the butter and shortening into the dry ingredients until the dough looks like crumbs. Work quickly to prevent the fats from softening into the dry ingredients. Make a well in the center of the dough and pour in the buttermilk. Stir with a fork just until the dough comes together; it will be very sticky.

Turn the dough onto a floured work surface, dust the top with flour, and gently fold the dough over on itself 5 or 6 times. Press it into a 1-inch-thick round. Using a 2-inch cutter, cut out the biscuits, taking care to push straight down through the dough. Re-form the remaining scraps of dough, working it as little as possible, and continue cutting out biscuits.

Place the biscuits on an ungreased baking sheet with their sides just touching. Bake until the biscuits have risen and their tops are light gold in color, 15 to 20 minutes.

I was amused by the remark that came along with this recipe from Marc Spooner, a former chef at Great Performances and *Chopped* champion: "Biscuits from the second pass will not be quite as light as those from the first, but hey, that's life." And that's cooking—it should be one thing we approach in the day without anxiety.

7. Peanut Butter and Jelly Power Muffins

This recipe comes from Ann Cooper and Lisa Holmes. Ann and Lisa are parents, authors, and educators who have focused their work on issues relating to children and their food—obesity, nutrition, and wholesomeness. Perhaps above all their concern has been the development of positive attitudes about good food. Their books have been useful references in our work at the Sylvia Center. I met Ann when the center was barely two years old; she's generously shared recipes, knowledge, and support.

PB & J is a favorite for just about any kid, not to mention more than a few of us elders. These muffins are nutritious, delivering a healthy balance of carbohydrates, protein, and fiber—and no cholesterol.   MAKES 28 MINI MUFFINS

¼ cup canola oil, plus more for the pan

1 cup whole-wheat flour

1½ teaspoons baking powder

1 teaspoon baking soda

½ teaspoon kosher salt

½ cup maple sugar (or brown, demerara, or turbinado sugar)

1 teaspoon cinnamon

6 tablespoons rolled oats

3 tablespoons raisins

¼ cup chopped raw peanuts

½ cup soy milk or regular milk

6 tablespoons pure maple syrup

1 teaspoon pure vanilla extract

½ cup natural peanut butter

1 tablespoon cider vinegar

2 medium ripe bananas, mashed

6 to 8 tablespoons strawberry jam

Preheat the oven to 350 degrees. Coat a mini-muffin pan with canola oil.

Sift the flour, baking powder, baking soda, salt, maple sugar, and cinnamon together into a large mixing bowl. Add the oats, raisins, and ⅛ cup of the peanuts.

Combine the soy milk, oil, maple syrup, vanilla, peanut butter, vinegar, and bananas and mash to blend well. Pour the wet mixture into the dry ingredients; stir just to combine, taking care not to over-mix.

Fill each muffin cup two-thirds full with batter and top with a dollop of the jam. Sprinkle the remaining peanuts over the muffins and bake for about 20 minutes, or until a cake tester or toothpick comes out clean.

Take care not to overfill the muffin cups or the jam will seep out and make them sticky, which in turn will make it difficult to remove the muffins.

These can be made ahead and frozen for about 2 weeks. Once defrosted, keep them at room temperature in an airtight container for several days of lunch-box treats or after-school snacks. This recipe yields a few more muffins than the 24 of a standard mini-muffin pan. You can make a second small batch with the extra batter.

PEANUTS

The most ubiquitous nut of all in this country is the peanut, which, strictly speaking, is a legume, the groundnut. For those who are not allergic to it, peanut butter is a good conveyer of vitamin E, magnesium, and other nutrients, along with monounsaturated fats, the good fats that help lower body cholesterol.

If you can erase from your mind visions of Elvis eating way too many peanut butter and banana sandwiches, they make a good lunch or snack for children. Make the sandwiches with whole-grain bread and avoid peanut butter brands that contain hydrogenated oils, salt, and sugar; those oils are added simply to keep the peanut oil from separating. When the oil in natural peanut butter does exude, simply stir it back into the butter and then store the jar in the refrigerator to prevent further separating. Besides health food and specialty stores, many supermarkets now carry unadulterated peanut butter.

Desserts

The payoff of baking is clear even to a two-year-old: make a cookie, eat a cookie. My collection of cookie cutters, from dinosaurs to rabbits and hearts to stars, numbers in the dozens and represents more batches of cookies than could be counted.

Just like those who wish that sweets were the first course of the meal instead of the grand finale, I believe dessert is the perfect starting place to introduce children to the magic of seasonal produce and how it can be transformed from fruit (an apple) to dessert (apple pie). Here I think like a typical farmer: the dessert course, like all others, is best built around whatever is seasonal and near at hand. That means an abundance of possibilities from early spring to late fall—from strawberries, rhubarb, peaches, and blueberries to apples and pears. I like simple dishes like cobblers and pies that emphasize rather than camouflage the fruit within. Cooking in season summons memories of my own childhood when peaches meant summer and apples meant fall—time to go back to school, and the Jewish New Year, when we dip apples in honey. In those days, berry season meant charging into the local orchards and picking my own fruit: one in the bucket, one in my mouth! We had a few short weeks of cherries. For rhubarb lovers, the three to four late spring weeks of those blessed stalks were heavenly, especially when they overlapped with strawberries.

When the warm weather and most fruit disappear, I still make mostly homey things like cakes and cookies. Chocolate, which rarely enters my mind in warm weather, returns to the repertoire.

This collection includes recipes from my family and some dear friends. I chose them with a busy home cook like myself in mind, one who always has the basics on hand—flour, baking powder, butter—and decent equipment. I am ready at a moment's notice when the peaches are irresistible or when a gang of teenagers in need of brownies suddenly shows up.

Of all the smells we remember, nothing is as powerful as the aroma of dessert. It seems to shout "I love you" to anyone who takes a bite.

1. Apple-Cranberry Pie

Throughout the year, I prefer fruit for dessert above anything, alone or in baked goods. So pies have become another way that we mark the changing seasons, sort of the way we move, almost without noticing, from grilling food to roasting or braising. Pies and tarts move along on a similar schedule—strawberries and raspberries to peaches and plums and then, suddenly, the first apples appear, and pie is right behind.   MAKES ONE 9-INCH PIE, SERVES 8

2 cups plus 3 tablespoons
   all-purpose flour, plus more
   for rolling the dough

1 teaspoon salt

1 heaping teaspoon light
   brown sugar

16 tablespoons (2 sticks)
   unsalted butter, very cold,
   cut into ½-inch cubes

3 to 6 tablespoons ice water

1 cup dried cranberries

⅔ cup granulated sugar

¼ teaspoon cinnamon

6 to 8 Pippin or Golden
   Delicious apples (2¼
   pounds), peeled, cored, and
   cut into ¼-inch-thick slices

1½ tablespoons brandy

1 teaspoon pure vanilla
   extract

1 large egg yolk

1 tablespoon heavy cream

For the crust, put 2 cups of the flour, the salt, and brown sugar into a food processor and pulse quickly to combine. Add the butter and pulse 6 to 8 times, until the mixture resembles coarse meal, with some pea-size pieces of butter still intact; do not overprocess. Add the water, one tablespoon at a time, pulsing just until the dough holds together; if you pinch some of the crumbly dough and it holds together, it is ready.

Remove the dough from the machine and place it on a clean, lightly floured surface. Carefully shape the dough into two thick disks, taking care not to overwork it—you should still see little bits of butter; this is the secret to flaky pastry. Wrap each disk in plastic wrap and place it in the refrigerator for at least 1 hour.

Position a rack in the bottom third of the oven and preheat the oven to 350 degrees.

Combine the cranberries, granulated sugar, the remaining 3 tablespoons flour, and the cinnamon in a large bowl. Carefully fold in the apples, then add the brandy and vanilla.

Remove one disk of pastry from the refrigerator and let it sit at room temperature for 5 to 10 minutes. Dust the dough with flour. Starting from the center, roll the dough out with a rolling pin, dusting it and the rolling pin lightly to prevent sticking, into a circle 12 inches in diameter and about ⅛ inch thick. As you roll, check to see if the dough is sticking by lifting it with a spatula; if it is, toss a few sprinkles of flour onto your work surface.

Gently fold the pastry in half and center it in a 9-inch pie pan. Unfold the dough and, without stretching it, gently press it down to line the pan, leaving the excess hanging over the edge.

Spoon the apple-cranberry filling onto the dough, mounding it slightly at the center.

Roll and fold the second disk of dough and gently turn it over the apples. Pinch the top and bottom crusts firmly together. Trim the excess dough with kitchen shears, leaving about ¾ inch. Fold the overhang of dough under itself to be flush with the edge of the pan. Crimp the edge of the dough, using your thumb and forefinger, or press it with a fork.

Stir the egg yolk and cream together in a small bowl. Brush this egg wash over the pie. Using a sharp knife or kitchen shears, cut 6 or 8 slits in the top crust to allow steam to escape. Place the pie in the oven and bake until the apples are tender—you can poke through with a cake tester—and the crust is golden, 50 minutes to 1 hour or so, depending on the type of apples used. Transfer the pie to a rack and let it stand for at least 1 hour; serve the pie warm or at room temperature.

2. Apple Crostata

The old-fashioned way of making dough for crostatas and other pastries is by placing the dry ingredients on a work surface, forming a well in the center, then working the butter and ice water (and sometimes eggs) in by hand until a smooth dough is formed. Pizza and pasta doughs also are made this way. It can be instructive for all concerned to get the feel of the dough as you go, and fun for kids to get their little fingers into the process; it may surprise you how focused and adept they can be. They may at some later point move on to faster and more efficient methods, but they will have developed a keen sense of how a good dough should look and feel.

The Cheddar cheese Americanizes this for me. In fact, it localizes it—our Hudson Valley apples are superb, and the region's cheese makers supply excellent Cheddars; do the same wherever you live—look for local Cheddars, and help support the great resurgence in American cheese making. MAKES ONE 9-INCH CROSTATA, SERVES 8

1¼ cups all-purpose flour, plus more for rolling the dough

¼ cup plus 2 tablespoons granulated or superfine sugar

½ teaspoon salt

12 tablespoons (1½ sticks) very cold butter, cubed

2 tablespoons ice water

3 large McIntosh or Golden Delicious apples (1½ pounds)

¼ teaspoon grated orange zest

¼ teaspoon cinnamon

1 cup (8 ounces) grated medium-sharp white Cheddar

For the pastry, place 1 cup of the flour, 2 tablespoons of the sugar, and ¼ teaspoon of the salt in a food processor. Pulse a few times to combine. Add 8 tablespoons of the butter and pulse 6 to 8 times, or just until the butter is the size of peas. With the motor running, add the ice water all at once through the feed tube. Continue pulsing to combine, but stop the machine just before the dough becomes a solid mass.

Turn the dough onto a well-floured work surface and form it into a thick disk. Wrap with plastic and refrigerate for at least 1 hour.

Preheat the oven to 450 degrees.

Peel, core, and cut each apple into 8 wedges. Cut each wedge crosswise into 3 chunks, place them in a bowl, and toss them with the orange zest. Set the apples aside.

Combine the remaining ¼ cup flour, ¼ cup sugar, ¼ teaspoon salt, 4 tablespoons butter, and the cinnamon in a food processor and pulse just until the mixture is crumbly. Pour the mixture into a bowl and, with your fingers, continue to work it into a crumbly mass, but do not overwork it.

Dust a rolling pin and a clean work surface lightly with flour and roll the pastry into a circle 11 inches in diameter and about ¼-inch thick. Transfer the dough to a baking sheet. Spoon the apples over the dough, leaving a ½-inch border.

Sprinkle the crumb mixture evenly over the apples. Distribute the Cheddar over the crumbs. Gently fold the border of dough over the apples, pleating as you go around; the crostata will now be around 9 inches in diameter.

Bake the crostata for 20 to 25 minutes, until the crust is golden and the apples are tender. Serve warm or at room temperature.

The Language of Cooking: *Crostata*

Crostata is simply the Italian word for pie, typically made with jam or marmalade, pastry cream, and fresh fruit or ricotta. When today's American professional or home bakers use the word "crostata" they usually mean a free-form, rather rustic sort of pie, similar to the Italian crostata or a French galette, which is pretty much the same thing.

Crostatas may be baked on a sheet like the one here, or in a tart or pie pan; they are appealingly homey and not necessarily perfectly round, with edges of dough folded or pleated over uncomplicated fillings. Crostatas or galettes are fun to make and by their nature, less intimidating—no one expects them to be perfect. It's part of their charm.

3. Lime-Honey Polenta Cake

Chefs often refer to flavored syrups as honey—they aren't truly honey but do add flavored sweetness. Here, the flavor is lime, which is deliciously compatible with cornmeal and almonds. MAKES ONE 9-INCH CAKE, SERVES 6 TO 8

FOR THE CAKE

1 teaspoon butter, melted and cooled, or vegetable oil

Zest and juice of 2 limes

18 tablespoons (2¼ sticks) unsalted butter, at room temperature

1½ cups sugar

3 eggs

1¼ cups ground toasted almonds, from about 4½ ounces blanched whole almonds

1 cup polenta or fine yellow cornmeal

¼ cup self-rising cake flour

1 teaspoon baking powder

Pinch of salt

FOR THE LIME-HONEY SYRUP

1 lime

1 cup sugar

½ cup honey

⅓ cup water

Vanilla ice cream or softly whipped cream, for serving

Preheat the oven to 350 degrees.

Brush a deep 9-inch round cake pan with the melted butter and line the bottom with a round of parchment paper or wax paper.

Beat the butter and sugar in the bowl of an electric mixer on medium-high speed until light and creamy. Add half the lime zest to the butter mixture and beat until thoroughly combined. Add the eggs, one at a time, beating well after each addition; the mixture will look quite curdled. Add 1 teaspoon of the lime juice, the almonds, polenta, flour, baking powder, and salt; mix on medium speed until the batter is smooth.

Spoon the batter into the prepared cake pan and smooth the surface. Place the pan in the oven and bake for 40 minutes, or until a cake tester or toothpick comes out clean.

Set the pan on a wire rack.

While the cake is baking, make the syrup. Combine the remaining lime zest and ⅓ juice with the sugar, honey, and water in a small saucepan.

Place the pan over low heat and stir, without letting it boil, until the sugar is completely dissolved. Raise the heat and continue to cook until the mixture comes just to a low boil; reduce the heat and simmer for 12 to 15 minutes, or until slightly thickened and syrupy. Strain the syrup.

Pour the hot syrup over the cake after taking it from the oven; let cool for 30 minutes before unmolding.

Cut the cake into wedges and serve warm with ice cream or softly whipped cream. This cake keeps for up to 3 days in an airtight container and can be gently warmed in a microwave oven.

4. Olive Oil and Thyme Peach Cake

Does it surprise you to see olive oil as an ingredient in a dessert? Lately, we're seeing olive oil in sweet dishes more and more, even in ice cream, which is delicious. I think it's a good thing to use this healthful ingredient as much as possible and it does make sense—the olive, after all, is a fruit.

This is a light cake with subtle, intriguing flavors, layered with whipped cream and dusted with powdered sugar and served with sliced fresh peaches to the side. This cake is especially nice still warm from the oven. MAKES ONE 8-INCH THREE-LAYER CAKE, 8 SERVINGS

1½ cups olive oil, plus more
   for greasing the pans
2 medium ripe peaches,
   peeled (see Note)
1 tablespoon cinnamon
1 tablespoon fresh lemon
   juice
¼ cup granulated sugar
1 tablespoon butter
¼ cup chopped thyme
2½ cups light brown sugar
4 eggs
3½ cups all-purpose flour
1½ teaspoons baking soda
½ teaspoon salt
1 pint heavy cream, whipped,
   for serving
Confectioners' sugar, for
   serving
3 or 4 fresh ripe peaches,
   sliced, for serving

Preheat the oven to 300 degrees.

Grease three 8-inch cake pans with olive oil.

Pit the peaches and cut them into small dice. Combine the peaches in a bowl with the cinnamon, lemon juice, and granulated sugar. Melt the butter in a medium skillet or saucepan over medium heat. Add the peaches and sauté to brown lightly, 6 to 7 minutes. Let the peaches cool to room temperature, about 15 minutes, and stir in the thyme.

Place the 1½ cups oil and brown sugar in the bowl of an electric mixer and mix at high speed until smooth and creamy. Add the eggs, one at a time, and mix for 5 minutes to incorporate well. On low speed, blend in the flour, baking soda, and salt. Add the peach mixture and mix for 3 minutes.

Pour the batter into the prepared pans, and bake for 30 to 45 minutes, or until a cake tester comes out clean and the cake is firm and springy to the touch. Take care not to overbake the layers; they should be only lightly browned.

Let the cakes cool to room temperature in the pans, about 1 hour, and then turn them out onto racks. Layer the cakes with the cream and dust the top with confectioners' sugar. Serve with sliced peaches on the side. The cake can be kept, well wrapped, at room temperature, for a day or two.

To peel the skins off peaches, bring a pot of water to a boil. Score the peaches at the smooth end and dunk them into the boiling water for about 10 seconds, then immediately drop the peaches into a bowl of ice water. This is where the kids come in. Once the peaches are cool enough to handle, let them slip the skins off. This is easy and lots of fun.

5. Carrot-Ginger Squares

This is my version of one of America's favorite desserts. I make it as squares rather than as a layer cake, but you could pour the batter into two 8- or 9-inch cake pans if you prefer, and the amount of frosting will definitely be enough. The affinity of carrots and ginger is well established, especially in soups; I've gone for a double threat, with fresh ginger in the batter and candied ginger jazzing up the frosting.

I've been told these are irresistible. MAKES 12 SQUARES

FOR THE SQUARES

Butter, for greasing the pan

1¾ cups all-purpose flour, plus more for the pan

1 cup sugar

1 teaspoon cinnamon

½ teaspoon allspice

½ teaspoon ground cloves

½ teaspoon freshly grated nutmeg

1 teaspoon baking powder

1½ teaspoons baking soda

3 eggs, lightly beaten

⅔ cup vegetable oil

1 cup shredded carrots (about 4 medium, page 360)

1½ tablespoons peeled grated fresh ginger

½ teaspoon salt

2 tablespoons Myers's rum or 1 teaspoon pure vanilla extract

2 tablespoons butter, melted and cooled

Preheat the oven to 350 degrees. Grease and flour a 9-x-13-inch cake pan and tap out the excess flour.

Mix the flour, sugar, cinnamon, allspice, cloves, nutmeg, baking powder, and baking soda together in a large bowl. Add the remaining ingredients and stir to combine well, but do not overmix.

Pour the batter into the prepared cake pan, place it in the oven, and bake until a cake tester or toothpick inserted in the center is nearly clean when removed, about 25 minutes. Carrot cakes should be a bit moist, so take care not to overbake. Allow the cake to cool in the pan, then turn it out and frost it.

Make the frosting: Beat the cream cheese, butter, and vanilla together in the bowl of an electric mixer on high speed. Lower the speed to medium and gradually beat in the confectioners' sugar; add more or less, depending on the consistency you like.

Spread the frosting over the cooled cake, let it set for 5 minutes, then cut it into 12 squares and garnish with the candied ginger, if using.

12 ounces cream cheese, at
    room temperature
2 tablespoons butter, at room
    temperature
1 tablespoon pure vanilla
    extract
About 3 cups confectioners'
    sugar
Minced candied ginger
    (optional)

CARROTS

Much to my delight more varieties of carrots can now be found in our markets. There are some newly developed varieties, along with heirlooms coming back into cultivation. Some small ones are often referred to as babies, though in fact they are mature but small, with thin skins that need only to be scrubbed. Short 'n Sweet and Baby Spike are slim, while the round little Thumbelina is as cute as it sounds; the elegant Cosmic Purple has an orange core. However, I am not enthusiastic about the chunky small carrots that come in plastic bags and are ubiquitous in supermarkets; they are carved down from ordinary large carrots and are curiously lacking in flavor.

Carrots are a good family garden crop, easy and rewarding, and even a very young farmer can know the thrill of pulling them out of the earth. However you get them, carrots have lots of vitamin A, more than almost any other food. Vitamin A is good for your heart and your lungs, and especially good for your eyes. Yes, your mother was right, carrots can actually help you see better—even at night.

6. Chocolate Chip Brownies

I believe in using the best ingredients I can find. Sometimes this means shopping at a farm stand and getting great value, like a box of peach seconds—excellent for pies and jams. Other times, it means paying a bit more. The difference between ordinary and superior chocolate is unmistakable and will show in desserts like this one. So spring for the best chocolate you can afford.

You may have a dozen brownie recipes at your fingertips, especially if your fingertips are near your computer, but I urge you to try this one. I worked hard to develop a brownie that would appeal to grown-ups as much as children and meet my criteria: deep, not overly sweet, chocolate flavor and fudgy texture.

This recipe provides a simple but important baking lesson that children might remember always, especially since it involves brownies. It is important to keep checking for doneness and not simply go by the clock: the difference between delicious brownies with just the right amount of gooeyness and not-so-wonderful dry ones is only a few minutes. The telltale change in the surface of the brownies will interest them, along with knowing that the brownies will retain internal heat and continue to cook as they cool.   MAKES TWELVE $1\frac{1}{2}$-INCH BROWNIES

Cooking oil spray or a neutral cooking oil like canola

26 tablespoons ($3\frac{1}{4}$ sticks) unsalted butter

12 ounces best-quality semisweet chocolate, coarsely chopped

4 ounces best-quality unsweetened chocolate, coarsely chopped

6 eggs

2 cups superfine sugar

1 tablespoon pure vanilla extract

Preheat the oven to 350 degrees. Lightly grease the sides and bottom of an 11-x-9-x-2-inch baking pan with the spray or oil, then line it with parchment paper.

Place the butter, semisweet chocolate, and unsweetened chocolate in a stainless steel or heat-resistant bowl over a saucepan of simmering water; the water should not touch the underside of the bowl. Melt the butter and chocolate, stirring from time to time, then remove the bowl and set it aside; let the mixture cool a bit.

In another bowl, beat the eggs together with the sugar and vanilla. This can be done by hand or in the bowl of an electric mixer fitted with the paddle attachment.

Pour the chocolate mixture into the egg mixture and beat well. Fold in the flour and salt, then stir in $\frac{1}{2}$ cup of the semisweet chocolate

1½ cups plus 2 tablespoons
all-purpose flour
1 teaspoon salt
1 cup best-quality semisweet
chocolate chips
About 2 teaspoons
confectioners' sugar

chips. Beat to combine well, scraping the sides. Pour the batter into the prepared pan, then sprinkle the remaining ½ cup chips on top.

Place the pan in the oven and bake for about 25 minutes. The brownies are ready when the top looks dry and crackly and has taken on a slightly paler color while the middle remains dark, dense, and gooey. Start checking after 20 minutes.

Cut into 12 squares while still warm, pile up on a large platter, and dust with confectioners' sugar, through a small sieve if the sugar is at all lumpy.

Lightly spray baking sheets or cake pans with cooking spray before you put on parchment paper—it will stay in place better.

A Short Guide to Cobblers, Crisps, Slumps, and Grunts

Many of these desserts are improvisations on English classics like steamed pudding and pie, modified for New World ingredients. They go by various down-to-earth, homey names but have a common theme: fruit and dough. And they can get us through a year of harvests, from peaches and blueberries to pears and cranberries.

A COBBLER is almost always simply sweetened fruit topped by a single layer of biscuit dough, cut into circles or squares (cobbles!) or dropped on more or less haphazardly. Less commonly, cobblers are made with pie dough, or even with a cakelike batter. But for me, a cobbler is defined by a biscuit top.

CRUMBLES AND CRISPS are nearly interchangeable; "crumble" may be the English name for the same dish. A crumbly mixture covers the fruit. Some recipes for crumbles include oats, while the ones for crisps tend to be simpler combinations of butter, flour, sometimes nuts, and even cookie crumbs.

GRUNTS AND SLUMPS are interchangeable and come from wherever in New England they happen to be. Slumps and grunts were New World attempts to replicate English steamed puddings. Their construction is more or less the same as for cobblers—fruit and biscuit dough—but they are cooked on top of the stove, covered, which results in a soft, dumpling-like, unbrowned top. Grunts supposedly got their name from the sound of the fruit cooking, but where the name "slump" comes from seems to be a mystery.

BROWN BETTY is another simple dessert, a Colonial American interpretation of similar English puddings. A Betty is usually made with apples, but other fruits are possible, and again, we see evidence of thrifty cooks—buttered crumbs, no doubt from day-old bread, are layered with the fruit. As a Betty bakes, the crumbs absorb fruit juices and thicken the pudding.

According to Richard Sax in his wonderful book *Classic Home Desserts,* the crust of a PANDOWDY was partially cooked, then cut into squares—"dowdied"—and pushed back down into the fruit to continue baking. Other descriptions refer to pandowdy as a kind of broken-up pie. The word "dowdy," in this context, is not clear, but if it started off as a not-quite-presentable pie, could it have come from the usual meaning, frumpy or shabby? And might it have been born by accident by a clumsy cook who made a mess of her pie? A traditional pandowdy is sweetened by maple syrup or molasses, making it a genuine American original.

7. Blueberry Cobbler

I doubt I'm the only American who, if pressed, would name cobbler as the one summer dessert she must have. (I've hedged here; where I live, strawberries, which lead to shortcake, appear in spring.) "Blueberry" would follow "cobbler" as night the day.   SERVES 4 TO 6

8 tablespoons (1 stick) cold
   unsalted butter, cut into
   cubes, plus more for
   greasing the pan
3 tablespoons cornstarch
½ cup sugar
6 cups blueberries, washed
   and picked over
2 tablespoons fresh lemon
   juice
½ cup packed light brown
   sugar
1½ cups all-purpose flour
1½ teaspoons double-acting
   baking powder
¾ teaspoon salt
1 teaspoon cinnamon
Vanilla ice cream or whipped
   cream, for serving

Preheat the oven to 350 degrees. Butter a 10-inch, deep-dish pie plate, 10-inch square baking dish, or a similarly proportioned oval oven-proof dish.

Sift the cornstarch and granulated sugar together into a large bowl. Add the blueberries and lemon juice and toss to combine them well, then transfer the berries to the prepared dish.

If the brown sugar is lumpy, push it through a sieve, then combine it with the flour, baking powder, salt, and cinnamon; add the butter, and blend the mixture with your fingers—my preferred method—or a fork until it resembles coarse meal.

Bring ¼ cup plus 2 tablespoons water to a boil; stir the water into the flour mixture just until it forms a dough. Drop the dough by about ¼ cupfuls all over the blueberry mixture. Place the dish on a baking sheet to catch any juices that run over, then put it on the middle rack of the oven; bake the cobbler for 30 to 40 minutes, or until the top is golden brown and the juices are bubbling.

Serve the cobbler warm or at room temperature with ice cream or whipped cream.

BLUEBERRIES

Blueberries are easy to grow, and great for a home garden. There are quite a few more varieties available than the familiar commercial ones, and they don't all ripen at the same time during the season, so you can select according to your needs. You may want to stagger your crops from early to late season to have the right size berries for different purposes: large for eating fresh, small for jam or baking. Choose a minimum of two plants per variety if you want to be a self-sustaining blueberry consumer.

8. Caramelized Peach and Ginger Crisp

I think of peaches and ginger just about as easily as peaches and cream. Peaches came to us from China, where ginger is a staple ingredient. Might this be one of the endless examples of things that grow together having a natural affinity for one another? SERVES 8 TO 10

8 tablespoons (1 stick) butter, at room temperature, cut into cubes, plus more for greasing the pan

½ cup sugar

3 tablespoons cold water

12 peaches, peeled (see page 357), cored, and quartered

⅛ cup thinly sliced candied ginger

1 cup all-purpose flour

⅔ cup packed brown sugar or maple sugar

1 teaspoon cinnamon

½ cup rolled oats

Preheat the oven to 375 degrees. Lightly butter an 8-inch square baking dish.

Put the sugar in a large, deep, nonstick skillet over medium high heat and stir in the water. Cook, stirring, until the sugar is dissolved. Stop stirring and leave the mixture on the heat until it turns a golden caramel color, 5 to 10 minutes. Lower the heat if necessary; do not let the mixture burn.

Toss the peaches and ginger into the skillet, stir to coat with the caramel, and heat gently for 3 minutes. Turn the fruit and juices into the prepared baking dish.

Combine the flour, brown sugar, and cinnamon in a large bowl. Cut in the butter to make a crumbly mass, then stir in the rolled oats. Sprinkle the topping evenly over the fruit.

Place the dish in the oven and bake until the fruit is very tender and bubbly and the top is golden brown, 35 to 45 minutes.

9. Apple Crisp

My friend Alex Guarnaschelli gave me this recipe. She's an accomplished cook but takes no credit for this crisp—it's the one she grew up with, and, presumably, the one her own daughter will be raised on as well. Alex is a true and indiscriminate lover of apples; for this recipe, she chooses good old reliable tart Granny Smiths.   SERVES 6 TO 8

8 tablespoons (1 stick) unsalted butter, cut into cubes, plus more for greasing the pan

About 8 (3 pounds) Granny Smith apples

2 lemons

1 orange

1 tablespoon molasses

¾ teaspoon kosher salt

1 cup light brown sugar

¾ cup all-purpose flour

½ teaspoon cinnamon

½ teaspoon ground ginger

⅛ teaspoon freshly grated nutmeg

Grease the bottom and sides of a 13-x-9-x-2-inch or similarly proportioned baking dish with butter.

Preheat the oven to 375 degrees.

Peel, core, and halve the apples, then cut each half into thin slices and put them in a large bowl. Zest the lemons and juice one; reserve the zest of the second lemon. Zest and juice the orange. Toss the apples with the lemon juice, orange juice, the zest of 1 lemon, orange zest, the molasses, ¼ teaspoon of the salt, and the brown sugar.

In another bowl, combine the flour, the remaining ½ teaspoon salt, the cinnamon, ginger, and nutmeg. Add the butter to the bowl; using your fingers, work the butter into the flour mixture until large clumps are formed.

Layer the apples and any juices in the dish and top evenly with the flour mixture. Place the dish on the middle rack of the oven and bake until the apples are tender when pierced with the tip of a knife and the top is golden brown, 35 to 45 minutes.

Set aside to cool a few minutes before serving. Sprinkle with the reserved lemon zest if desired.

Fun Chores

Buy an apple peeler, the kind you clamp down to a table top. Between that and a 6-sectioned apple slicer, your young assistants will have hours of fun. Kids invariably love apple "machines" and I guarantee you will too!

10. Strawberry Shortcakes

Claudia Fleming is a brilliant baker and the proprietor of the North Fork Table and Inn, nearly at the end of Long Island. The area reminds me of where we are in the Hudson Valley; Claudia is surrounded by luscious farmland, small growers, poultry farms, cheese makers, and wine makers, all suppliers to her restaurant and inn.

Claudia has come up with an ingenious variation on biscuits—she makes her dough with hard-boiled egg yolks, with rich and tender results. I urge you to try them, even if shortcake is not on the menu—they may very well become your house biscuit. But don't miss the moment to celebrate the short season for local strawberries, and get the best cream you can find to go with them. SERVES 6

FOR THE BISCUITS

1⅔ cups all-purpose flour, plus more for kneading the dough

3½ tablespoons sugar, plus more for sprinkling

1 tablespoon plus ½ teaspoon baking powder

2 hard-boiled egg yolks

⅛ teaspoon salt

6 tablespoons cold unsalted butter, cut into cubes

2 teaspoons grated lemon or orange zest (optional)

⅔ cup plus 1 tablespoon heavy cream

Mint leaves, for serving (optional)

To make the biscuits, combine the flour, 3 tablespoons sugar, the baking powder, egg yolks, and salt in a food processor. Pulse to combine. Add the butter and zest, if using, and pulse until the mixture resembles coarse meal. Add ⅔ cup of the cream and pulse just until the dough comes together.

Turn the dough out onto a lightly floured work surface and gather it into a shaggy mass. Knead it a few times, until it becomes a cohesive mass, and then pat it into a rough circle 6 to 7 inches in diameter and ¾ to 1 inch thick. Do not overwork the dough.

Using a sharp knife, cut the circle into 6 wedges and arrange them on a parchment-lined baking sheet. Alternatively, you can cut rounds or other shapes with a biscuit or cookie cutter. Chill the dough pieces for at least 20 minutes (or up to 2 hours).

Preheat the oven to 350 degrees.

Brush the tops of the biscuits with the remaining tablespoon of cream and sprinkle them lightly with the remaining sugar. Bake until risen and golden brown, 18 to 20 minutes. Turn the sheet around halfway through to ensure even cooking.

Remove the biscuits from the oven and let cool.

While the biscuits are baking, prepare the filling: Toss the strawberries, sugar, and lemon juice together in a bowl and set aside for

½ pound strawberries, hulled
and quartered

1 tablespoon sugar

1 tablespoon fresh lemon
juice

1 cup heavy cream, beaten to
soft peaks, for serving

several minutes. If the strawberries are extremely firm, let them stand for around 30 minutes.

Split the biscuits in half horizontally. Place the bottoms on individual dessert plates and heap the strawberries on top. Spoon the whipped cream generously over the strawberries and cover with the tops; if you like, place a mint leaf next to each. Serve immediately with any remaining whipped cream on the side.

Save some strawberries for later! When strawberries are in their short peak season, buy a few extra quarts and freeze them. Hull the strawberries and then lay them out in a single layer on a baking sheet and place it in the freezer. When the strawberries are frozen, gather them in plastic bags, squeezing the air out completely. You will find lots of great uses for them in the dead of winter: smoothies, apple/strawberry sauce, chocolate-covered frozen strawberries, and even shortcakes.

11. Summer Pudding

Matthew Tivy is the American chef of Café du Soleil, a popular neighborhood French bistro in New York, but the dessert closest to his heart is this one from his English mother. This "pudding" is a variation of the trifle and one of the most wonderful and gorgeous of all summer desserts. Use bread with a tight crumb; day-old is a good idea as well. The berries soak through the bread to turn it brilliant scarlet in color and give it a cakelike consistency. If you come upon some fresh currants, use them in this. In season, they may be available at farmers' markets or roadside stands in the countryside.

A narrowly slanted pudding bowl is ideal for this, but you will have good results in any case.

SERVES 8

6 cups raspberries

6 cups blueberries

2 cups fresh red currants (optional)

¾ to 1 cup sugar

2 tablespoons port (optional)

One 1-pound loaf thinly sliced firm white bread, crusts removed

1 pint heavy cream, whipped, for serving

Mint leaves, for garnish (optional)

In a large saucepan over medium heat, gently simmer the raspberries, blueberries, currants (if using), sugar, and port for about 5 minutes, just enough to break the berries down a bit and dissolve the sugar. Use the full cup of sugar if you are including the currants.

Line a deep 6-to-8-cup bowl with plastic wrap. Line the bowl with the bread slices, making sure to leave no gaps between them, trimming to fit if necessary. Cut a piece of bread to fit the bottom. Press all the edges of the bread together to form a complete mold inside the bowl.

Spoon half the berry mixture into the bowl. Cover the berries with a layer of bread, add the remaining berries, and cover with a final layer of bread. Place a plate that fits neatly into the bowl over the pudding and place a weight—about 3 pounds; canned goods are good for this—on the plate. Refrigerate the pudding overnight.

About an hour before serving, take the pudding out of the refrigerator and remove the weight and plate. Pour off and reserve any juices that have exuded. Unmold the pudding just before serving and pour the juices on top. Garnish with mint leaves. Serve the pudding, cut into wedges, with the whipped cream.

12. Arborio Rice Pudding with Coconut

A domestic risotto variety, like one of the very good ones from Texas or Alabama, can be substituted for the Italian rice called for here, or you might try a short-grained Asian "sushi-style" rice.

This pudding is best served warm or at room temperature. SERVES 6

2 quarts whole milk

2 cinnamon sticks

1 cup Arborio rice

One 13.5-ounce can unsweetened coconut milk

¼ cup sweetened condensed milk

2 teaspoons vanilla extract

½ cup sugar

½ teaspoon grated lemon zest (optional)

½ cup shredded sweet coconut

Combine the whole milk, cinnamon sticks, and rice in a large saucepan over medium-high heat. Bring just to a boil, then reduce the heat and simmer, stirring frequently, until the rice is tender and the liquid is thick and creamy, about 30 minutes.

Remove and discard the cinnamon sticks; stir in the coconut milk, condensed milk, vanilla, sugar, and lemon zest, if using, and simmer, stirring occasionally, until the rice is very tender and the liquid is thickened, about 15 minutes. Set the pudding aside to cool slightly.

Meanwhile, put the coconut in a small skillet or saucepan over medium heat and stir it constantly until it is fragrant and golden, about 3 minutes. Transfer the coconut to a plate to cool.

Serve the pudding with the coconut sprinkled on top.

The Language of Cooking: *Arborio*

Arborio is the name of a small Italian town as well as one of the varieties of the particular rice known primarily as "risotto" rice. In general, these are short-grained, pearly, and starchy varieties.

13. Lemon-Rosemary Custard Cakes

Thirty years ago my friend Rozanne Gold was served what she describes as "a remarkable apple tart" at the three-star restaurant Maison Troisgros in Roanne, France. I am sure there were many reasons that this tart was special, but one was that it was made with fresh tarragon. Rozanne was already an accomplished cook and food professional, but this was a kind of epiphany: herbs do not need to be confined to savory dishes. Rozanne went on to slip fresh herbs into desserts whenever it made sense; in this case, the familiar pairing of rosemary and lemon give a fresh twist to an old-fashioned favorite.

Make this with your children and you have a choice: you can perpetuate the myth of a kitchen fairy who waves a wand and turns a simple batter into two desserts, a yummy top layer of airy cake and a bottom layer of soft, saucy custard. Or you can seize the opportunity to teach a bit of food science: the batter includes just a little bit of flour, far less than most cakes, which keeps it very light. Then the beaten egg whites, full of air, expand the mixture even more, the way a balloon does, in the heat of the oven. So part of the batter rises to the top. At the same time, the heavier ingredients, the egg yolks, milk, and butter, sink beneath to make the pudding.

This recipe is easy and fast, with a number of the usual kids' chores included: cracking and separating eggs and beating them, juicing lemons, mixing, and dusting the custard cakes with sugar. MAKES 6 CUSTARD CAKES

3 large eggs, at room
    temperature
Salt
¾ cup sugar
2 tablespoons unsalted butter,
    at room temperature
¼ cup flour
1 teaspoon grated lemon zest
¼ cup fresh lemon juice
1 teaspoon finely minced
    rosemary, plus sprigs to
    garnish
1½ cups low-fat milk
Cooking spray for ramekins
1 tablespoon confectioners'
    sugar

Preheat oven to 350 degrees. Place a pot of water on to boil.

Separate the eggs. Beat the whites and a large pinch of salt in the bowl of an electric mixer until foamy. Add ¼ cup of the sugar, 1 tablespoon at a time, and continue to beat until stiff peaks form, about 5 minutes; set aside.

In a separate bowl, beat the remaining ½ cup sugar with the butter on medium speed until well blended, about 3 minutes. Add the flour, lemon zest, lemon juice, rosemary, and a dash of salt and beat at low speed. Add the yolks and milk and beat well. Gently fold a quarter of the beaten whites into the batter, then gently fold in the remaining whites.

Coat six 6-ounce ramekins or custard cups with cooking spray. Divide the batter evenly among the cups; place the cups in a baking pan. Add the boiling water to a depth of 1 inch. Place the pan in the oven and bake for 45 minutes, or until the tops are light golden brown and the puddings are just set; they should still be a bit wobbly. Remove the cups from the pan, let them cool, then refrigerate until cold. Unmold the puddings, sprinkle with the confectioners' sugar, pushed through a sieve, and garnish with small sprigs of rosemary if you like.

There is a good, old-fashioned, and very efficient method for separating eggs that kids like. Show them how to crack the eggs, and then, with a hand over a bowl, have them cradle the yolk and let the whites slip through their slightly parted fingers, taking care not to squeeze the yolk. This combines the thrill of yucky and slimy with a job well done.

LEMON-ROSEMARY CUSTARD CAKES   377

14. Jamaican Bread Pudding

Newton Pryce is one of the best pastry chefs I've ever known, classically trained and a real authority. I had the joy of working with him every day for ten years. This recipe reflects Newton's expertise as well as his Jamaican background—the rum in the custard is a clue.

If you can plan ahead, do soak the bread overnight for really lovely silky custard, but even half an hour will be fine. As rich as bread puddings are, they take nicely to embellishments like ice cream, whipped cream, or custard sauce.   SERVES 6 TO 8

One 1-pound loaf day-
   old white bread, crusts
   removed

4 cups whole milk

½ cup sugar

¾ teaspoon cinnamon

¼ teaspoon ground nutmeg

¼ cup dark rum

4 tablespoons (½ stick)
   butter, melted and cooled

6 eggs, well beaten

½ cup sweetened condensed
   milk

½ cup raisins

Break the bread into small cubes in a large mixing bowl. Add 2 cups of the whole milk and let the bread soak overnight, or for at least 30 minutes.

Preheat the oven to 350 degrees. Grease an 8- or 9-inch square baking dish or similarly proportioned gratin dish.

Add the sugar, cinnamon, nutmeg, rum, and melted butter to the bread mixture; crush any lumps with a fork. In a separate bowl, whisk together the eggs, remaining 2 cups whole milk, and the sweetened condensed milk and gently combine this mixture well with the bread mixture. Stir in the raisins and pour into the prepared baking dish. Place the dish on a baking sheet to catch any spills and place in the oven.

Bake the pudding for 1 hour to 1 hour and 15 minutes, or until a knife inserted in the middle comes out clean, but do not bake it until it is dry; you want a custardy texture. Serve warm or at room temperature.

15. Max's Famous Chocolate Chip Cookies

Shula Bergman has been a dear friend since she had Sylvia as a prekindergarten student in 2003. They would often have play dates on days when school was closed and spent hours in the kitchen. To say that Sylvia had a sweet tooth would be an understatement. Together, Shula and Sylvia baked and chatted, leaving the cleanup of chocolate-covered bowls and spoons to Sylvia.

Max is Shula's son. He began making these cookies when he was just three years old—it was his favorite pastime. Max and Shula bake dozens at a time and always have a freezer full. These delicious cookies are egg, dairy, and nut free to accommodate Max's food allergies, and are equally good warm from the oven, at room temperature, or frozen.

MAKES ABOUT 3 DOZEN COOKIES

16 tablespoons (2 sticks) margarine, at room temperature (look for brands low in trans fats)

¾ cup granulated sugar

¾ cup packed brown sugar

1 teaspoon pure vanilla extract

3 tablespoons water

3 tablespoons vegetable or canola oil

2½ cups flour

2 teaspoons baking powder

1 teaspoon baking soda

1 teaspoon salt

2 cups chocolate chips

1 heaping tablespoon soy nut butter

Cooking spray

Preheat the oven to 375 degrees.

Beat the margarine and both sugars together in a large bowl until well blended; stir in the vanilla, water, and oil. In a separate bowl, combine the flour, baking powder, baking soda, and salt, then add them to the wet ingredients and blend well. Fold in the chips and soy nut butter.

Spray cookie sheets lightly with cooking spray or brush them with canola oil or a similar mild-flavored vegetable oil. Drop tablespoons of the dough onto cookie sheets and bake for 8 to 10 minutes; the cookies should still be slightly soft when you take them out of the oven. Set the sheets on wire racks. Let the cookies cool for about 5 minutes on the baking sheets, then transfer them directly to the racks.

If, like Shula, you like to emphasize the contrast between sweet and salty, add an additional pinch of salt. You can also adjust the quantity of chips, including more or less, as you like. And regular peanut butter can be used in place of the soy nut butter.

16. Meringue Kisses

ere's a meringue, give Mama a kiss!" These have become my specialty. I am often called on to bring them to celebrations like baby showers; I add a drop or two of food coloring—blue or pink if the baby's gender is known, or I separate and color two batches if it is still a surprise. For a chocolate version, I add about ¼ cup unsweetened cocoa to the mixture. Lemon extract can be substituted for the vanilla. Tiny kisses make a pretty decoration on cakes and tarts as well.　MAKES 18 TO 24 KISSES

3 large egg whites, at room
　　temperature
Big pinch of cream of tartar
Pinch of salt
½ cup superfine sugar
¾ to 1 teaspoon pure vanilla
　　extract

Preheat the oven to 200 degrees and line a baking sheet with parchment paper. If you have a nonstick sheet, you don't need to line it.

Put the egg whites, cream of tartar, and salt in the bowl of an electric mixer fitted with a whisk attachment; mix on low speed to combine, then increase the speed to high and beat until the whites thicken.

Continue beating while gradually adding the sugar; add the vanilla and beat until stiff peaks form. Spoon the mixture into a pastry bag fitted with a fluted tip. Twist the bag and pipe the meringue onto the parchment paper, into 1-inch or slightly wider peaks about 1 inch high, about 1 inch apart.

Place the baking sheet on the middle rack of the oven and bake the kisses for 8 hours or overnight; they will be completely dry and crisp.

The kisses will keep well in a tightly closed container; I put sheets of parchment paper between layers. I store the containers in new hiding places every time; otherwise, they disappear overnight.

17. Oatmeal Pecan Cookies

MAKES 4 TO 5 DOZEN COOKIES

16 tablespoons (2 sticks)
  unsalted butter, plus more
  for greasing baking sheets
1 cup sugar
1 cup light brown sugar
2 teaspoons vanilla extract
2 tablespoons milk
2 eggs
2 cups flour
1 teaspoon baking powder
1 teaspoon baking soda
½ teaspoon salt
2 cups quick-cooking oats
1½ cups roughly chopped
  pecans

Preheat the oven to 350 degrees. Lightly grease two large baking sheets or line them with parchment paper.

Cream the butter with the sugars in the bowl of an electric mixer until well blended and fluffy. Add the vanilla, milk, and eggs and mix just until well blended.

In a separate bowl, combine the flour, baking powder, baking soda, and salt. Add to the egg mixture and mix well. Stir in the oatmeal and pecans.

Spoon the batter out by teaspoonfuls onto the cookie sheets, in several batches if necessary. Bake until the cookies are lightly browned, about 9 minutes. Cool the cookies on racks. These keep well in a cookie jar or covered container.

It is almost always a good idea to toast nuts before using them, even when they are to be baked or ground up. Toasting brings forth flavor and refreshes nuts that have been around for a while. I usually put them into a 300-degree oven for about 10 minutes. Pine nuts can be done in a skillet over medium heat—take care because they brown quickly. If you can, buy nuts loose, from a store that does a brisk business or caters to a Middle Eastern community—there is a good chance they will be of high quality and bought and replenished rapidly. Do not buy nuts in great quantities; besides the risk of losing their flavor, their oils can become rancid and spoil whatever you make with them. Store nuts in tightly closed glass jars or in the freezer.

Not so many years have passed since fat of any sort was on the banned list, particularly for heart health. Strict—you almost could say cultish—adherents to such regimes struggled to keep the fat content of their diets at 10 percent or less. Research now indicates that some of those foods on the "Don't Eat!" list contain fats that are not only not harmful, but beneficial. Nuts are a great example of a food that has moved back onto the "Good to Eat" list. The high oil content of nuts makes them efficient little sources of monounsaturated fat, which helps to lower blood cholesterol levels. Pecans, walnuts, macadamias, almonds, and Brazil nuts are 50 percent to 70 percent oil and 10 percent to 30 percent protein. With the exception of the chestnut (which really is the fruit of the chestnut tree), nuts also are low in starch. It may be true that nuts are relatively high in calories, but if you are moderate with this as with any other food, nuts will not upset your weight regime. And they are low in carbohydrates and much better for you than chips or sweets.

Here are some easy ways to work nuts into your daily diet:

- Toast and add them to homemade granola (page 280), or sprinkle them over your morning yogurt and fruit.
- Add to salads, vegetable stir-fries, fish, and vegetables like green beans, spinach, and broccoli.
- Eat them out of hand as a snack. Make your own tidbits to serve with drinks. Spread almonds, pecans, Brazil nuts, or walnuts (or any combination you like) on a baking sheet. Toss with a light drizzle of olive or canola oil and herbs like thyme or spices like cumin,

chili powder, paprika, and sea salt and roast in a 400-degree oven, turning from time to time, for about 20 minutes. Let cool and store in jars.

- Serve them with a perfect piece of cheese and fruit. Walnuts, sliced ripe pears, and blue-veined cheeses are a classic combination, and they make a sublime salad with endive or frisée lettuce dressed with sherry vinegar and walnut oil. The traditional cheeses of choice for this are Roquefort or Gorgonzola, or try one of the very good American varieties (page 388).

18. Oven-Baked Apples

This is the dish to make if you don't make dessert. Toss a pan of these in the oven as you sit down to dinner on a crisp fall evening and let the fragrances warm the room. These apples are perfect for company as well. SERVES 6 TO 8

8 to 10 apples (about 5 pounds), such as Golden Delicious, Granny Smith, Baldwin, Empire, or other baking variety (see page 319)

¾ cup sugar

¾ teaspoon cinnamon

1 tablespoon grated lemon zest

2 tablespoons fresh lemon juice, plus more for serving

6 tablespoons unsalted butter, melted

Vanilla ice cream or whipped cream, for serving

Preheat the oven to 350 degrees.

Peel, halve, and core the apples.

Combine the sugar and cinnamon. Toss the apples in a large bowl with the sugar mixture, then add the lemon zest and juice. Pour the melted butter over the fruit and toss again. Let the apples rest for 5 minutes to release some of their juices.

Pour the apples into a baking dish and bake on the middle rack of the oven; baste and stir the apples every 10 minutes or so with the accumulated juices, using a bulb baster or, with the pan tipped, a large spoon. The apples are ready when they are tender when tested with a sharp knife but still hold their shape and are just lightly colored, after 35 to 45 minutes.

If the pan juices are not syrupy, pour them into a small saucepan over medium-high heat to boil down rapidly. Pour the syrup over the apples and serve warm or at room temperature with ice cream or whipped cream and a squirt of lemon juice. For a variation, in this case on a classic American theme, omit the cinnamon from the ingredients and grate some good, sharp cheese over the apples while they are still warm.

19. Homemade Apple Roll-Ups

As long as there are juicy apples in the market, I turn them into sauce (see page 318). I have wonderful memories of Grandma Nellie making applesauce from the apples that grew on our tree in the country. I am careful to cut out bruises or blemishes, but Grandma didn't believe in wasting anything—it all went into her pot.

I also like to turn applesauce into fruit roll-ups. I've been doing this since my children were little, and now that they are grown, I still send roll-ups to them at school and overseas! No one's ever too old for a homemade natural treat.

To begin, I usually opt for large apples to cut down on the time needed for peeling and coring. As for variety, any apple works for me. The harder ones will yield a chunkier sauce; for a more uniform, smoother sauce choose apples that break down more readily, like McIntosh.

Peel and core 12 to 15 apples and roughly chop them up into 1-inch chunks. Pour a cup of water or apple cider into a large heavy pot and toss in the apples. Place the pot over low heat and cover.

Stir the apples after 20 minutes, and test by mashing the apples with a spoon. You'll want a smooth applesauce, so cook the apples for roughly another 20 minutes. Then pass the sauce through a food mill or mash it by hand.

For roll-ups, I use my dehydrator, with the liner inserts on the drying rack. I spread a thin layer of smooth sauce from edge to edge and then follow the directions for drying fruit. With my machine, it takes about 12 hours to completely dry. Then I peel off the fruit, lay it out on a large piece of plastic wrap, and roll it up. That's it.

You can make roll-ups with peaches or any other fruit (pears, plums, berries) that will reduce into a thick sauce.

Five pounds of apples, chopped into 1-inch pieces, will yield approximately 4 quarts of chopped fruit. When cooked, they will yield about 7 cups of sauce. For my dehydrating tray (which is 12 inches wide around, with a 3-inch hole in the middle), 1 cup sauce yields 6 roll-ups.

Roll-ups will keep well for at least three weeks at room temperature. I store them in resealable plastic bags.

20. Balsamic Roasted Pears

Roasting brings out the deep flavors of autumn fruits like pears, and balsamic vinegar adds sweetness and spiciness. Ice cream, whipped cream, or crème fraîche can be dolloped next to these in place of cheese. This is the time to use an aged balsamic vinegar.

Otherwise, this recipe is open to lots of variations; the list below will probably inspire some of your own. Walnuts are a classic accompaniment to pears—especially if you make the version with some sort of blue cheese—but you may want to try other nuts. SERVES 4

3 tablespoons unsalted butter

4 firm but ripe pears, preferably Bosc, halved lengthwise and cored

¼ cup balsamic vinegar

Freshly ground pepper

¾ cup (3 ounces) walnut halves or pieces, toasted

1 to 2 tablespoons finely chopped fresh rosemary

Cheese (optional; see Note)

½ cup honey (optional; see page 388)

Preheat the oven to 400 degrees.

Have ready a roasting pan or baking dish that will just barely accommodate the pear halves in a single layer; use two if necessary. The pears should fit snugly or the sauce may scorch during roasting. Put the butter in the pan and place it on the middle rack of the oven until melted, about 3 minutes. Arrange the pears, cut sides down, in the butter. Return the pan to the oven and roast the pears until almost tender, about 10 minutes, depending on their ripeness.

Spoon the vinegar over the pears, add pepper to taste, and roast for 5 more minutes. Immediately transfer the pears, cut sides up, to serving plates. Toss the walnuts and rosemary over the pears and ladle the juices from the baking dish on and around them.

Arrange the cheese, if using, on the plates, drizzle the honey on top, if using, over, and serve at once.

Try these cheeses for different flavors.

Blue cheese: Crumble about 1 ounce over each pear half just before serving. I am partial to local choices (page 388), but French Roquefort and Italian Gorgonzola are classic partners to pears. The choice is yours, but keep in mind that there are many more blues than even ten years ago.

Goat cheese: Place a spoonful of soft goat cheese next to each pear half just before serving; this is especially good with a drizzle of honey.

Mascarpone: Place a spoonful next to each pear half just before serving. The warmth of the pear will melt the mascarpone slightly so it will mingle with the juices from the baking dish; this also is especially good with honey.

Mascarpone and Blue Cheese Sauce: Place about ½ cup of each in a bowl, mashing to combine them well. Spoon the sauce over each pear half just prior to serving.

Granny Smith apples can be substituted for the pears.

AMERICAN BLUES

By some estimates, there are now fifty or so domestic blue cheeses, some made from cow's milk, some from sheep's, some from a combination. A lot of this growth has taken place in the last decade or so, and the production of some of these cheese makers is quite small and distributed narrowly, if at all, outside the dairy itself (or online). However, local blue cheese can be found from Vermont to California.

Maytag Blue is an exception; it was established more than 60 years ago and is widely distributed. Humboldt Fog, Old Chatham Ewe's Blue, and Point Reyes Farmstead Blue also have pretty sizable productions.

HONEY

The array of honeys now available is almost dizzying. What a change from just a few years ago, when only one or two big commercial brands could be found. Beekeeping seems to be a growing hobby, even on Brooklyn rooftops, now that beekeeping is legal in New York City. There also are many interesting and elegant imports.

What is most interesting about single-flower honeys is how distinctive their flavor can be, unlike some generic types that taste mostly just sweet. Honey from rosemary or chestnut flowers, for instance, may startle you with the clarity of their flavor. We have just started beehives on the farm, locating the hives close to the pond and fields. We cannot wait to jar our own honey and we wonder just how it will taste.

21. Blackberry, Rhubarb, and Basil Compote

Serve this with pancakes, waffles, pound cake, or ice cream, or in the morning with yogurt.

MAKES ABOUT 3 CUPS

¾ cup sugar, organic if
   available

1 teaspoon grated lemon zest

1 pound rhubarb, ends
   trimmed, cut crosswise
   into ¾ inch pieces

4 ounces (about 1 bunch)
   basil leaves and stems

1 tablespoon water

1 vanilla bean, split

2 pints blackberries, cut in
   half if extremely large

Place the sugar and zest in a small bowl and rub them together to let all the wonderful lemon oil flavor the sugar.

Toss the rhubarb with the sugar until it is well coated. Set the rhubarb aside for about 15 minutes, until the juices begin to release.

Put the basil, water, and vanilla bean into a large saucepan; add the rhubarb and sugar. Bring to a boil, then lower the heat to medium, and simmer, stirring, until the rhubarb begins to break down, about 5 minutes. The compote should be somewhat chunky.

Remove the pot from the heat and allow the rhubarb to cool completely. Remove and discard the basil and the vanilla bean. Fold in the blackberries. Store the compote in a covered container for up to a week.

Rhubarb

We planted our first rhubarb in 2010 and harvested our first crop two years later. It is a sight to behold. Each leaf grows as a tightly closed bud, almost prehistoric-looking, and then unfurls into an enormous fan. To witness this once is enough to understand why the leaves are so wrinkled. Imagine your white button-down shirt all squished into a tiny ball for months before you unfold it. The baby rhubarb stalks are sweeter than the full-grown ones, benefiting from the cold weather as they bridge the transition from cold/cool spring to warm/hot summer. In the height of rhubarb's season, children are always amazed at the giant red leaves of the mature plant and shudder on hearing that the leaves are "poisonous." Funny how they inevitably tease one another about tasting some!

SUGAR

Learning to taste is important; it helps us think about what is in our mouths, and the simple language we apply to the exercise literally expands our understanding of food. Even with sugar, which above all is sweet, distinctions can be perceived, especially among the less processed types.

Table, confectioners', and superfine are white sugars that vary mostly in texture.

Brown sugar is less highly refined than white and retains a hint of molasses in its flavor. Light or dark brown sugar is defined by the amount of molasses it contains, and, of course, dark brown sugar has a deeper taste.

Agave is a syrup made from the Mexican succulent plant sometimes called the century plant, and is a relative of the blue agave, which is used to make tequila. Agave is around one and a half times sweeter than cane sugar, which is one of the reasons its popularity has been growing. Agave comes in a range of colors from nearly clear and tasteless to amber to dark, with progressively deeper caramel flavors.

Turbinado sugar has larger crystals than white table sugar and a trace of molasses as a result of being less processed. The name comes from the turbines that are used in the process. Demerara sugar is similar, with smaller crystals than turbinado, a slightly paler color, and correspondingly less intense flavor. Because so much commercial brown sugar is, in fact, white sugar that has had molasses added back in, turbinado and demerara are considered to be more "natural."

Keep in mind that refined sugar is refined sugar; some, such as honey, may have traces of vitamins or minerals, but not enough to make much of a difference, especially not at the dentist.

22. Watermelon Salad with Lime and Fresh Mint

A true summertime treat at Katchkie Farm is enjoying this dessert with melons from our own garden. The vines spread through the children's garden. We like to pair it with mint (peppermint and spearmint), which is abundant in the herb garden. For many of our visiting children, this is the first time they have seen watermelon growing naturally. Ours are the sweetest watermelons I have ever enjoyed. I bring them home and my son simply scoops out large spoonfuls as soon as I cut one in half. SERVES 6

⅓ cup sugar

Zest and juice of 1 lime

1 small or ½ large
   watermelon

¼ cup thinly sliced mint
   leaves, plus more for
   garnish

Stir the sugar, 2 tablespoons water, the lime zest, and 1½ tablespoons lime juice together in a small heavy saucepan over high heat until the sugar dissolves and the mixture comes to a boil. Remove from the heat and let the syrup cool to room temperature, then refrigerate for several hours, or at least until cold (overnight is good too).

While the syrup is chilling, cut the flesh of the watermelon into large chunks and put them into a serving bowl.

Strain the chilled syrup into a small bowl and stir in the mint. Allow the mint to infuse for at least 5 minutes. Strain the syrup again and pour it over the watermelon chunks, garnish with mint leaves, and serve.

ACKNOWLEDGMENTS

Sylvia's Table has had the loving help of many dear friends, family, colleagues, and professionals. Without them, the dream of this cookbook would not have become a reality.

Long ago, Rozanne Gold helped me to articulate my concept: to engage adults and children around delicious meals and seasonal ingredients. I wanted it to tie in with our work at the Sylvia Center and the lessons we were learning at Katchkie Farm. Best of all, it would be a part of my daughter Sylvia's legacy. "It's *Sylvia's Table*," Rozanne said. From that moment, the book came alive.

I am indebted to Jennifer Baum, a public relations maven and my good friend who introduced me to my agent, Judith Weber. Judith is an elegant woman with vision and culinary passion who believed in the project and was willing to take a chance on a novice writer. I am very grateful for her guidance and patient stewardship of this process and for her early appreciation of nurturing connection between children and healthy food, the concept at the heart of *Sylvia's Table*. There has been nothing more delightful than bumping into Judith in the Greenmarket and upstate at the farm, sharing notes on culinary trends from food trucks to cookbooks.

Judith is also a skilled matchmaker, leading me to the extraordinary Carole Lalli, who helped breathe life into each page with her food knowledge and writing. Like Judith, Carole has inspired her own children and grandchildren to connect with life through food. We spent hours and hours together, over food, of course, working on content and refining recipes, a task enriched by comparing notes on our fluffy cats and shopping expeditions to farmers' markets. Her humor, intelligence, and passion for food are reflected in the soul of the book. My only regret in completing our work together is the end of our breakfast meetings of oatmeal and coffee.

The remarkable Judith Jones acquired the book for Knopf—what an honor it was to capture her attention. Judith's career has been rooted in classic cuisine, distinctively simple and unpretentious, and over her career she published some of the best and best-selling cookbook authors of all time. And Judith recognized the significance of bringing children into the kitchen; she understood the effect the contemporary food scene could have on families. Judith's insights guided the selection of recipes and encouraged us to use storytelling to achieve the goal of *Sylvia's Table.*

After Judith's retirement, the book fell into the capable hands of Lexy Bloom, an attentive editor and food enthusiast. I knew she was the right person when we ended up in long conversations extolling the virtues of vegetables before we even discussed the book. Her love for this project helped guide it through final stages of editing and design. I hope one day we get the chance to actually cook together!

I am grateful to the unique culinary team at Great Performances who shared their extensive expertise, creativity, and technical skills with me. Besides the recipes they had developed as professionals, they offered recipes and personal family cooking experiences; I think these are some of the best recipes in *Sylvia's Table.* Chefs Matthew Riznyck, Marc Spooner, Christopher Harkness, and Newton Pryce spent hours with me discussing techniques and flavors, always willing to answer questions or solve problems. Without their involvement, this collection would not have been as delicious.

My friends in the greater culinary community were eager to support the mission of this book. I am grateful to them for the outstanding recipes they contributed. You might recognize them as some of the leaders in their fields. But besides being star chefs and authors, they understand the importance food plays in family life and in the health of the next generation. It is no coincidence that they are among the leaders of today's important food movements, from getting good food into public schools to supporting local farms to working with anti-hunger programs and community access to wholesome food.

The Sylvia Center provided the ultimate test kitchen for many of our recipes. Whether in our open-air field kitchen at Katchkie Farm, or in New

York City community centers and schools, Sylvia Center chef-instructors have learned how to make magical connections between children's palates and fresh vegetables. They engage children in the cooking process, from teaching basic knife skills and cooperative learning to setting the table for a shared meal. And as each meal is prepared and progresses, it is the children who teach us.

Anna Hammond, Executive Director since 2009, has nurtured the organization with love and commitment. She is inspirational to the staff and works tirelessly to grow the Sylvia Center. Nina Simmons, who was part of the original core of chef-volunteers, helped guide much of the culinary material we use in programs today. Julie Cerny is the Educational Coordinator on the farm, nurturing the two-acre Children's Garden, reaching out to the community, and overseeing close to a thousand visitors each summer. They have been supported by Miranda Lievsay, Lilly Nanh, Jackie Chang, Stacy Ciaravella, and Whitney Reuling, as well as chefs and volunteers, too many to mention.

The board of the Sylvia Center is comprised of unique individuals who have the patience and vision required to grow a seedling into a thriving creation. Board members past and present—Richard Aaron, Joel Cooperman, Rabbi Anne Ebersman, Trudy Gottesman, Dean Martinus, Dr. Dodi Meyer, Amy Todd Middleton, Michael Pollack, and Chaim Wachsberger—have made this work possible. They have been enthusiastic about the book, sharing their own culinary insights and inspirations.

Through the Mayor's Fund to Advance New York City, we were awarded a grant from Rachael Ray's Yum-o! organization. That grant helped the Sylvia Center pioneer critical work in the New York City Housing Authority. Thank you to Fund President Megan Sheekey, along with Nina Freedman and Jenny Sharfstein Kane.

A lot of nitty-gritty work went into making this book happen. Sally Parham, my right hand for five years, kept order over the paperwork—gathering recipes and establishing lines of communications with the contributing chefs and authors and their agents, organizing meetings and probably all sorts of details I'll never even know about. None of this was in her job description and I am grateful to her. Susie Cover, an author in her own right as well as culinary instructor, worked with me to test every recipe and set them up for photography in our makeshift studio. Thanks to Anastassia Batsoula for her eleventh-hour culinary efforts as well. It was delicious fun! And thanks to Johannes Courtens for his photographic contributions. Dean Martinus deserves an extra hand for letting me work on this book when I should have been working.

Final thanks go to three sources of never-ending inspiration.

First, to the farmers I have met who let me walk their fields, visit greenhouses, photograph crops, and share stories. These have been the most life-affirming and enriching experiences. A special shout-out goes to our Kinderhook neighbors Jean-Paul Courtens and Jody Bolluyt of Roxbury Farm for introducing me to Bob Walker and helping us get off to a good start. And to Farmer Fuad Azziz of Ryder Farm, who first introduced me to the distinctive flavors of organic produce and the joys of CSA and who also guided my way to Kinderhook. Green Sparks Farm in Cape Elizabeth, Maine, with their magnificent produce and beautiful market stand, has been a magnet for the past four years and their veggies star in several of the book's photos.

Without Bob Walker, the dream of Katchkie Farm and the Sylvia Center might never have taken root on our sixty acres in Kinderhook. Farmer Bob's dedication, knowledge, and giant heart are the greatest gifts he so generously shares year after year. The summer of 2013 will be our seventh harvest—and the farm continues to grow in the most wonderful ways.

And last but truly first, my children—Nell, Katie, and Sam—and my husband, Chaim, the source of my strength, motivation, and inspiration. We shared a terrible loss. Here is just one small reminder of Sylvia laughing in the kitchen, licking the batter bowl, or picking berries in the field. This book represents our belief in hope, love, and life.

A very special thank you to the wonderful chefs, authors, and other food professionals who contributed to this book: Michael Anthony, Dan Barber, Erik Blauberg, Guiliano Bugialli, Bahija Cherkouai, Ann

Cooper, Dana Cowin, Norma Jean Darden, Claudia Fleming, Rozanne Gold, Alexandra Guarnaschelli, Lisa Holmes, Jenifer Lang, Beth Linsky, Deborah Madison, Sara Moulton, Michael Romano, Eric Ripert, Mark Strausman, Bill Telepan, Pierre Thiam, Matthew Tivy, Corrine Trang, and Jonathan Waxman.

And to my family and friends, for sharing their recipes as well: Ronnie Davis, Dinah Herlands Foer, Max and Rosie Harnoy, Cynthia Hayes, Nannette Herlands, Rachel Neumark Herlands, Steve Hertzling, Soonjo Lee, Dodi Meyer, Grandma Debby Neumark, Eytan Shalev, Miriam Shalev, Nina Simmons, and Miriam Stern.

INDEX

PERMISSION ACKNOWLEDGMENTS

Grateful acknowledgment is made to the following for permission to reprint previously published and unpublished material:

Michael Anthony: "Barley Risotto with Carrots and Spiced Nuts." Used by permission of Michael Anthony.

Dan Barber: "Mushroom-Hazelnut Stuffing" and "Spicy Cranberry Sauce" originally published in *New York Magazine* (November 2004). Used by permission of Dan Barber.

Erik Blauberg: "Oven Roasted Wild Heritage Turkey with Cornbread and Andouille Sausage Stuffing." Used by permission of Erik Blauberg.

Giuliano Bugialli: "Pasta with Artichokes and Eggs." Used by permission of Giuliano Bugialli.

Ann Cooper: "Peanut Butter and Jelly Power Muffins" from *Lunch Lessons* by Ann Cooper and Lisa Holmes (New York: William Morrow, 2006). Used by permission of Ann Cooper.

Dana Cowin: "Sylvie's Stars and Moon Soup" from *Soup's On!* by Leslie Jonath (San Francisco: Chronicle Books, 2007). Used by permission of Dana Cowin.

Norma Darden: "Norma Jean's Fried Chicken," originally published in *Harlem World Magazine* (June 2008). Used by permission of Norma Darden.

Claudia Fleming: "Strawberry Shortcakes" from *The Last Course: The Desserts of Gramercy Tavern* by Claudia Fleming (New York: Random House, 2001). Used by permission of Claudia Fleming.

Rozanne Gold: "Lemon-Rosemary Custard Cakes" from *Eat Fresh Food* by Rozanne Gold (New York: Bloomsbury USA Children's, 2009). "Onion Soup with Apple Cider and Thyme" from *Radically Simple* by Rozanne Gold (New York: Rodale Books, 2010). Used by permission of Rozanne Gold.

Alexandra Guarnaschelli: "Potato and Brussels Sprout Gratin" and "Apple Crisp." Used by permission of Alexandra Guarnaschelli.

Steven Heinzerling: "Bertha's Chicken." Used by permission of Steven Heinzerling.

Jennifer Lang: "Mom's Own Fish Sticks" from *Jenifer Lang Cooks for Kids* by Jennifer Lang (New York: Harmony Books, 1991). Used by permission of Jennifer Lang.

Soonjo Lee: "Kimchi." Used by permission of Soonjo Lee.

Beth Linskey: "Blueberry Jam." Used by permission of Beth Linskey.

Deborah Madison: "Fresh Spring Pea Soup." Used by permission of Deborah Madison.

Sara Moulton: "Creamy Cauliflower Soup with Chorizo and Greens" from *Sara's Secrets for Weeknight Meals* by Sara Moulton (New York: Clarkson Potter, 2005). Used by permission of Sara Moulton.

Eric Ripert: "Salade Monique" from *A Return to Cooking* by Eric Ripert and Michael Ruhlman (New York: Artisan Books, 2002). Used by permission of Eric Ripert.

Mark Strausman: "Tuscan Pot Roast." Used by permission of Mark Strausman.

Bill Telepan: " 'Fried' Black and Gold Rice." Used by permission of Bill Telepan.

Pierre Thiam: "Black-Eyed Pea Salad" from *Yolele! Recipes From the Heart of Senegal* by Pierre Thiam (New York: Lake Isle Press, 2008). Used by permission of Pierre Thiam.

Matthew Tivy: "Summer Pudding." Used by permission of Matthew Tivy.

Corinne Trang: "Crescent Moon Dumplings." Used by permission of Corinne Trang.

A NOTE ABOUT THE AUTHORS

LIZ NEUMARK is CEO and founder of Great Performances, rated Zagat's top catering company in New York City. Originally intended as a staffing service for women in the arts, Great Performances has evolved into one of the nation's most recognized and trend-setting catering companies. Liz's commitment to supporting sustainable agriculture and good earth practices led her to establish Katchkie Farm, her sixty-acre organic farm in upstate New York, in 2006. As well as providing fresh produce for catering events, Katchkie Farm is home of the Sylvia Center, a garden-to-table culinary-based program that inspires young people to discover good food and flavors on the farm and in the kitchen. Liz's experience in the food world has shaped her advocacy efforts: she serves on the boards of several groups on food policy and the food system, such as Just Food and GrowNYC, and she is the recipient of numerous awards, including Food Arts Silver Spoon Award and Crain's 100 Most Influential Women. In her spare time, Liz can be found exploring farm stands and food shops, and spending time with her husband and three grown children.

CAROLE LALLI has worked as a food writer and as an editor specializing in cookbooks at Simon & Schuster and Rizzoli; she also was editor in chief of *Food & Wine* magazine and is the author of three cookbooks.

NOTES

NOTES

A NOTE ON THE TYPE

This book was set in Celeste, a typeface created in 1994 by the designer Chris Burke. He describes it as a modern, humanistic face having less contrast between thick and thin strokes than other modern types such as Bodoni, Didot, and Walbaum. Tempered by some old-style traits and with a contemporary, slightly modular letterspacing, Celeste is highly readable and especially adapted for current digital printing processes which render an increasingly exacting letterform.

Composed by North Market Street Graphics
Lancaster, Pennsylvania

Printed and bound by C&C Offset Printing
Shenzhen, China

Designed by Soonyoung Kwon